BIRTH *your* GREATNESS

BIRTH *your* GREATNESS

You're Carrying Something

CHRISTOPHER WILLIAMS

Faith Works
AN IMPRINT OF FAMILY TIES PUBLISHING

Faith Works

An Imprint of Family Ties Publishing

Published in Chicago, Illinois, by Faith Works, an imprint of Family Ties Publishing

Faith Works books may be purchased for educwational, business, or sales promotional use. For information, special discounts for bulk purchases or questions, please contact : info@familytiespublishing.com

ISBN: 978-0-578-91888-4

FIRST EDITION

10 9 8 7 6 5 4 3 2 1

To my father, Innman Christopher Williams "POPs".
Words cannot express how much I thank and appreciate
him. Without him I would not be the man I am today, for
which I owe him my entire career. I know he is in heaven
right now smiling down on me. I love him with all my heart
and miss him more every day.

To my beautiful mother, Florida Williams. I thank her
and I appreciate everything she has done for me. Without all
her sacrifices, love, wisdom, discipline and support she has
given me I do not know where I would be today. Thank you.
Thank you. Thank you.

P.S. "I love you and it ain't a thang you can do about it."

I dedicate this book to my superhero parents.

CONTENTS

INTRODUCTION

WHERE THE JOUNEY BEGAN

Allow me to take you on a journey called, "The Birth of Greatness." I will begin with how this baby was actually conceived. Before I disclose to you the secrets of its development and growth. This maybe a shock, but I conceived a baby then I conceived a book. I know this may be a head scratcher for you, but this baby I am referring to was indeed conceived in me. So yes, I a man, conceived and birthed a baby. Although this was obviously miraculous and amazing, it was also unexpected.

At this point you are probably wondering how something like this could have happened to me. First, there was a marriage or a joining together in covenant as my pastor would put it, and then on the night of the wedding, a few unexplainable things happened. Unconditional love, knowledge, and spiritual intercourse took place. In other words, one thing led to another and a baby took form; yet this was not a planned baby. Let's just say that this was an unintended pregnancy. In fact, one might even think that it was a mistake; surely, I was not ready for such a tremendous responsibility. This pregnancy was something that I had not even imagined in my wildest dreams.

Yet, as I sat on the couch pregnant and confused, I began to panic. Just like you, I wondered how this conception had happened in the first place. Countless questions flowed into my thoughts. Such as, what would all of my friends say? Was this normal, especially for a man? Up until this moment, I was pretty sure that I was not designed to conceive. Up until the moment of conception, I believed that carrying life was a women's job–not a man's job. So, I began to research my dilemma, starting with what I like to call the dilemma solver, Google. Yet, no matter how long and hard I searched, I could not find a single answer as to how this was remotely possible. Unfortunately, this heightened my confusion and ignited my worries.

Just as I was about to label the situation "hopeless," I remembered how I solved problems in the past–by "beginning at the beginning." So, I decided to revisit the source of this pregnancy, going back to the person who first introduced me to the person who reshaped my life for the rest of my life; in hopes that we would begin a relationship and one day marry. That wonderful matchmaker was my mother. Frantically, I picked up my phone to call her, trying to disguise the distress in my voice. At the same time, I knew that I had to confront her for introducing me to whom which would impregnate me. Because I was now carrying something inside of me that I once thought was impossible. "Why?" I whispered, as the tears streamed down my face.

Despite her silence, I could imagine my mother sitting on her couch, sighing on the other end of the phone, waiting for me to calm down. Although she understood my frustration, she must have known that my somewhat irate demeanor stemmed from a place of fear. Surely, she realized that I was experiencing a fear of the unknown. Sadly, the thought of me being a parent someday soon terrified me.

Knowing exactly what I needed, my mother hung up the phone and without warning, showed up at my front door. She sat me down and said, "Son, I understand what you are going through."

"But how could you know, Mom?" I replied.

She responded by saying, "I introduced you to Jesus because I believed you needed to get to know Him so that you could have a real relationship with Him and so that you could experience Him for yourself."

"But, but…," I stuttered.

"No buts", she says.

"I knew that when you were ready, you would trust and commit yourself to Jesus. You are not the first person He has impregnated, and you will not be the last." She ended with the words from the great Maury Povich, "Son, you are the father" and it is your job to carry and birth this baby called GREATNESS."

Staring into her eyes, I was able to catch a glimpse of myself. I said, "Mom, I do not understand." "I know it sounds crazy, but I know you can handle what Jesus has in store" she said, gently patting my head. I remember it like it was yesterday, the way she leaned in towards me and wrapped her loving arms around me. She posed a question that reshaped the rest of my life. She had asked me if I was ready to birth greatness?

At that moment I felt a tremendous amount of pressure. My forehead started to sweat profusely, and my hands were shaking. As I stood up slowly, legs trembling. A part of me wanted to run and hide but I remembered my father telling me, before his passing, that pressure creates diamonds. I stopped in my tracks asking myself, was I meant to create diamonds? At that moment, my spirit started to ease. Yet, I still pondered this greatness that my mother was so confident about. Personally, I was anything but confident. At this moment I really did not want to hear anything else. However, because of the respect and a little sprinkle of fear, I sat back down and continued to listen.

After this life changing talk with my mother, I knew that I had to fall on my face before God. Nervously, I began to speak, although I was not really sure where to start. I just began to cry out to God in prayer, asking for His guidance, His grace, His wisdom, and most importantly His presence. Even in my ignorance, I knew that carrying greatness, let alone birthing greatness, was something that I could not do alone.

Surprisingly, God responded in a way that only God can respond. He said to me, "All are given greatness, but much is required to access it." With my head hung in humility, I received that word over my life that day. Yet, I still did not know how to access this greatness that was being spoken of. From that moment, I spent years learning how to prepare my mind, body, and soul to carry and birth greatness. It was not only important to me that I become the best vessel possible, but to also help those in need of birthing the greatness on the inside of them, such as yourself. Trust me, the process was not, and is not easy; however, I assure you that it will be well worth the wait.

My question to you is, "Are you ready to birth the greatness that is on the inside of you?" Are you ready to allow God's vision to come to pass in your life? If you do not learn anything else beyond this point, you must know that you are a *game changer* and that what is on the inside of you makes you a *world changer*. Now, I must warn you that this process will be an intense journey, but in the end, I promise you that this book will prepare you to birth *something great*. So, if you are ready, fasten your seatbelt, and get ready for the journey to "Birth your Greatness."

DOCTOR VISIT

I must admit that I am like most men in the world; I dislike going to the doctor. In addition, I dislike filling out the intake form, to me it is just tedious drawn-out paperwork. And do not get me started on the wait that seems like forever while listening to that god-awful waiting music. And did I forget to mention how I despise sitting on that examining table, waiting for the doctor while the nurse examines me? I know I sound like a grumpy old man; nevertheless, I do know the importance of going to the doctor.

Against my better judgement, I made a doctor's appointment because I was not feeling like myself. As a matter of fact, I was not myself. I was living a life that was not designed for me. I was trying to be someone I was not. I was just unhealthy. Now I did not want to go to a typical doctor; I needed the best doctor that money could buy, or should I say the best doctor that no amount of money could buy.

My actions of me not being myself caught the attention of my mother. She saw how unhealthy I was. She believed that I was not the same son she once knew and on top of that she claimed that I was unrecognizable to her. I knew then that something was wrong with me. So, she recommended me to the best doctor that she knew. His name was Doctor G-O-D. When

I met this doctor, I told Him that I had heard such great things about Him. Such as how He healed a blind man, cleansed a man of leprosy and how He even helped a 90-year-old woman give birth to a healthy baby. Trust me, I did my homework, and his work was known across the world. I knew I was at the right place, getting help from the right person. I could see that he was excited to see me, but I was not entirely sure why. "How can I help you", he asked?

I simply replied, "I'm not feeling too well, Doc."

I continued, stating that "I am constipated, nauseous, fatigued, and I get these god-awful cramps, and don't get me started on my mood swings doc."

He proceeded to ask me. "How long have you been having these symptoms?"

"Throughout my life," I replied. "These symptoms have come and go, and they have usually been noticeably light, but in the last year they have come and have never left. Doc, in the recent weeks, they have more of an impact on my day-to-day life than ever before." I was nervous because it became silent. With a smile on his face, He was looking at the intake form and to be honest, I did not see anything to be smiling about.

While drumming his fingers on the desk He proceeded to

say, "It says here that your significant other's name is Jesus; is that correct?" "Yes!" I told him. "I have known Jesus since I was eight years old. My mother introduced me to Him; in hopes that we would begin a relationship and one day marry. Surprisingly, we did end up dating and ended up getting pretty serious. However, throughout my life we have had an off and on relationship; it was my periodic wrongdoing that caused our many breakups. The crazy part is that He never stopped loving me. He always wanted to be a part of my life, but I was always being stubborn and disobedient."

He asked, "When was the last time you two were intimate?"

I dropped my head as I recalled the time. "It was when my father passed away in March of 2015. I was an emotional mess and the only person I could turn to was Him. He was there to pick me up and dust me off. He gave me words of encouragement and strength. And from then, my love grew for Jesus and one thing led to another and let's just say spiritual intimacy took place, doc. I can honestly say that was my first time I truly gave myself to Him."

He shook his head as if He understood. He followed up by asking me to break down the symptoms that I was having, so He could further diagnose the problem.

"Doctor G-O-D, where do I begin?" He stopped me and said, "Just call me God." Well, God let's start with these crazy mood swings that have been taking place in the last month. One day I am passionate about my vision and then another day I am depressed because I do not know how to ignite my passion, so I can make it my career. It is mentally challenging to see other people living out their passion when I am sitting here with a passion but not knowing where to begin.

"Begin at the beginning," He said.

As I continued to explain, my eyes filled up with tears. "God, I am a Bible reader and in Proverbs 18:16 it says, "That your gift will make room for you", but it is frustrating when those doors have not been opened yet. It is frustrating when you get to those doors, knocking and beating, desperate to get in, to get on the other side; yet nobody is opening them to give you an opportunity." I took a deep breath and started to pace the floor of the room.

"Why don't you sit down and relax?"

"I cannot, Doc. My life is falling apart."

"Who told you that?" He asks.

"My body, it is the way I feel. Sometimes when I turn on the television or look on Social Media and it appears to me that people are using their gifts while I am still sitting at home, trying to figure out how to unwrap mine."

God nodded and scribbled onto my form.

"I could go on and on about this, but this is no time for complaining, but a time for answers."

"Maybe you should keep talking until you have talked it through. Let your guard down." God replied.

Well, if you insist.

I consider my mood swings to go hand in hand with this god-awful cramp I have been having. It is like someone is twisting the inside of my body. These cramps are not only physical, but mental, and spiritual as well. I sat down and put my head in my hands. "God, it takes a toll on my thought process because I know I am destined to succeed in life, but it is a struggle. Or how about when I see other people living out their dreams, but it feels like I am still dreaming? The cramps sometimes take over my body and make me not want to move or to get up and go after it." God looked directly at me without blinking. "What about this time for intimacy you mentioned before?"

"Yes, I realize now that it also affects my intimate time with Jesus. He does not mind hearing my problems though; He actually encourages me to bring my problems to Him," I said. "But sometimes I find a way to blame Him for my problems, so it hinders our time of intimacy."

"And why do you believe these things are happening to you?" He asked.

"I do not know why, but I believe that all of these physical, mental, and spiritual things that are happening in my life are causing me to feel fatigued. God, I am always feeling tired; as a matter of fact, I am tired of being tired. This makes me not want to do anything and sometimes makes me want to give up. It causes me to separate myself from all of my friends and family as if isolation is better for me at this particular time in my life. In fact, I am even tired of talking to you about this now. I am just sick and tired of being sick and tired. I guess you can say that I'm nauseous." I bowed my head, filled with shame that I had never felt before. *"Why was I such a failure?"* I asked myself. God replied, "I think I know the problem, but before you end and before I give you a solution as to why you are having these symptoms, I need you to tell me about your constipation."

I immediately lifted my head, thinking that this was a ridiculous question. Yet, after a moment, it seemed like the most natural question to answer. "God, this is my biggest struggle out of all of these symptoms. I know I have so much inside of me that the world needs to see but it is so hard to get it out. So much potential, talent, passion, gift, an abundance of purpose, wisdom, intelligence, and the list go on, but it is so hard for any of those things to come out." God sat there with a smile on his face. "I see a lot of patients with these same symptoms. And I believe the answer I gave my other patients will be no different for you."

As I was anxiously awaiting my results, I was also praying that there was nothing seriously wrong with me. Then God entered the room and said, "I have great news."

My face lit up with anticipation. He says, "Congratulations, you are pregnant."

PREGNANT!?

That was certainly the last thing I expected to hear. I did not even know that it was remotely possible, that I, a man, would be able to conceive. I was in shock. I cried out to God in both frustration and fear. I did not know what to say, think, or do. So, in my vulnerable moment, I decided to ask for direction, "God, what I am supposed to do?

God replied, "All are given greatness, but much is required to access it."

Suddenly, I frantically I woke up from my sleep, sweating because my dream seemed so real. I started to touch my stomach in belief that I was pregnant. No, this could not be true; that was what I told myself. I was still in doubt that I was not designed or equipped to conceive. No matter how I tried to force myself to wrap my mind around it, I still believed that carrying life was a women's job- not a man's job.

After I laughed off the dream, I tried to mentally prepare myself to start a productive day. However, I slowly felt myself becoming immersed in my thoughts about life. Feeling overwhelmed, I ducked down under the covers. I had never imagined that my life would be like this; there had to be some mistake. Battling an array of emotions, wrestling with the excitement of knowing I could somehow change the world, I tried to embrace what God had placed in my heart. I tried to embrace the thought of becoming a motivational speaker. Hiding under the covers did not work because I could not hide from myself. Instead, I pulled the covers back and sat upright. In what seemed like only glimpses of the future, I envisioned myself changing lives, one stage at a time. Yet, by the same token, I struggled with the thought of where to begin. Doubt and questions continued to creep in. "Am I capable? Smart enough? Experienced enough? I felt myself filled with an abundance of emotion. The burning desire to succeed and to impact people lives around the world ran deep inside of me.

But at this very moment I struggled to impact my own life which was painful. Before I knew it, I was trying to cover my pain like an addict. I was addicted to social media, not because I liked posting about my own unentertaining life, but because I could not stop looking at the lives of others and comparing them to mine. Other people seemed to be living out their dreams and their passions online; yet I could not fulfil my own purpose. This disappointment in myself caused depression. I was hurt. I wanted my eyes and ears to be tuned to the people. Yet, that seemed so far away.

Again, I screamed out to God for direction until I heard a soft voice whisper, "Begin at the beginning." That authority of the voice startled me. It sounded all too familiar, as if I had heard them before. It sounded like the words God spoke to me in my dreams. I began to replay my dreams and realized that these were the exact words spoken to my situation. At this moment, I wondered if I was losing my sanity. "There is no way that dream was real," I said to myself as I paced across my floor.

"Am I really displaying a mood swing right now?"

At this point of my life, I was filled with so many emotions. I had lost my father in March of 2015 and then on top of that I have the nerve that same year to want to be an entrepreneur and I was not sure where to begin. I was twenty-one years old, the age when boys are considered men. I was a young man without a father. The same young man that had to witness his mom take on the role of a widow and a single mom. Although I was heartbroken and confused, the only thing I knew was that I was a young man with a passion. A passion to change the world one stage at a time, but I was lost. I sat day after day holding onto a gift that I did not quite understand how to unwrap. Pastors, strangers, family, and friends would identify my gift, but I still could not fully see it. I was tired of hearing that I had "potential," that I was going to "be somebody," or my favorite line, "I cannot wait to see you become a success." One of my favorite holidays was Christmas and the most frustrating thing about this holiday was having your eye set on a gift you want to unwrap but having a hard time unwrapping it. Well, that was how I felt about my God given gift. I was eager to open it. Other people knew what was inside, but I had no clue and on top of that I was struggling to open it. Sadly, everyone was talking about this gift that I could not ignite.

Against my better judgement, I started to listen to that voice that said. "Begin at the beginning." So, the next Sunday I went to my safe haven, the place I called my spiritual home, the church. I was nervous because I had an off and on relationship with Jesus. My stubbornness and disobediences made me nervous to step back into His house. However, I knew that I needed answers from my spiritual daddy and I also knew that the only place to get the answers I was looking for was in the church. Now I have attended many churches in my lifetime, but I was not certain about where my new church home should be. My close friend by the name of Rodney Barber invited me to his church, New Harvest Ministries International presided over by the shepherd of that house by name of Pastor Otis Burns. This man of God spoke into my life, telling me that that I had something great on the inside of me that I may not understand but that the world needs to see.

Nervously, I listened and received what he was saying. In fact, at that moment it sounded like he said that I was pregnant. There was that word again-the one I had been struggling with. Even though I felt like my life was falling apart Pastor Burns confirmed what God spoke into my life about me becoming a motivational speaker. Desperate to be obedient to the Lord, I took a big leap of faith and took a temporary leave from school so that I could follow my assignment as a motivational speaker. With not a since of direction nor guidance I was truly struggling. I felt lost and alone after the loss of my father, trying to find a way to turn this dream of mine to a reality. So, I can turn my girlfriend into a fiancé, while struggling to keep a roof over my head- let alone put a ring on her finger. Yet, the Bible said that my gift will make room for me. Yet, it looked like my gift appeared to be stuck in a box.

As I continued to fight the thought that I might be spiritually pregnant, the "symptoms" told me differently. Suddenly, I felt this pain in my stomach as if someone were twisting my insides out. Weeks later I felt a pain in my head like no other pain I had ever experienced, and it started to affect my mental state. These pains felt so severe that I started to do what most people do; I begged God to get rid of these pains while promising Him I will do no wrong in the future. These pains went on for weeks but there was still no sign of God. I did not see any healing in sight. What about how He healed the blind man or healed a man of leprosy? Surely, He was able of healing me.

"Where is my miracle, Lord?" I shouted.

I felt my physical, mental, and spiritual well-being taking a drastic hit. At this point I was at an all-time low. I started to feel tired all of time, I had no energy, I guess you can say I was fatigue. That caused me not to want to do anything, not get up and go after it nor find answers to my problems. This also put a big strain on my relationship with Jesus. It was no one on one anymore, I felt like this was all His fault and He did not care about fixing it. How can you give me a passion for something but do not give me instructions on how to ignite it? How can you give me a gift, but make it virtually impossible to unwrap it? How can you create doors and do not open them for me when you hear me knocking? How can you allow me to be sick, almost to the point of nausea and do not heal me? I felt spiritually, mentally, and somewhat physically constipated. The feeling of having so much inside of me but not knowing how to get it out.

At this moment I did not need to say another word. I started to really listen to what I was complaining about. I hear myself talking about having world wind of emotions, *mood swings*. Then I am talking about me being tired, *fatigue* and feeling *nauseas*. And having theses crazy pains I feel spiritually, physically, and mentally, *cramps* that cause me to lack one on one time with Jesus, *intimacy*. Aw, and did I mention how *constipated* I felt sometimes, having so much to be let out to the world but having a hard time releasing it.

After years of battling with this thought of me being spiritually pregnant, I finally cave in and admit that I am indeed pregnant. There was no need of denying nor hiding from that fact that Jesus place something inside of me that the world needs to see. Just like myself, I believe God has been trying to get your attention. I believe situations and circumstances that has been happening in your life are for a reason. I am here to tell you that there is always a reason for your season.

So, if you been having the same symptoms that I have experienced then I believe you are carrying something great. Let us take this journey together and find out if indeed that you are carrying something.

CHAPTER 1

1

I THINK I'M PREGNANT

Maybe your cycle is a few days or a few weeks overdue. Or maybe your cycle is not scheduled to arrive yet, but you can tell that there is something brewing on the inside of you. Maybe you have been intimate with Jesus for months or years now yet, you still have not had any luck with "birthing greatness" is concerned. Perhaps, you have not wanted the responsibility of carrying anything but despite your attempts to not conceive, you miraculously have something "baking in the oven." Nevertheless, no matter your age, gender, faith walk, relationship with Jesus, situation, or circumstances in your life, you are still on the edge of your seat, wondering: Am I pregnant?

Do not worry this is a question I have asked myself many of times. As you read earlier my relationship with Jesus was off and on due to my periodic wrongdoing. Throughout our relationship, my faith walk was not what it should have been. To be honest I had trust issues. Even though at times I was not a fan of His and at points in the relationship He got on my nerves, I always found myself going back to Him. In the mist of my trust issues, disobedience, and wrongdoing, He somehow saw the best in me, and because of that, He wanted to put a spiritual "baby bun" in the oven. At that point in my life, I was not trying to receive what He was trying to put in me. At the same time, I believed that it was impossible for me to conceive so it was easy for me to try to deny His blessing. Although He was trying to put something inside me that He knew would change my life forever, my belief was that this responsibility was not what I needed at that stage of my life.

However, this spiritual pregnancy was something that I could not run away from anymore. Just like me, you are probably running away from what Jesus is trying to do in your life because it sounds and looks uncommon. It feels unconventional because what was prayed for seems so uncertain. I am here to tell you that the harder you try to run from His blessing, the closer you will get to His open arms.

Trust me, carrying life that you have created with a partner is a big responsibility, but carrying a spiritual baby called "greatness" is an even bigger responsibility.

"But how do I know if indeed I am pregnant", you ask?

SIGNS & WONDERS

The alarming sign that a woman receives alerting her to the possibility that she might be pregnant is usually a missed *period or cycle*. The only way that she can be positively sure that she is actually pregnant, is to obtain a positive pregnancy test. When it came to me being pregnant, I knew who the father was, but I was nervous because I did not know how active He would be in our lives. Deep down inside I had my doubts. I did not believe God when He told me that I was pregnant, because I did not think that it was possible. What made my doubts slowly fade away is when I missed my *period/cycle*. Now just like you I thought it was impossible for me, a man, to conceive. Through my ignorance, I asked for clarity and soon realized that this was not a normal pregnancy, but a spiritual pregnancy. Now the missing of a spiritual period or cycle is quite different from the experience than the average women go through naturally.

- **Cycle**: *a series of events that are regularly repeated in the* *same order.*

- **Period**: a length of portion of time

I was going through a cycle of wrongdoing. I was hanging out with people that were just eating off my table instead of bringing things to the table. In the mist of my ignorance, I kept those people around because I did not want to be alone nor eat alone. At the time I did not understand that sometimes in order to be elevated, you must be isolated. Do not have people come into your life that always have their hands reaching out but have people in your life with their hands reaching up. You want people to stand in the gap for you, praying and praising for what is to come into your life.

Unfortunately, at that particular time in my life, I was in relationship with the type of people that when the well ran dry, they ran away. Yet, I continued this cycle of wrongdoing and wrong choices. For years I was living a life that was not designed for me. I became numb to the feeling of not being who I was called to be. My dream of becoming a motivational speaker was not my choice; I quickly learned it was an assignment given by God. However, just like I did in school for years, I did not study to pass my assignments and on a bad day, I chose not to show up to class to receive my assignments. I was not raised to be disobedient; I knew that I could and should be doing better, but this false life, this deception facilitated a downward cycle.

I started seeking material things and people that were not designed or placed in my life. I began to run away from the assignment that God gave me and started to focus on the assignment that man gave me. I felt my life falling apart. While I was watching my father suffer from a horrific sickness; called cancer and pneumonia. One day visiting my father to show him love and support. I found myself falling to my knees in prayer by my father's hospital bed, asking God to have my father suffer no more. In addition, I started to ask God for another favor and that was to make me over again. I asked Him to show me and guide me on how to become the man I was created to be.

This prayer took place the last few days in February. Sadly, eight days later I received the call that my father had passed away. Forwhatever odd reason, I felt the urge to become a motivational speaker. I felt in my current mess it was a message. "But where do I begin", I asked myself? I had never heard a motivational speaker before, did not know how much they got paid, nor did I know where or how to start. By the grace of God, eight months later I got my first gig as a motivational speaker.

I finally understood when my mother would say, "God works in mysteries ways." The number eight is an incredibly significant number for me. Eight means new beginning, I did not realize that my father's passing eight days after my prayer meant that I was about to have a new beginning and that my father was going to suffer no more. The number eight also means "a new order" or "creations" also meaning a man's true "born again" moment. I did not know in those eight days God was making me over again. I was not aware that after those eight days, my *period/cycle* was a few days overdue. As days went by, I began to realize that my life was different, that it was not like the old days. Life was changing right in front of me. People that I thought were my friends started exiting stage left. The urge for material things went away. I stopped listening to man's assignment and started listening to God's assignment. I started to show up to class to receive my assignment from God and studied to show myself approved. After accumulating a few days of a life that I was not familiar with, I was able to recognize that my patterns were different, that *my cycle* was way overdue.

Scared out of my mind because at that moment I was one hundred percent certain that I was pregnant, I did not know what was to come. I never dreamed about carrying life. I never tried to get pregnant; again, I thought that was impossible to begin with. So, do not be alarmed that you missed your cycle; do not be sorry that you do not want to do the same things over and over. A teacher once told me that the definition of insanity is doing the same thing over and over and expecting a different result. I know that you may be nervous, but I am glad you missed your period because that period of your life only came to make you stronger. I am glad that you missed your cycle because that cycle you were going through was only to help you navigate back to God loving arms.

Allow me to inform you of the meaning of *Signs and Wonders*. Signs and wonders are special miracles that "signify" that something miraculous is about to occur. They are always intended on making people "wonder" about the important things instead of remaining numb to them. Your missed period or cycle was and is a special miracle that signifies that something miraculous is about to happen. However, there are a few signs that Jesus has placed in your life that will make you "wonder" about the importance of them instead of remaining numb to them. As you read earlier, the alarming sign that a woman receives alerting her to the possibility that she might be pregnant is usually a missed *period or cycle*. I believe that this is the most obvious "sign". Other than this, women might have noticed some changes in their body or in your spiritual case, you might have noticed some changes in your life and started to "wonder," could I be pregnant? Or you might not have experienced your period or cycle being late, but you are still "wondering" if indeed you are pregnant.

The early days and weeks of spiritual pregnancy are the

beginnings of the journey to birth greatness and there is much unexpected anticipation. However, at this stage you may not be aware that you are pregnant. Subsequently, in the first few weeks of being pregnant you may not notice early signs and wonders of pregnancy, but trust there are many miracles going on inside of you that will affect the rest of your life.

PREGNANCY TEST

Spiritual pregnancy is the most exciting and breath-taking experience you can go through. This is also one of the most extreme emotional roller coasters that you will undergo in your lifetime. The thought that another life is growing inside of you is amazing. Spiritually speaking, you are bringing a new life into this world. That life is called greatness. The most amazing thing about this experience is that greatness is forming inside of you just as if you were carrying a human being. Your greatness is forming its own five senses as well as getting bigger by the weeks and months. It is something that only God can create and something that only you can birth. Carrying greatness can produce anxiety and uncertainty but it is certainly a fulfilling and worthwhile experience.

So, the big question is "Are you pregnant?

There are two types of pregnancy tests when it comes to natural pregnancy; one uses a urine sample, the other a sample of blood. Most women use the urine sample test; there are around 97% accurate when done correctly and it only costs as low as $7.99. However, when it comes to spiritual pregnancy there is only one test and it is 100% accurate. This might be surprising, but it does not require any finances to discover; however, it does require your commitment to the Lord Jesus Christ. God once told me "all are given greatness, but much is required to access it." One of those requirements is giving your life over to Christ, which is easier said than done.

Taking a spiritual pregnancy test requires what most people do not do first or at all and that is to check or qualify the blood. In the natural, it is the blood sample test. God gave His commitment to us by dying on the cross, and through that process He shed *blood* from the crown of His head to the soles of His feet. So, if you been through hell and back while shedding blood, sweat and tears through the process; I am here to tell you that your experiences were not negative. In fact, that means your pregnancy test shows positive. A Spiritual pregnancy test is essentially a life test. The measure of whether or not you are pregnant with greatness depends on how you react to life when it decides to throw curve balls at you.

It may feel like life is bullying you and although you are

trying to push and fight back, it seems like nothing is working. I want to tell you to keep pushing; **P.**ush **U.**ntil **S.**omething **H.**appens. Everyone has greatness inside of them but not everyone is willing to take or go through a spiritual pregnancy test. There are so many obstacles and there is such required commitment that people would rather be normal than great. I believe you want to be great. I also I believe that you are reading this book because you took many of the tests but when you looked at that pregnancy test stick, you saw it as negative. That is how you view certain situations and circumstances that happened in your life- negative.

After today I need you to look at your life not through your natural eyes, but through your spiritual vision. The test that has been thrown in your life has set you up to birth greatness. You must take a look at your life and your future through your "vision" lenses, not your eyes. When you do, you will soon realize that spiritual pregnancy test stick actually says positive. So, congratulations, you are expecting! Now I need you to have an expectation that your life is going to get better. I need you to expect that you are going to be a great parent to your greatness. I need you to expect that your greatness is going to change the world and make the world a better place, because you will not accept anything less. And the irony of all of this is that Jesus is going to exceed all of your expectations. I heard the world-renowned motivational speaker and author, Les Brown say, "Life has no limitations except the ones you make." Do not limit your greatness. Speak life into your greatness. The Bible says in Proverbs 18:21, "Life and death are in the power of the tongue and those who love it will eat its fruit." What you speak over your greatness is what you will receive and watch how God multiply the fruits of your labor.

So, the life you have lived so far was not in vain. It was just a spiritual pregnancy test. A test that was designed for you and only you. What you have experienced is different than what anybody else has experienced. Jesus chose you to impregnate, not only because He trusts that you can handle it, but because He has something great in store for you. I believe that God gives the tough battles to strong soldiers. If you have been through what my mother calls, "hell and high waters" then I have great news for you. You are pregnant!

CONGRATS!

Congratulations, on finding out you are pregnant! I know you may be in shock that you are pregnant. Especially after believing that this was impossible to begin with. Or maybe you are in shock that you are actually carrying something of value. Whether you are completely filled with joy about being a parent to your child called greatness, or are still getting used to the idea, now is the time to start planning and getting informed on what to expect as well as how to birth greatness. Now I know it is going to take some time for you to adjust to the idea of you being pregnant, let alone your mind, body, and soul which must adjust also. But while you are adjusting to the idea of you being pregnant, your greatness is dividing into layers. The new life that is inside of you has been busy. Just like a natural woman's pregnancy, the baby starts as a fertilized egg and it swiftly divides into layers of cells, some of which become an embryo. That embryo is very tiny, surprisingly it is only about 0.04 inches long. Did you know that embryo is the size of a poppy seed? Well, that is how big, or should I say how small your baby is at 4 weeks.

This may come to you as a shock, but when it comes to a spiritual pregnancy, your embryo is even tinier. In fact, the greatness inside of you does not start with a fertilized egg. It starts with a fertilized seed and that seed is about 0.03 inches and that seed is called a mustard seed. The Bible says in Matthew 17:20 (NSA) "Because of the littleness of your faith; for truly I say to you, if you have faith the size of a mustard seed, you will say to this mountain, 'Move from here to there,' and it will move; and nothing will be impossible to you." Your pregnancy starts and ends with faith. And through this pregnancy your faith will be tested. Faith, at its core, is deep-rooted in the expectation of good things to come. In Hebrews 11:1 (NKJ) says, "Now faith is the substances of things hope for and the evidence of things not seen." Unfortunately, some people do not believe in things they cannot see. So, when Jesus impregnates us it is hard to believe because we cannot see what He has placed in us.

That is why the first trimester of your pregnancy is going to be one of the hardest stages of this spiritual pregnancy. While this pregnancy can be hard at the best times, faith is the engine that helps you believe that it will get better. In life faith is just as important as the air we breathe. In your pregnancy, faith gives breath to your child called GREATNESS; faith is the air your greatness breathes. That type of oxygen is the key that nourishes the development and growth of your greatness. And just like any seed that is planted, it must be watered, given sunlight, and the right nutrients to grow.

PREGNANCY DIET

Speaking of nutrients, who says eating healthy is only for people that are overweight? Those individuals are wrong. Eating healthy is particularly important to your mind, body, and soul. In the words of the great author and motivational speaker Jim

Rohn, "Take care of your body. It is the only place you have to live." Well, this quote is especially important when it comes to your spiritual baby called greatness. You must take care of your body because your body is the only home for your greatness. When you are pregnant with greatness, what you accept inside your body including your eating habits become more important than ever. Yes, you even must take care of your body before conception. Why? Because the right food gives not only us energy and nutrients to grow and develop but it does the same for the greatness inside of us.

Ironically, a pregnancy diet is not about weight loss. When it comes to a natural pregnancy, some doctors suggest that the last thing you want to do is lose calories while pregnant. However, when it comes to your spiritual pregnancy you indeed want to lose weight. Now it is not body weight, but it is an array of natural things you do want to lose. Now all pregnancies are different, and certain individuals have different amount of weight that they need to shed off. Whether what weighs you down in your life needs some minor *tweaks,* or you need to take a huge leap in creating a heathier diet in your life, this will give your greatness the best opportunity to be healthy.

While I was pregnant with greatness I soon realized how "overweight" I actually was. I realized that I had people in my life that were bringing negativity into my life; that caused me to feel weighed down. Remember that there is a seed on the inside of you; a seed which is growing. Therefore, if you intake negativity you will hinder your greatness growth. One of the perks of carrying greatness is that it forces you to outgrow certain friends. Through this process you will change as well as your friends. Imagine if you can buy greatness for .50 cents but you only have a $1.00 bill. Would you still buy it? What happens is that when you "invest" in greatness, in return you get change. Some people do not like carrying change so even if greatness will *change* their life, they still will not accept *change.* People that birth greatness realize that there is value in *change.* They understand that all are given greatness, but much is required to access it. I was aware that when I sought greatness in return, I will have *change(d).*

If you know that the people who you label "friends," are not adding value to your life, but are only waiting for a handout, then do you and your greatness a favor and cut those friends off. Especially, those who are holding you back, who are knowingly or unknowingly sabotaging your diet. Because it is making you look a bit overweight in certain areas. It took me a long time to realize that bad company played a part of my weight gain, but that was just the beginning.

Life sometimes throws us curve balls which makes us feel like the world is out to get us. You want to know something funny? Sometimes it is not life, but it is our perspective on life. I thought life was hard but in reality, it just has it challenging moments. Those moments were designed to make us stronger. Yet, at one point in my life I was stressed about those moments. And when I found out that I was expecting; I, a man, my stress level was sky high. I had to find answers to those problems. So, I turned to my Bible, which provides the guidelines for problem solving. The answer to my problem, according to the Word of God was to seek out wisdom. In Proverbs 4:7 (KJV) says, "Wisdom is the principal thing; therefore, get wisdom: and with all thy getting get understanding."

I started to change my perspective on stress. I quickly understood that stress is an annoying alarm clock that I desperately needed. When I was not where I wanted to be in life it somewhat stresses me out, but that alarm clock woke me and pushed me to get up and do something, to make change to my situation. Stress will decrease the chance for you to have a health pregnancy if you allow stress to use you. Do not let stress use you. Change your perspective on stress and use what transpires as a lesson; stop allowing it to add weight to your life; stop allowing it to weigh you down. Burn those unnecessary calories.

It took me a long time to understand the importance of eating healthy and burning those unnecessary calories. I want you to understand that this is the time to start eating healthy. Start thinking about what you put into your body, mind, and soul. Why? Because your greatness depends on it. A healthy eating plan is a necessity when it comes to birthing greatness. When birthing greatness, I did not realize the importance of the process and every process needs a plan. Stop unhealthy habits right away because they will quickly derail the plan and process. When it comes to natural pregnancy, doctors and books inform you to quit certain habits such as smoking and to replace alcohol with water to help you prevent birth defects. Similarly, with spiritual pregnancy, there are precautions.

I am here to tell you to stop certain habits, or your greatness will have birth defects. Stop internalizing negativity, laziness, doubt, bad company, and much more. Remember this pregnancy is a process and more importantly, it is a marathon-not a sprint. Take your time, relax, and keep your mind set on birthing a healthy "greatness."

I know that this type of conception is new for you and that it will be challenging. Remember it starts with just a little faith, the size of a mustard seed. Although that faith is small you can always exercise your faith. Being healthy does not mean you have to be big and strong. Nevertheless, you do want exercise because exercising your faith will increase the circulation of the blood between you, your greatness, and Jesus. For the human body, exercising helps improves your energy level and helps you to feel emotionally well. There is no difference when it comes to spiritual pregnancy. Remember take care of your body because that is the home of your greatness. Support your health and help the new life that is growing on the inside of you. At this point, I hope that you understand the importance of preparing your body for pregnancy and childbirth or should I say the birth of greatness. You must pay attention to your overall health and how it contributes to your mind, body, and soul.

CHAPTER 2

2

PRENATAL PRAYER

When it comes to a natural pregnancy, doctors would refer you take a multivitamin supplement to ensure that your body has the nutrients that it needs. Your current condition requires that you follow a specific regimen for months to come; this protects the overall health of you and your child. However, spiritual pregnancy does not require any supplements or prenatal vitamins. But it does require "prenatal prayer." Although a healthy pregnancy diet can help to keep you well nourished, sometimes you need a little extra help.

During pregnancy, your body needs even more prayer than

when you are not pregnant. And although you are about to embark on a journey of eating healthy and implementing a stricter diet, I still suggest that you consider using "prenatal prayer." Now for natural pregnancy, there are a wide range of over-the-counter prenatal vitamins available to women. To be honest there are a wide range of "prenatal prayers" available as well, even if you are a man or a woman. When it comes to a natural pregnancy, it is recommended that you should ask your healthcare provider to recommend which vitamins you should take.

Now I believe that my job here on earth is to be a G.P.S., Gods Personal Servant. It took a lot of training, but my job is to Guide. People to. Salvation. So, look at this part of the book as if you are at the counter in the pharmacy. As His servant I suggest that you take these five types of "prenatal prayers." Through conception there are going to be occasions when things seem like they are not working in your favor. And you will go back to the page in this book where I said, "Push Until Something Happens;" at times you will see no tangible or life changing events. However, when life is pushing at you and you are truly pushing back, you will be pushed to your knees. This situation will make you Pray Until Something Happens. That *something* in many cases is your ticket to peace. Trust me, when you pray until peace manifest into your life then no matter the circumstance or situation, everything is going to be alright. The Bible says in Isaiah 54:17 (KJV),

"No weapon formed against me shall prosper..." It just requires a little P.U.S.H.

Now before we move on let's make something clear; God is your Doctor, but as His servant I recommend five types of "prenatal prayers" that will help not only your health but will also help insure the best possible start in life for your greatness.

FIVE PRENATAL PRAYERS

Before I begin, first allow me to define what prayer is. There is a lot of deep meaning to prayer that you can search or read about. However, to define prayer is quite simple in my mind. **Prayer**: *It is how you have direct communication with God.*

Prayer allows you to talk to God; it is a free phone service with unlimited minutes and great service. No matter where you are in the world you can always reach God through prayer. While being spiritually pregnant, I do recommend that you use what I like to call "prenatal prayers." In particular, I believe that you should use these five types of prenatal prayers. I want preference that you do not have to do these in any particular order.

- **Communion Prayer** (All day, all the time)

Probably to your surprise I am not referring to the service where Christian's worship as bread and wine are consecrated and shared. What I am referring to is the sharing or exchange of intimate thoughts and feelings on a spiritual level with God. One of my favorite teachers, authors, and pastors of all time, Rick Warren said, "You will never develop a close relationship with Jesus by just attending church once a week or even by just having a daily quiet time. A relationship with God is built by sharing *all* your life experiences with him." God is the greatest listener of all time. He created His son Jesus just to impregnate you. He knows problems will occur throughout this process of birthing greatness. That is why it is important to take advantage of your direct line of communication to God and one of those ways is **Communion** prayer. You must get in the habit of praying to no end. Meaning, in 1 Thessalonians 5:17-18 (NIV), "pray continually, give thanks in all circumstances; for this is God's will for you <u>in Christ Jesus</u>." I know carrying greatness is tough, but I need you to **Pray Until Something Happens**. Do not stop praying. Converse with God while you ride in the car, taking a shower, or cleaning the house. Invite God in all day and all the time.

"But how do I pray", you ask?

Prayer is just a conversation between you and God. I know what you are thinking. Trust me, God does not want you to change who you are. He wants you to continue to be you; He desires to have a relationship with you. I remember meeting and talking to my fiancés mother on the phone for the first time. I was trying hard to impress her, but it did not work. I can honestly say that I did not win an Oscar for that horrific performance. So, when it was time for me to meet her in person for the first time, I knew things had to be different. I expected to impress her, but as you suspect, it did not work. But what did happen is that she sat me down and said to me, "Son, be true to yourself, because that is why my daughter fell in love with you." One of God's desires is for you to simply be yourself, because that is why His son Jesus fell in love with you. To this day, I keep in touch with my fiancé's mom as well my mother every day. I dare you to keep in communication with your spiritual daddy and see what happens. **Communion Prayer.**

- **Supplication Prayer** (Lifting up your needs)

Supplication (also known as petitioning) is a form of **prayer**, wherein one party, which is you, humbly or earnestly asks another party, whom is God, to provide something. The Bible says in Philippians 4:6-7 (NIV), "Do not be anxious about anything, but in every situation, by **prayer** and **petition**, with thanksgiving, present your requests to God. And the peace of God, which transcends all understanding, will guard your hearts and your minds in Christ Jesus." Now before you continue, I really want you to become accustomed to **Communion Prayer;** since it is just having a conversation with God, it helps with your communication with your heavenly father. Communication is key to any relationship especially when a child is involved, or in your case, when greatness is involved. Because when two people come together to create a child, you get to know your partner a little bit better.

Sometimes you find out things about your partner that makes your heart melt, but on the other hand, you may find out things that make your headache. When it came to my relationship with Jesus, I was nervous that He would not be in my life while I was on this journey of birthing greatness; oh, how naïve was I. However, through the process I felt alone, and at times you will probably feel alone, but I learned, and I want you to realize that God is omnipresent. Meaning God is present everywhere at the same time and He sees and knows what you are going through. He is just waiting for you to lift your needs up to Him. This is called, **Supplication Prayer**. Remember, life and death are in the power of your tongue. And one of ways you can speak life is by communicating what you need through prayer. The revelation I had through my pregnancy is that God allowed me to go through things because He wanted to see me in a certain position.

God does not care about titles. He does not care whether you are a CEO, or you carry the title as Manager in retail. He cares about position. He wants to know if He is the center and priority point of your life. Habakkuk 2 (AKJ) says, "I will stand upon my watch, and set me upon the tower, and will watch to see what he will say unto me, and what I shall answer when I am reproved." In this verse, there was a test; in your life there is a test and God's test is given in order to get you into position. That position is on your knees in prayer so that you can hear from God. He responded in Habakkuk 2:2-3 saying, "And the Lord answered me, and said, write the vision, and make it plain..." He continued in verse 3 by saying, "For the vision is yet for an appointed time, but at the end it shall speak, and not lie..."

The answers to your problems are in your greatness. Pregnancy is a process, and it will take some time for you to birth greatness. Indeed, the appointed time will come when God believes that you are ready to birth greatness. He says that your greatness "shall speak and shall not lie," but you must be in position, **Supplication Prayer**.

- **Spiritual Warfare**

Now I must warn you that anytime you are in a high or pivotal position, there is someone sitting close or afar hating and trying to see how he or she can knock you off of your position. Most of the time we help those people, including Satan, knock us off our position because we believe we are not worthy of God's blessing. Sometimes we cannot fathom why Jesus wants a relationship with us. This leads to feelings of doubt and inadequacy; we ultimately believe that we cannot carry and birth greatness. Remember that God gives the tough battles to strong soldiers and you are a strong solider. One of my favorite Gospel Artists is Kirk Franklin and he has a song entitled "More Than I Can Bear."

The song simply implies that God does not allow situations to transpire in your life that we cannot handle. When situations occur in your life, that is just a sign that it is war time. Anytime a solider goes into battle he must be equipped with armor. Through this spiritual pregnancy you will need to be equipped with the best armor that no amount of money can buy and that is the Armor of God. Ephesians 6:13 (NIV) says, "Therefore put on the full armor of God, so that when the day of evil comes, you may be able to stand your ground, and after you have done everything, to stand." When you are in position, use the

Supplication Prayer so that you are prepared to be on not only defense but as well as offense. The devil never takes a break on attacking you so do not take a break from fighting back.

Through this process you will encounter **Spiritual Warfare**, but you must fight back because your greatness depends on it. The great news is, as long as you are equipped, you are one step ahead of Satan. The devil must disarm you to defeat you. Stay equipped! However, for some of us we allow doubt to creep in which takes us back three steps. You cannot allow our negative thoughts to dictate your actions.

One of the devil's goals is for us to pay attention to the problem, not the promise. God promised us in Leviticus 20:24, "But I said to you, "You will possess their land; I will give it to you as an inheritance, a land flowing with milk and honey." I am the LORD your God, who has set you apart from the nations." Remember that all are given greatness, but much is required to access it. You are a rare breed. Not everyone is willing to do what it takes to birth greatness. That is why God promised you Milk and Honey, which symbolizes riches. That is why you will encounter and experience at some point in your journey **Spiritual Warfare** because Satan understands what is on the other side of your faithfulness and consistency and that is milk and honey.

The devil is determined to send his demons out to do these

three "D's"; Distract. Destroy. Devalue. Stay Equipped!

Ephesians 6:14-18 (NKJ) says, "Stand therefore, having girded your waist with truth, having put on the breastplate of righteousness, and having shod your feet with the preparation of the gospel of peace; above all, taking the shield of faith with which, you will be able to quench all the fiery darts of the wicked one. And take the helmet of salvation, and the sword of the Spirit, which is the word of God, praying always with all prayer and supplication in the Spirit ..." Allow me to help you understand what you are wearing while in your **Spiritual Warfare.**

In Ephesians 6:14 it says, "grid your waist with truth". This allows you to discern when the devil sends his demons or certain people in your life and tell you lies. But also arming your waist with the truth will allow you to discern what individuals that John 16:13 (NIV) speaks on. That scriptures says, "But when he, the Spirit of truth, comes, he will guide you into all the truth. He will not speak on his own; he will speak only what he hears, and he will tell you what is yet to come." This person sometimes come as a preacher, a prophetess or what you believe to be a random person with no title. While in **Spiritual Warfare** girding your waist with truth is just the beginning.

Ephesians 6:14-18 also mentions that having a breastplate of righteousness. In Roman times soldiers wore breastplate armor to protect themselves in battle. While spiritually pregnant you also need a breastplate for protection. Your body is a temple of the Holy spirit and we are called to take care, protect, and honor God's temple. When you are in position, people will try to come after you. For those who are spiritually pregnant such as yourself. The breastplate is the one piece of armor that guards one's heart. Let me make something clear I do not expect you to be walking around with a breastplate through your neighborhood. The breastplate of righteousness is something not seen, but provides spiritual strength, with an abundance of confidence, but more importantly, it is a holy lifestyle that every Christian must personally depict.

In order to deal with the battlefield that is going on in your head and in your life, you must face the **Spiritual Warfare** that you are in or will endure. I know it may come to you as a challenge which will affect your peace, but that is why you need to stay equipped. Also, in Ephesians 6:14-18, it mentions you "having shod your feet with the preparation of the gospel of peace." Have you heard of the story of the "Battle of Jericho?" If not, I am going to break down the power when you shod your feet with the preparation of the gospel of peace.

The "Battle of Jericho" can be found in Joshua 6. In this chapter, there were people behind this massive walled city that were in great fear for their lives and their country. Scouts from the Israelites crept behind the walls of the city of Jericho, hiding behind a house owned by a woman named Rehab; she was known as a prostitute. She helped the scouts hide from the king's soldiers; it is amazing the people that God uses. Again, God does not care about your title. God instructed Joshua to use an unorthodox strategy for the battle of Jericho. He told Joshua to have his army march around the city once a day for six days straight. While marching, the soldiers played their trumpets. My question to you is, if God asked you to do something that looked ridiculous to people, would you do it?

The instructions that God gave to Joshua were very thorough. Likewise, the instructions Joshua gave to the army of Israel and accompanying priests were extremely specific. For six days, they were to circle Jericho's walls one time without speaking. On the seventh day, they were to circle seven times, blow trumpets and shout. Although they were in the midst of a battle, they were walking with peace. Why? Because His peace surpasses all understanding. And on that seventh day the walls came tumbling down. When you shod your feet with the preparation of the gospel of peace, I promise you that God will direct your path.

However, it requires something and that something is called faith. That is what you are going to need throughout this spiritual pregnancy and after. That is why one piece of the

Armor of God is a "shield of faith". I hope you did not think that the breastplate of righteous was the only equipment that was going to protect you. In battle Romans use shields to protect them from attacks such as arrows being thrown. In **Spiritual Warfare** the devil is out to kill, steal and destroy. To protect yourself, the faith shield is required. That is why in Ephesians 6:16 (NIV), it states that "Above all, taking the shield of faith with which, you will be able to quench all the fiery darts of the wicked one."

Your body is a temple, and it is your job to protect the temple and the gift that God places in the temple. Again, the shield is not a physical piece of armor, but rather a spiritual one, and the only thing that will hold your shield together is your faith. It is a caveat to having faith; it requires a series of test. That test might come as situations and circumstances or it might come as and through a person. If you were never tested, then there would not be a need for you to exercise or even have faith. Faith is the things hoped for and the evidence of things not seen. Through my journey of spiritual pregnancy, the only valuable thing I had when the world threw me curve balls was faith. When relationships have rocky moments, most people give up. When Jesus told me to use faith, that proved my commitment to Him. It also showed God that I was willing to fall backwards because I trust that He will catch me. I dare you to take Jesus at His word when He says, "He will never leave you nor forsake you." That shows that you are holding up the shield of faith in the time of **Spiritual Warfare**.

I need you to understand that the devil is smart. The devil knows that it will be hard to defeat you when you activate your faith. That is why he will attack you mentally; the kryptonite to people's faith is their thoughts. That is why I believe that one of the most important defense equipment you should have is the "helmet of salvation." Helmets are designed to protect us from head damage. When the devil runs out of ideas for how or what to destroy, he turns to attack your head. In Roman times the helmet protected not only their heads, but also the eyes of the soldier, enabling him to maintain physical vision. When it comes to your spiritual pregnancy, your spiritual vision allows you to fix your eyes on the goal, which is birthing greatness. It also helps you to press forward without distraction or detours that your natural eyes would not be able to do. You need a clear mind, there is no space for doubt or negativity. The helmet of salvation will deliver you from harm, ruin, or loss. It will not prevent you from being hurt; remember that God will not put more on you than you can bare. So, do not be alarm when you get nicked up and brushed. God has your back; that is the definition of Salvation.

Salvation means being saved—receiving deliverance. You

are probably wondering how you receive salvation? Ironically, salvation is not something you work to receive. Instead, it is simply given to us, regardless of our flaws. No matter what walk of life you come from, whether you have had a troubled past or a smooth one, Jesus died for all of our sins. Nevertheless, no matter what happens, you have control over your thoughts. Your mind is the battleground of your life. Again, stay equipped!

However, you cannot go into battle with just defense equipment and protection, you need equipment to fight with. In Ecclesiastes 3:8 (KJV) it says, "A time to love, and a time to hate; a time for war, and a time for peace." God equipped you with the sword of the spirit, which is the word of God. A weapon is needed in **Spiritual Warfare** against the devil. Spiritual battles are not won by just playing defense; you must also hit Satan where it hurts. You must speak the word of God over all attacks. Do not be afraid to add a little fasting, prayer, praise, and worship. The revelation that I had during my spiritual pregnancy was that when it comes to **Spiritual Warfare** the only way, I could truly win each battle is by using the Sword of the Spirit. Then and only then was I able to defeat Satan. I want you to always enjoy defeating the devil, but you must promise to always watch and pray. Continue to be a watchman over your temple.

Through your spiritual pregnancy it is important that you count your many blessings that God has given you. Personally. prenatal prayer was an important part of my journey and helped me to overcome adversity; as a result of prayer, God brought me through. From the words of Pastor and Gospel artist Marvin Sapp, "I never would have made it." So, "I will bless the Lord at all times: his praise shall continually be in my mouth", Psalms 34 (KJV).

- **Prayers of Thanksgiving** (Count your Blessings)

Through my spiritual pregnancy there were many trials and tribulations, but I was reminded again and again how much thanking God always changed my outcome. Not only did it change my perspective, but it also changed my situation and gave me peace throughout my mess. I am here to tell you that **Prayers of Thanksgiving** will bring you through especially when you are feeling overwhelmed. The Bible says in Hebrews 13:15 (NIV), "Through Jesus, therefore, let us continually offer to God a sacrifice of praise—the fruit of lips that openly profess his name."

We must remember as we pray and communicate with God, it is so important that we also remember to always give thanks. Giving thanks in all circumstances, through the good and the bad is crucial. God wants to know that you are thankful for the small things to see if He can trust you with bigger blessings. But the big test that God gives us is to see if we will praise Him through the bad times. It is hard to thank God through the bad, but when I did not have anything to my name, no money for rent, no food, and no feelings of self-worth, I only had one thing left to do. Through my brokenness, the only thing that I could do was to give God thanks. Why? Through all of my mess, He somehow kept me. He protected me. Although I did not have any money for rent, no food, or transportation I still had breath in my body. So, I do not care what is going on in your life, if you still have breath in your body to praise God, do it. I dare you to give Him praise and watch how He will turn your situation around for your good. He made a way out of no way for me. I know that He can do the same for you.

- **Intercessory Prayer** (On the behalf of others)

The hardest vitamin to swallow or should I say the hardest prayer to swallow is, **Intercessory Prayer**. Now for some, they have no problem with this. However, for others it is difficult to pray on behalf of someone else when you are going through struggles yourself. It is difficult to pray for someone when you have been told that you are pregnant with greatness and you have neither a clue as to how to carry, nor a clue as to how to give birth to greatness. Prayer is the most potent arsenal that we have because God gave us the ability to have the power of life and death at the tip of our tongues.

The power of prayer is something that God invites us to use, not only for personal gain and transformation, but for the transformation of others as well. An *intercessor* is who you are when you partake in **Intercessory Prayer or the Prayer of intercession.** An intercessor is also someone who takes up a burden of another individual's life and tries to transform that situation through prayer. Intercessors or people interceding through prayer in my life, contributed greatly to my own success. God allowed them to feel that my spirit was being hindered. **Intercessory Prayer** encourages prayer in union with the mind of God which makes you powerful beyond measure. God loves when your heart goes out for other people. When you pray on another person's behalf because you realize that their greatness is not being realized, you will be blessed also. This book is a result of **Intercessory Prayer;** intercessors prayed for this moment. I pray that your life will change after reading this book. I challenge you to pray for someone in your prayer time because when praises go up, blessings come down.

HOW YOU FEELING?

Before we continue, I must ask how are you feeling so far? Are you jumping for joy of thought of being pregnant? Are you in shock still, or feeling a mixture of both? Listen, I know this maybe a bit overwhelming. The thought of being spiritually pregnant, especially if you are a man reading this can be me more than a bit overwhelming. Trust me I understand but do me a favor and take a breath. You got this! Let me continue to guide you through on how to carry and birth the great inside of you. Trust me when I say that this book was written and design not only to teach you but also to support you every step of the way to a healthy spiritual pregnancy.

WHAT SENSE DOES THAT MAKE

There is no turning back. There is no changing to the results; you are pregnant. No matter if you are scared out of this world or excited about being pregnant, now that we have the results in that you are pregnant your life is about to change, if it has not already. I know you are wondering what changes that are about to happen to your life and body. Well wonder no more I am about to inform you what to expect when expecting. When my nerves started to fade away, and the excitement of me being pregnant started to creep in, the unexpected started to happen. My body started to undergo changes. Now I understand when it comes to a natural pregnancy it is normal for a woman's body to undergo changes.

However, I could not quite understand how my body could change especially me being a man during a spiritual pregnancy. To be honest it never crossed my mind that my body could change. I found myself saying through this process, "What sense does that make?" The thought of being spiritually pregnant is hard to digest at times. You will find yourself asking yourself, "What sense does that make?" To be honest, after I came to the conclusion that I was pregnant, and it still did not make that much sense to me. My mother use to always remind me of Proverbs 3:5, "in all thy getting, get understanding." So, in prayer I talked to God and asked him for clarity, and He broke it down in such that was mind blowing. Sit back and read this.

SPIRITUAL SENSE

In my time spent with Jesus I found Him attractive, and I know the feeling was mutual. I know what you are thinking, how can I find Jesus sexually alluring? This might come as a surprise, but I am not talking about anything sexually appealing. When I say attractive, I am referring to how He was pleasing and appealing to my senses. Allow me to explain. We have five natural senses: hearing, smell, touch, sight, and taste. All of our senses help us navigate through life.

However, if we surrender our natural senses and if we accept that we cannot do this thing call life alone, then God will ignite our five spiritual senses. The types of senses do not change, but our senses do become repurposed. I believe that one of God's favorite senses is hearing and I believe that in the beginning of our relationship, He was frustrated with me. Why? Because I was on my knees calling out for help, but I never stayed in position long enough to **hear** the answer. One of the biggest problems with people, including myself, is that our faith is messed up because our hearing is messed up.

I used to think I had a faith problem, when in reality I had a hearing problem. The Bible says in Romans 10:17, "Faith comes by hearing." I used to think that the lines of communication with God were messed up, but instead it was my hearing all along. It is not that God does not speak, because He speaks all the time; in fact, God is talkative. However, it is hard for us to hear what He is saying because we are too distracted and impatient. Earlier I told you that I was addicted to social media, not because I liked posting about my own life. Oh no!

It was because I was too busy looking at other people's lives, wishing that I had what they had; I was distracted. My loving fiancé used to tell me that I was too busy trying to connect to people on social media instead of trying to connect to God so I could *hear* what He wanted me to do.

At that point in my life, I was trying to listen with my eyes and not my hears. Circumstances and situations that were occurring in my life were telling me that I was not going to succeed. And sometimes when we allow the volume of other things or other people to be louder than God's voice, it makes us hard of hearing. My biggest problem, since before conception, was that I allowed people to block my connection with God. For the longest I thought that I was on the block list of God's phone. That is one of the main reasons why you see people living their lives without ever being in the presence of or in the house of God; they are too busy allowing others to block their connection with God. Stop allowing people to disconnect your service.

Yet, there are some of you that are reading this book that do not have a hearing problem but a doing problem. The Bible says, "Faith without works is dead." When I finally got my act together or should I say, when I hit rock bottom and when nothing I did was successful, I started to listen. I decided to try that thing called faith out. I activated my belief system, but I did not activate my doing. You may have heard what God is going to do to and for your life but when are you going to play your part and do?

This brings me to your second sense, your **sight**. The reason why people do not put work to their faith is because they look at their future with their natural eyes instead of with their "vision" lenses; that sense is called *sight*. Faith is things hoped for and the evidence of things not seen. You must put in the work for the things you cannot see in order for your vision that God gave you to be revealed. Right now, some of you cannot see what God is going to do but when you activate your faith by using one of the senses God gave you, *hearing*. Then things will look much clearer. I know it sounds strange but allow me to explain and teach you how you need your hearing to help you see God's vision for your life.

In Mark 10:46-52 there was a blind man by the name of Bartimaeus sitting on the side of the rode begging in this city called Jericho. There were tons of people in the city of Jericho trying to see this rock star named Jesus. There were also tons of people passing this blind beggar, but offering him no assistance, nor money nor food. While he was sitting there, a loud outburst alerted the people that Jesus was leaving the city. The blind man quickly shouted, "Jesus, have mercy on me!" The blind man did not know that he was at the right position, at the end of the city where Jesus was planning to exit.

Many people told him to be quiet, to shut up, but that made the blind man shout louder. Sometimes there are going to be people in your life that will try to block your communication with God because they do not want you to be blessed. Again, the blind man did not know that he was in the perfect position. Yet, he had faith as small as a mustard seed that Jesus would notice him and help. All of a sudden Jesus stopped and said, "Call him."

I learned quickly during my conception that God will make your enemies your footstool. Jesus proceeded to order his disciples to "get" the blind man. They ordered the blind man to stand on his feet and to go to Jesus. By surprise, he stood on his feet and started walking by faith and not by his physical sight. Jesus then asked, "What do you want me to do for you?" The blind man did not know that *hearing* the name Jesus would lead him to a blessing. The blind man said, "I want to see." Jesus replied, "Go." Immediately he began to use his vision lenses.

When he used a little faith and took a few steps forward

Jesus said,

"Your faith has healed you." Immediately after he received his *sight,* he followed Jesus along the road to assist Jesus. The revelation I want you to get out of this story is that God is waiting on you to get in position, to have faith, to communicate with him, but more importantly to *hear* Him when He gives you instructions, because when you do, your third sense has no choice but to come forth. That sense is **taste.**

The Bible says in Psalms 34 verse 8, "Taste and see that the Lord is good…" I learned this simple revelation when I was pregnant. Before we taste anything, we must eat something, right? Before eating something, we must "see" the food, right? And if you are blind physically or spiritually, we must have faith in what we *hear,* and in what we taste; we must know that the food that we are about to consume is good. However, how do we "taste and see" that the Lord is good?

First, for full disclosure, I do not mean taking a bite out of God physically. When you taste something, you are getting a sample of something to see if you like it or not. Everyone who finds out that they are pregnant with greatness starts off spiritually blind. This is a test to see if you are going to *hear* God when He tells you about your greatness. It is also a test to see *what* He is going to say or for some of you, *what* He has already said. It will sound so good that you are going to think that it is too good to be true. This sets you up for the second step of this test which is to see if you are going to activate your faith. What you *heard* can only be seen through your "vision lenses". And when God is pleased with your diligence in developing a true relationship with Jesus, He will start to sprinkle blessings throughout your life.

The purpose of this is so that you can taste and see that the Lord is good. When God activates your spiritual taste buds, He trusts that you will have the ability to discern what is of good, *taste.* Jesus' plan was not to impregnate you and leave. He desires a personal relationship with you. God wants to know that you are hungry to get to know Him better and to love Him more. God gave you a taste and you see that He is good. I dare you to seek more of Him and when you do, I promise that you will find out how great He really is.

Through this process I was thinking. I do not know about you, but I find it fascinating how God created the human body. Through my experiences I concluded that He created our natural senses to navigate us through life, but He created our spiritual senses as tracking device to let us know how to navigate back to God's loving arms. The wonderful thing about our senses is that they all work together.

However, there are levels to each of our senses. As we just discussed you have to *hear* from God and your hearing activates your "vision lenses", which is your *sight*. Then your faith starts to get tested differently which leads to your *taste*. But one sense that tends to get overlooked in the natural as well as in the spiritual, is your sense of smell. We heard of someone being hard of hearing and blind.

However, have you ever heard of someone being "hard of smelling?" In most cases we never hear someone lacking the ability to smell. Unfortunately, there is someone in the world that lacks this particular natural sense, which is smell. The sense of smell is a vital key to our human body. The sense of smell is closely linked with memory more so than any of our other senses. The things we smell go straight to this place in our brain known as the olfactory bulb; let's just call it our brain smell center. So, without hesitation the smell of something can immediately trigger a detailed memory. Just like our natural senses God gave us the spiritual sense of smell for a reason. That reason is for us to only be able to smell a certain *scent*. Allow me to explain.

According to "The Message Bible", which breaks down the King James Version to a simple read, 2 Corinthians 2:14-16 informs us that God lead a group of His people from place to place in one everlasting victory parade. Through His people, He brings knowledge of Christ. In verse 14 it says "Everywhere we go, people breath in the exquisite fragrance. Because of Christ, we give off a sweet scent rising to God, which is recognized by those on the way of salvation."

Salvation means the preservation or deliverance from harm, ruin, or loss. It also means the deliverance from sin. The reason for God giving His people, who are pregnant with greatness, a special scent is because sometimes people, believers and non-believers struggle to *hear* from Him. Sometimes they cannot see with their vision lenses what God is trying to do in their lives, *sight.* This hinders them to *taste* their blessing because they lack hearing and are too blind to see what God is trying to do. So, by God giving you a *scent,* you become what The Message Bible describes as an exquisite walking fragrance. This scent is designed to diffuse His presence around us, and to awaken the spiritual senses of others. Why? Because if your communication with God is prone to static, then God will get your attention through your sense of smell. God knows that your smell will trigger your memory.

The scent of the favor of God will remind you who brought you out of those dark places. It will remind you that without God, you would not have gotten through those situations and circumstances that transpired in your life. God allowed situations and circumstances to occur in your life for a reason. He brought you out of your dark places as evidence that He is real, but more importantly, as evidence that He loves you, that

He will never leave you, nor forsake you. One of the meanings of *scent* is, a trail of evidence, or other signs assisting someone in a search or investigation. That someone is *you.* God gave you the sense of smell so that you can search Him.

He knew that some of you would struggle to hear his voice. He knew that some of you would struggle to see what He has planned for your life. Additionally, He knew that some of you would struggle with both seeing and hearing which would hinder your taste buds. So, God left a scent so that you could always find yourself returning to Him. You are coming out of those situations and circumstances of your past is your trail of evidence that will lead you to God. When you truly love Jesus, you will know that you need Him to help you birth greatness; you will find yourself searching for Him, with His *scent* leading the way I am so fascinated at how God took His time when creating us.

His thought process while He was creating us must have been so interesting. Just imagine, He thought of our ears so that we can *hear* Him. He considered providing us with our eyes so that we can have *sight,* so that we can see what He has done in our lives and what He is going to do for our lives. I am grateful that He has given us a *taste* of His favor; that is more than I can ask for. I am even fascinated by Him giving us the sense of *smell.* He knew that we would someday have the desire to find

His love. But there is one last sense that we have not discussed and that is the sense of *touch*.

When God took His time to construct every part of us, He made sure that every part of us had a purpose. When He created our eyes, He created them to see. When He created our feet, He created them so we can walk. When He created our hands, He created them to touch. When God gifted us the ability to touch, it came with what I like to call a few natural powers. One of those powers is that when we decide to touch something, we will have the ability to feel. For some people, knowing that someone is pregnant, but more importantly seeing someone who is pregnant brings a level of excitement.

It does not matter if that woman is one month pregnant or nine months pregnant, many people feel as if it is their duty to rub or touch the woman's stomach. One of the ways to access that excitement is through touch. Now if you are anything like how I used to be, then you do not like being touched and I get it. Perhaps people have germs and diseases, and you do not want any parts of that. In fact, germs and diseases are the last thing that you want your unborn child, or in your case, your developing greatness to be exposed to. So, in retrospect you do not touch people because you want to give them the same kindness and courtesy that you desire, and that is to not be touched.

Over time, I have learned that touch is not my love language. When I was carrying greatness, Jesus always had His hands on me, and I never knew why. To be honest, at times I did not like it. I felt conflicted, because through my mess, He still touched me, and it made me feel uncomfortable. He knew that I had something inside of me that the

world needed to see, and more importantly that I needed to birth.

However, I remained with one foot in and one foot out in my relationship with Jesus. That was one of the reasons why there was no one on one intimacy time with Jesus. It is hard to touch someone when you are doing wrong or with whom you have trust issues with. It was hard for me to believe that something was great on the inside of me. It is probably safe to say, that just like me, you have had your doubts about there being something great on the inside of you, but I am here to tell you to believe the truth. Do not talk yourself out of the greatness that is on the inside of you. Yet, in order for you to birth something great, you have to touch Jesus. Remember I do not like being touched so I do not like touching people. However, the Bible says, "if two shall touch and agree on about anything you ask for than it shall be done." Your sense of touch was repurposed for a dual purpose.

If you have not realized it yet, Jesus' love language is touch.

He not only likes touching but He loves being touched. To your surprise, Him liking to touch and the enjoyment He gets of being touched has nothing to do with Him. The reason that He enjoys the spiritual sense of touch is because He put a power in touch. In Luke 8:40-59, He displays the power of touch. In the verses 40-48, Jesus was in a country by the name of Gerasene. Jesus being the rock star that He is, the crowd welcomed Him, for they were all waiting for Him.

While people were welcoming Jesus, there was a man by the name of Jairus, who was a ruler of the synagogue. And this man knew that Jesus did not care about titles; He cared about position. Quickly this man falls to Jesus feet, begging for Jesus to come to his house because his one and only child was dying at the age of twelve years old. Because of that man's position, Jesus began walking to the man's home. As He was walking, a woman who had a discharge of blood for twelve years and who had been told that she could not be healed, approached him. She had *heard* that Jesus was in town and when she *had seen* Him walking, she *touched* the fringe of his garment, and immediately her discharge of blood stopped.

This is why Jesus' love language is touch because it has power when you touch and agree with Him. In verse 46, He was trying to find out who touched Him because He felt a power shift. The lady that touched Jesus falls down before Him and declared in front of everyone that she had touched him, and how she had been immediately healed. In verse 48, Jesus said to her, "Daughter, your faith has made you well; go in peace." I told you earlier that it starts and ends with faith. Sometimes you will not understand the outcome of you touching and agreeing with God, but you have to lean on your faith. Jesus loves being touched because it is a power shift when you touch and agree with Him.

CHAPTER 3

3

EXHAUSTED!?

Again, I ask, how do you feel now that you are actually pregnant? Does exhaustion sum it up for you? Again, I know that it may seem overwhelming to take in. What you are learning and experiencing so far is everything that people who are carrying greatness experience in a short period of time. I do not know about you but everything leading up to this moment of conception has been exhausting. Trying to come to grips with the fact that I, a man was pregnant, drained so much of my energy.

Not only was I battling this unorthodox concept, but I was also stressing about life. When I initially doubted my pregnancy results, I started worrying about my diet, while battling with stress about everything that comes along with being spiritually pregnant. Oh, did I forget to mention that while all of this was going on, I was struggling to pray myself through this process. All of this plus more wore me out during the first four weeks or so of my spiritual pregnancy. Listen, I was EXHAUSTED! However, I had to remind myself and I want you to continue to remind yourself although all are given greatness, much is required to access it. You have to go through, to get to where you are trying to go. In addition to that, I had to remember that "God does not put more on us than we can bare."

I do not know about you, but I was one of those who was not trying to get pregnant, so when the results came in, I was petrified. I was so scared that it started to take a toll on me mentally, physically, emotionally, and especially spiritually. After a while I realized that Jesus impregnated me for a reason. It took me some time, but I learned that what is inside of me is not for me, it is for the world. But that did not stop me from being exhausted.

TIRED OF BEING TIRED

Before and sometimes during this journey of carrying and birthing greatness, I was living a life that was not designed for me. Not only was I trying to be someone that I was not, but I was also doing wrong when I knew what was right. I can honestly say that I was a mess. I realize that not being myself and living a false life was tiring and draining. But do you want to know something? Although that lifestyle was tiring, I was more tired of myself. I was tired of not living up to my potential. I was tired of not going anywhere in life while I was watching people pass me by.

I was tired of not going after my passion. I was sick and tired of myself not unwrapping my God given gift. Keeping my dreams captive and not living them out was exhausting. I was so tired of seeing people that appeared to be living their dreams out on social media while I was still trying to find the key to unlock mine. I was so tired. But the most sickening feeling was disappointing my parents. Although they never said they was disappointed in me, I felt that not birthing the best of me was disrespectful to them. This led me to realize that I was just tired of being tired.

As expected, carrying and birthing greatness took a toll on me mentally, physically, emotionally, and spiritually. Sadly, this process made me not want to do anything and sometimes made me want to give up. I thought that I was tired before, but this pregnancy wore me out. I promise you that you have not experienced being tired until you are pregnant. Do not believe me; just ask a mother. Essentially, when you are a mother you are a mobile home for your child. You must carry around a child that is growing every day on the inside of you.

Well, it is no different when you are spiritually pregnant. Carrying around greatness is draining and heavy, not only for your body but for your heart and mind. So, do not be surprised if you feel completely depleted. It is normal to feel *fatigue;* that is one of the symptoms that you will experience throughout this process, especially in the first trimester. Your mind, body and soul are dealing with an increase of anointing. When carrying this gift, your assignment is to birth it.

Inevitably, this can leave you feeling more tired than usual.

For a natural pregnancy it is normal to feel this lack of energy throughout the duration of your pregnancy and unfortunately, there is no difference when it comes to a spiritual pregnancy. The reasons why most of us experience fatigue during this time is because we have allowed the devil to come into our minds. Remember, one of Satan's goals is to delay you. When people are delayed, one of the reasons may be because they were tired. During your journey of being spiritually pregnant, this tiredness might be a sign of you having low blood pressure. I know that it may come to you as a shock, but yes, you can experience low blood pressure while being spiritually pregnant. Naturally speaking, there are a wide range of reasons why your blood pressure may be low during pregnancy. However, there are three things that the devil tries to attack which causes you to experience low blood pressure.

Heart Problems:

Satan loves when he can come into your life and cause you to have heart problems. The Bible says in Proverbs: 4:23, "Above all else, guard your heart, for everything you do flows from it." Satan knows that if he attacks your heart, he just interrupted the blood flow between you and Jesus. Without blood flowing, your greatness suffers. The devil knows the importance of your blood pressure lining up with God and his power. Satan's job is to steal, kill, and destroy. Do not do the devil's work for him. Stay prayed up. Your greatness has high value. The Bible says in Matthew 6:21, "For where your treasure is, your heart will be also."

Dehydration:

Dehydration can have a significant impact on blood pressure. That is why the devil tries to convince you that you do not need to thirst for Jesus anymore. Us millennials use a term called "thirsty." "Thirsty" means overly joyous about or overly anxious for something or someone. In relationships this is considered love to some people. Spiritually speaking to be thirsty for God is indicating that He is the root of our being. In other words when we thirst for God, we imply that He is more important than the water we drink. Low blood pressure indicates that we can be dehydrated. God said in John 4:14, "Whoever drinks the water I give them he will never thirst. Indeed, the water I give them will become in them a spring of water welling up to eternal life." The devil tries to convince us to get comfortable. Comfortability is an indicator that something is wrong spiritually. Comfortability creates dehydration. We should never be dehydrated. Matthew 5:6, "Blessed are those who hunger and thirst for righteousness, for they will be filled."

Infection:

This may be a shock but when you are spiritually pregnant, the number one thing that causes low blood pressure is an infection. There are many infections that you can get while you are naturally or spiritually pregnant. However, spiritually speaking this infection is what I like to call confused motivation. Before and while I was spiritually pregnant, I was confused. I had the desire to grow and succeed, but sometimes it got mixed in with negative thoughts or lesser motivation.

A few of my motivations to birth greatness was so that my mother could live in her dream house, be proud of her son, and no more worries. Another motivation I have too birth greatness is so that I can turn my fiancé into my wife, then into the mother of our future children, while giving her the option to work or not. Last but not least, my motivation for birthing greatness is just making God proud that He was able to trust me with greatness.

However, sometimes I got off track. I started getting infected with the thoughts including the wish to be loved by people, wishing to be special in people's eyes; when I felt I was not accomplishing that I started to feel like a failure. I also started to focus more on the money that comes with success. None of these motivations were what I should have been thinking. But I allowed Satan to come into my mind and interrupt my focus. I allowed him to throw me off from my true motivation of birthing greatness. I want you to write down your motivation for birthing your greatness and continue to remind yourself of the importance of why you need to birth your greatness. To help you avoid spiritual heart problems, dehydration, and infections; thank God continually, stay close to Jesus and do not stop being intimate with Him. And always remember that you have the victory. You have got this!

I'M SICK OF THIS

I know I said you got this, and I genuinely believe you do have this. But I can also completely understand if you are sick of this pregnancy already. Trust me, I know how you feel. It is the feeling as if you are standing at the bottom of what I like to call, "Mount Expectation." And as you are standing there at the bottom, you can see how virtually impossible it seems to reach the top of those people-set expectations. I know how it feels to wake up in the morning and feel like you should not even bother trying to birth greatness because of so many things that you must go through.

I understand that isolation feels weird. You want to hang out with your friends and family and to do the things you all used to do, but this spiritual pregnancy is telling you to give them a rain check. I know that you are sick of this. I was sick of this. During this time period, a few pregnancy symptoms will appear. Through this spiritual pregnancy you might feel mood swings, morning sickness and fatigue. Spiritual pregnancy symptoms are signs to let your body and your entire life know that greatness is upon you.

What you are experiencing is what some people go through in their natural pregnancy and that is, *morning sickness or nausea.* Some go through morning sickness and some do not. The same thing goes for spiritual pregnancy; some go through the things that you may have been going through in the beginning of your pregnancy and some may have gone through less or even more. Spiritually speaking, queasiness may strike you at any time, not just in the morning.

Depending on what stage of your spiritual pregnancy you are in or in other words depending on God's timing, you may feel mildly nauseated, or you may vomit. Do not be alarm. There is nothing wrong; in fact, other individuals who are in quest of birthing greatness will go through some level of *morning sickness.* Naturally speaking, approximately eighty five percent of women go through morning sickness during their pregnancies. Depending on how you take this, you may regard the following as bad news; one hundred percent of people that are spiritually pregnant go through *morning sickness* or what I like to call, "I am sick of this." Now some of you may not think that this stage is bad news and trust me, I understand. However, morning sickness is just God doing a daily cleaning. He is just getting the bad out of you so the good have room to live on the inside of you.

When it comes to a natural pregnancy *morning sickness* or *nausea*: the sight of food, the thought of food or even the smell of food will sometimes make you want to vomit. Spiritually speaking though, when you are not smelling with the right sense that we spoke on earlier or when you are allowing someone, or something to distort your sight and are even allowing negative thoughts to creep in, then it will cause you to feel nauseous or vomit. You are probably wondering if it is all worth birthing greatness? The answer is yes. I do not know about you but many of times I have asked myself and God, "Why do these things have to happen to me in order to birth greatness?" The answer simple, but mind blowing. He said to me, "Why not you?" From that moment I woke up every day ready or at least I thought I was ready for the things that come along with my personal journey to birth greatness. I want to inform you that the things you will and are going through including nausea are normal. Trust the process and what you are experiencing shall pass.

MOOD SWINGS

Other symptoms you may have noticed and experienced while being spiritually pregnant include *mood swings*. I was and to be honest sometimes I still experience moodiness. I am an emotional wreck at times. I expressed earlier in the book that sometimes I will be on Social Media, looking at other people's lives or dreams that appear to be fully living their best life. They seemed to be using their gifts while I was still sitting at home, trying to figure out how to unwrap mine. I know that the Bible says that my gift will make room for me.

Yet, often it seemed as if my gift appeared to be stuck in a box. I was so emotional, feeling as though this stagnant phase was all God's fault, that he did not care about me, or care about fixing my problems. I found myself being so frustrated with God at times because I believed that He gave me a passion without giving me instructions on how to ignite it. During my period of struggle, it seemed as if it was. virtually impossible to unwrap my gift. In my own arrogance, I imagined that although God created doors, He forgot to open them for me.

When I tell you that it seems like I found myself crying more than smiling, that is an understatement. During the first and third trimester your emotions will be wildly all over the place. Spiritually speaking, they are wild because you are experience something new in the beginning that you did not know was possible to begin with. Towards the end, which is in your third trimester, you are moody because you are excited and anxious that all of the hell you have been going through is now about to pay off and you want and need everything to be perfect.

So, no you are not crazy for your having wild emotions. At times I know that I had experienced a phase of what I like to call dramatic mood swings. I believe women experience this phase in natural pregnancy as well. For me, it was moments when looking at the clouds, certain stories, or even certain songs made me cry. I believe most of us have gone through this in life where we hear certain songs that make us *boo-hoo.* I want to tell you a quick story; my fiancé knew that I was spiritually pregnant, so she knew my emotions were all over the place.

However, she never seen me cry before until after a peaceful conversation that we had about the wedding planning. All of a sudden, a burst of tears streamed down my face. She had a look of confusing all over her face, she did not know why I started to cry. However, because she loved me, she attempted to calm me down, but I grew even more hysterical and then I randomly stopped; *do not judge me.* But can you say DRAMATIC? My point is that throughout this spiritual pregnancy, mood swings are common. Do not stop the tears.

Fellas, it is ok for you to get emotional and cry; it is part of the process.

Now on a serious note. Most of my mood swings stem from a weak foundation. I continue to allow the devil to enter my floor plan and I allow him to damage my foundation. I am not a construction worker, but I do know that a building structure will not survive on a bad foundation. This does not apply to the natural but to the spiritual. When you are tossed, driven and or confused by your emotions, you are what I like to call "a salve" to your moods or emotions. I need you to know that you are the master of your moods; do not allow the devil to come in your mind and rearrange your emotions. Take control of your emotions.

The Bible says that in 1 Peter 1:13, "Therefore grind up the loins of your mind, be sober, and rest your hope fully upon the grace that is to be brought to you at the revelation of <u>Jesus Christ</u>." Moods are very closely connected to our thoughts. When we feel bad, we think bad. When we say we feel sad, we think sad thoughts. Closely examine your moods, then shortly after, examine your thoughts. So, I ask, what are you feeling? What are you saying to yourself? What are you thinking about? Do they contribute to birthing your greatness? Do they line up with the Word of God?

While the spiritual pregnancy is developing, you must learn

how to walk with Jesus, and how to control your mood swings. Moodiness weighs you down. Lose the weight of moodiness which will cause you to look a bit overweight. Remember that a healthy body is a healthy home for your greatness. Now we have all had bad emotions.

Emotions are used as gauges, not guides. When we allow our emotions to guide us, they direct us on where to go and what to do. For example, when our emotions tell us that we are angry, then the average person reacts to a situation in the wrong way which may cause permanent outcomes for a temporary problem. I learned that wildly and uncontrollable moods that are not tamed can become an unnecessary and a sinful weight for us. When we allow that to happen, our moods damage our identity, our belief and alignment with God. It is time for you to take control of you.

I'M SO PROUD OF YOU

I am proud of you for sticking around and continuing to read. I pray that you are being fulfilled with an abundance of information. As you continue with the process of carrying greatness you soon see a baby bump. Spiritually speaking it is called a spiritual pregnancy bump. I am excited and cannot wait to see your spiritual pregnancy bump! And yes, even though you are spiritually pregnant you can still physically "show."

That is why everybody notices when you are doing well or when you are down and out. Spiritual pregnancy shows in the face and body as a whole. We will talk more about "showing" a little later in the book. Nevertheless, even though you are still in the early stages of your spiritual pregnancy, there are tremendous changes taking action inside of your body and inside of your life. By the way, not am I proud but I am thankful that you are still reading this book. I am even more proud that you are taking your life seriously and are trying to learn how to birth the greatness that is on the inside of you. I just had to take some time to tell you that I am so proud of you!

Now that we have taken a step further in this spiritual pregnancy process, I must inform you of something in case you have not noticed. You and your greatness are developing new features. During this stage of a natural pregnancy, the six-week time period is an important milestone. Inside of a women's body there is a such thing called a neural tube. That tube begins to close over what will become the baby's spinal cord. Spiritually speaking there is not much difference.

During this stage, your greatness will start to develop a backbone and spinal cord, which will strength your backbone and spinal cord. You will start to believe that no weapon formed against you nor your greatness shall prosper. At this particular stage of my spiritual pregnancy, I started feeling a bit overly confident. I imagined myself as a superhero in a movie and although villains (the devil) attacked me,

which made it seemed as if I was close to being defeated, I remembered that I have a weapon that no person or devil can stop. That the undefeated weapon is JESUS.

This stage of your life is important. Situations, people, and circumstances will come into your life to try to defeat you, but I need you to say, "It shall not prosper!" Now I need you to say it with conviction, out loud, and with passion, "IT SHALL NOT PROSPER!" You and your greatness are starting to develop, and the devil is jealous; he will do anything to try to kill, steal, or destroy you and your greatness.

THE ATTACK

During your spiritual pregnancy, your body will feel tender or achy, no different than a natural pregnancy. The reason for these pains is because of the increase of blood flow between your greatness, you, and God. It is normal that the devil will attack the thing which is developing; and you will feel discomfort. Naturally speaking the reason for tenderness or aches is normal because a women's body is preparing for breastfeeding.

It is recommended that women wear a supportive bra which can help with the extra weight. Well in your case; male or female you want to gather people around who support you. A bra supports a women's back and chest. Your support system will support your back and your chest, in other words your heart. This journey may be something that you can only experience alone, but not something you have to go through alone. I knew I was on to something great.

While I was getting attacked, I started to experience constipation. I knew that something great was developing on the inside which I desperately needed to get out. I know that you are aware that you have something great on the inside of you as well. You are itching to get it out and it is causing you daily soreness. However, at this moment it is not the time for you to release it. I know that you are feeling pain and I know that you want this to be over.

The Bible says is in Ecclesiastes 3:1-8, "There is a time for everything, and a season for every activity under the heavens: A time to be born and a time to die, a time to plant and a time to uproot, a time to kill and a time to heal, a time to tear down and a time to build, a time to weep and a time to laugh, a time to mourn and a time to dance, a time to scatter stones and a time to gather them, a time to embrace and a time to refrain from embracing, a time to search and a time to give up, a time to keep, and a time to throw away, a time to tear and a time to mend, a time to be silent and a time to speak, a time to love, and a time to hate, a time for war and a time for peace.

Right now, this is your season. Right now, this is your time to plant the seed of greatness and soon it will be time for you to uproot. Right now, it is the time to carry your greatness and then it will be a time to birth your greatness. You must allow your greatness to develop. In natural pregnancy, this is the early stage when the baby's nose, mouth, ears, and lungs are just starting to take shape.

Spiritually speaking, your greatness is taking shape and it is developing lungs so it can take its first breath. But in order for that to happen, your spiritual development on earth must take place. I know that it is a lot to take in but take a deep breath; you have got this. It is early, but this a marathon- not a race. Natural pregnancy takes 9 months, however spiritual pregnancy is on God's timing. For some it takes years and for others it takes months. During pregnancy, natural or spiritual symptoms continue to get added on. It is time for you to get prepared.

CRAMPING MY STYLE

Around six weeks of pregnancy, all women experience cramping. It is a sign that her uterus and the surrounding tissues are expanding to make room for the baby. In your case you are experiencing a spiritual cramp. Your body and life are making room for your greatness. First allow me to explain what a spiritual cramp is. "Spiritual cramping" is just a spiritual pain involving your feelings of anxiety or distress.

A spiritual cramp occurs when you are struggling to find the sources of meaning for what and why you are going through. This pain will have you struggling to find hope, love, strength, and comfort. This spiritual cramp will have you reevaluating the essence of life and it will have you deeply thinking about your relationship with Jesus and people. These cramps will make you feel alone because you have no one to really turn to; no one will quite understand your quest of birthing greatness.

Everyone that has experienced spiritual cramps or spiritual pain experiences it differently and has had different outcomes. People who usually experience spiritual cramps are facing a particular life crisis. Your crisis or situation happens to be the birth of greatness. Now this pain that you are enduring might make other symptoms worse. For me, my spiritual cramps affected my mood swings; for you it might be different.

Naturally, a woman that experiences cramping can take over the counter pain medication. Doctors also recommend resting, taking hot baths, exercising, or even putting a heating pad on your belly or lower back. However, spiritually speaking, there are other remedies to help ease the pain. Remember spiritual cramps are occurring because your body is making room for your greatness. So, you will experience pain like no other during this process; mentally, emotionally, physically, and spiritually. Through my experience, I found it extremely helpful to do things that I enjoy such as: reading, spending time with my mother, or shooting pool. Although your body is making room for your greatness, that does not mean that you have to be a couch potato. Do things that ease your mind and do things that will soothe you.

Now there is another type of spiritual pain that people go through. Some people experience spiritual cramps because they worry about being a hindrance to others because they expect a lot or great things from the people who are in their lives. Or like me I started straying away from others because I sought out peace during my time of being spiritually pregnant; I isolated myself.

As a result of my belief that my isolation was damaging my relationships, I began to carry other people's feelings and attitudes instead of focusing on the greatness that I was carrying. I am here to tell you that no one will ever understand what it feels like carrying your greatness except you. However, it is crucial that you get emotional and spiritual support during your spiritual cramps. Sometimes activities such as reading or shooting pool will not work for you. Every person's tolerance for pain is different. Mine was exceptionally low so I could not stand those god-awful cramps.

I put people around me that tailored to my needs, beliefs, and values. Yet, I did not have yes men around me that only told me what I wanted to hear. Although the people I had around me never been through what I have experienced, I made sure that they "kept it real" with me, gave me spiritual advice, and lent an ear for me to vent. Talking about how you feel, what you are going through, and asking questions is key; it may help you get through whatever you are going through. You cannot, and I mean cannot do this alone. You are the one that is going to experience that trial and tribulation, but you do not have to go through it alone. Do not be embarrassed, especially my fellas, about talking about your spiritual pain. But who do I talk to? Is it friends, family, pastor, significant other?

There is no right or wrong answer on who you talk to, but as I stated before they need to be able to tell you what you need to hear and not what you want to hear. Sometimes it may feel and get uncomfortable, but I learned that you can only grow from an uncomfortable state. Some of these people may give you an uncomfortable answer or advice that you need to help you grow.

So, if that person is your friend, family, significant other, or even a spiritual leader, the goal for you is to make sure their words are acceptable unto Christ. My fiancé tells me all the time that having cramps is no joke and that she dislikes the process and the feeling with a passion. I know that it is not the same, but spiritual cramps are not something that I would want to experience again.

So, far you have experienced cramps, aches and pains, mood swings, fatigue, nausea, exhaustion, and the list go on and on. I know that it is a lot to take in, but I have great news. In the natural, when you are around six weeks pregnant, it is possible that you will experience no symptoms. Yes, you read that correctly. NO SYMPYOMS! All women are different when they are pregnant, and some have experienced no symptoms during this six-week time period.

For you and your spiritual pregnancy there is no particular time frame, but there will come a time where you will not experience any symptoms. Unfortunately, I cannot tell you when that will come; that is in God's timing. What I can tell you is to remember what the Bible says in Ecclesiastes 3:1-8, "There is a time for everything, and a season for every activity under the heavens: A time to be born and a time to die, a time to plant and a time to uproot, a time to ill and a time to heal, a time to tear down and a time to build, a time to weep and a time to laugh, a time to mourn and a time to dance, a time to scatter stones and a time to gather them, a time to embrace and a time to refrain from embracing, a time to search and a time to give up, a time to keep and a time to throw away, a time to tear and a time to mend, a time to be silent and a time to speak, a time to love and a time to hate, a time for war and a time for peace."

In other words, there will be a time where you will go through hell and high waters, but there will also be a time of peace, *no symptoms.* God loves you too much to allow you to go through hell every day, all day. Naturally, there are only a lucky few that will not experience morning sickness, mood swings, and nausea free days without any worries. However, for you spiritually speaking there is no such thing as luck especially when you are carrying greatness. Your experiences or lack of experiences is not lucky. You are not lucky; you are blessed and highly favored. My mother used to say this to me all the time, "Favor is not fair." So, when you finally get some peace, cherish that time, and use it wisely. For me that was the perfect time to talk to God.

PREGNANCY JOURNAL

Before we move on there is something, I would like for you to consider. I know that you have been through a lot since finding out that you are spiritually pregnant. With that being said, I want you to do yourself a favor; when you have concerns, feelings of being overwhelmed and let me not forget to mention when you have racing thoughts, I need you to get what I like to call a "Spiritual Pregnancy Journal." Yes, I said pregnancy journal, fellas. This is essentially a notebook for a spiritually pregnant person like yourself. I want you to write down your inner powerful, private, and sometimes uncomfortable thoughts on what you have been experiencing during this process. During and definitely after pregnancy your mind, body, and soul will never be the same. With that being said, I want you to face whatever you are going through head on rather than ignore the issues, situations, or circumstances that come up during this time.

I know that you are probably wondering how you should get started on writing in this spiritual journal. Well, first I need you to purchase a journal or diary. Then I need you to set aside specific days and times to write. Now what I am about to say next is important; this journal is sacred. This means that you need to regard this with great respect while being connected with God. Time, peace, and privacy is key in this process. Now I know that you have a busy life, but you need to find time to write, because your mind, body, soul, and greatness depends on it. I do not care if it is for ten minutes or for a half an hour. Just make sure that it was a productive time, well spent. I have to be honest about how I struggled with writing out my thoughts during my time of pregnancy. I was judging my experiences and thoughts as well as trying to plan out my thoughts during this process. I do not want you to go through those same struggles. I want you to just write. Do not write with your flesh, write with your heart and soul. Allow your tears from your situations, circumstance, and experiences to write for you. The purpose of this assignment is for you to dig out what you are thinking and feeling from what you went through and are going through. Remember that some people are not going to understand so your time spent writing is your safe haven and judge free zone. Trust me when I say that there is no right or wrong way to write in your spiritual pregnancy journal. Your journal or diary is your private place, where you can talk how you want to talk. A place where you can write anything and everything that you want to write about.

Now you are probably wondering what you should write

about. Every individual's issues are different. So that means that what you write about is going to be different from what the next "spiritually pregnant" person will write about. You may want to talk about how your body is changing, or the fears that you have experienced when you initially discovered your condition. You may want to write about how all of the symptoms that you have experienced through this process. There are countless things that you can write about. Tweet me your experience on Twitter @Chris_Empowers. I want to know how this exercise has helped you. I also want to know your outcome through this process. The beauty is that when I did this exercise, I found out that no one could tell me what and what not to write about. I want you to jot down your thoughts and experiences throughout this spiritual pregnancy. You never know whether what you have written can help the next person in their journey of birthing greatness.

CHAPTER 4

4

I'M CRAVING

I know that it is still early but trust me, this pregnancy is going to be worth all of the things that you have endured and that you will endure. If you are feeling anything like I was feeling during my spiritual pregnancy, then we can agree that these symptoms are both tiring and annoying. Trust me, I get it. However, I have good news for you. You are very close to entering your second trimester which means that you will soon be at the halfway point of your spiritual pregnancy.

Currently, you are in the middle of your first trimester where your greatness is in its development stage; thankfully, greatness will continue to develop even after you give birth. The only way that your greatness will slow down or stop developing is if you have slowed down or stopped developing. Remember that your greatness depends on *you*. I trust that you will neither slow down nor stop. To be honest, you cannot afford to stop. Naturally speaking, a little after six weeks the baby's digestive system and lungs are developing.

This includes tiny facial features which are starting to take shape, more each and every day. The interesting thing that I learned about the woman's body during pregnancy is that after six weeks, the formation of the umbilical cord starts to take place. This cord creates a connection between the woman and the development of the baby.

Similarly, your spiritual umbilical cord creates a connection between you and your greatness, held together by your faith. There goes that faith word again.

Throughout the woman's natural pregnancy, that cord allows nutrients and oxygen to flow to the baby as well as eliminates the babies waste. Well, there is no difference for you when it comes to your spiritual pregnancy. That faith cord is essential to allowing the right nutrients that comes from God to flow between you and your greatness. Although faith is a key part of birthing greatness, you still must play your part and watch what enters your body. Remember that a health body is key for your greatness to live and to thrive.

When it comes to the oxygen that flows from you to the baby, the Bible says in, Luke 13:19, "It is like a grain of mustard seed, which a man took, and cast into his garden; and it grew, and waxed a great tree; and the fowls of the air ledged in the branches of it." Allow me to break this down. The man in this scripture is you. The grain of mustard is your faith. In the beginning of the book, I said that in your spiritual pregnancy, you do not carry a fertilized egg; instead, there is a fertilized seed which is called faith. He planted this mustard seed, *faith*, into the garden. The garden represents the inside of you. In the scripture it says that that mustard seed grew into a great tree. Essentially, your faith developed to your greatness. The scriptures demonstrate that the air, which is the oxygen you get from God, helps you to develop the branches. This helps your greatness grow, develop, and take form.

Just like any tree that is planted, it goes through seasons. Your seasons are sometimes situations, circumstances or sometimes disguised as symptoms. One symptom that you may experience around this time is what I like to call spiritual craving or spiritual aversions. Aversion means; a strong dislike for something. During a woman's natural pregnancy, she may start to crave foods such as ice cream, pickles, chips or even chocolate at any part of the day.

A woman may have those cravings for breakfast, for lunch

or for dinner. Interestingly enough, sometimes a woman can have a strong dislike for the taste or smell of certain foods. When it comes to your spiritual cravings, you do not crave for food, but you crave for things that you may not have desired in pre-pregnancy. I assume that you want to achieve success. During your pregnancy you may start seeking and craving for knowledge. You may also start craving God's grace and mercy so that you may start seeking and craving for the word of God. Personally, I could not stop craving for Jesus and His word, wisdom, peace, mercy, and grace. I cannot pinpoint what exact cravings you will have during your time of spiritual pregnancy, but what I can say is that some of you will start craving more of something you already love and for some, you may start craving things that you never thought you would ever like.

Now I must warn you that not every craving is healthy for you and your greatness. As a matter of fact, Satan believes that this is the perfect time to creep in and play with some of your cravings. When I accepted that I was pregnant with greatness, I soon began craving for success. Seeing that, the devil thought it was the perfect time to come into my thoughts. He had my mind stuck on the excitement of the end goal instead of on the necessary steps in the process to achieve my goal.

The Bible says in Proverbs 11:14, "Where there is no guidance, a people fall, but in abundance of counselors there is safety." When I began to crave knowledge and guidance, my goals became much clearer; my mind was at ease. Yet, the important key was finding someone who could help to guide my thoughts. Just so you know, the devil did not stop there. As I was craved Jesus' love, the devil had me looking for love in the wrong places and in the wrong people. The Bible says in 1 John 4:1, "Beloved, do not believe every spirit, but test the spirits to see whether they are from God for many false prophets have gone out into the world."

This applies to love and guidance, but I did not realize that there were some people who merely wanted to get a piece of my greatness for themselves. They were not willing to help me birth it for the right reasons. Romans 12:2 says, "Do not be conformed to this world, but be transform by the renewal of your mind that by testing you may be discerning what is the will of God, what is good and acceptable and perfect."

Spiritual craving will happen but make sure that you test those cravings and people beforehand; do not accept everything that people say to you or give you. You do not want to be addicted to the wrong cravings. When it comes to a natural pregnancy you do not want to be hooked on cravings because every food that you want may not be good for you. However, during spiritual pregnancy, it is okay for you to be hooked on cravings. I was hooked on God wisdom, but I did not just lean on His wisdom as if I were crippled. I am going to teach you how to cope with cravings and how to not allow them to cripple to you. But first I must inform you of some important information.

DEVIL'S SNACK ATTACK

Have you ever felt like you absolutely need some love from some place or someone? I have. Spiritual pregnancy can be lonely at times; subsequently, I sometimes felt myself craving for love. Believe me when I say that your spiritual cravings are not a sign of weakness. The devil is just feasting on your life because he sees your development up close; he does not attack anything or anyone that is not growing. There is no fun in attacking those who are already on his team. That is why I call this the "Devil's Snack Attack."

He knows no matter how healthy you are, you still love snacks. The word snack means a small amount of food eaten between meals. In your spiritual case, it means a small number of things consumed throughout your spiritual pregnancy. Now there are many different things that we crave throughout this process, but one thing that everyone craves, believers or non-believers, physically pregnant or spiritually pregnant, and that is love.

The devil likes to attack people who have this particular craving called love. Trust me, I get it. I was one of those people and if you are one of those people you may experience headaches and insomnia, which is the inability to sleep, mood changes, and sometimes depression. I experienced all of these things while craving love. The devil tries to make you feel as if no one will ever understand you which can trigger the headaches or depression.

He can also enter your thoughts and make you feel as though no one loves you. The biggest reason why I could not sleep was that I felt like no one was on my side. I believed that no one was interested in helping me to birth greatness. It truly felt as if I was alone. So, I craved love from people; yet I could not find it. I later learned that I was allowing the devil to win because I felt as though I needed approval or love from man. The truth was that God was all I needed; He will provide all the love that we need. In John 3:16 it says, "For God so loved the world, that he gave his only begotten Son, that whosoever believeth in him should not perish, but have everlasting life." If that is not love, then I do not know what is.

Now it is important to identify and distinguish whether your cravings are affecting your mental or physical state. Remember what was said about emotions earlier in the book? Controlling your emotions throughout your spiritual pregnancy is vital. Emotions play a big part in cravings, naturally and spiritually. Rebecca Wilborn, director of the Midtown Diet Center in New York City says, "When we are stressed, anxious, frustrated, lonely... all those feelings can trigger our cravings." I could not say it any better; this even applies to spiritual pregnancy as well. Whenever you are stressed, you start seeking love and attention. Similarly, when you are anxious, frustrated, and lonely, you will crave so much that it can start being unhealthy for you. Again, a healthy body is a healthy home for your greatness.

CRAVE FOR JESUS

Earlier I mentioned how I used to crave Jesus and His word, wisdom, grace, peace, and mercy. Likewise, in any relationship you need to love your significant other. During your spiritual pregnancy, your significant other is Jesus; He is the one who impregnated you. Allow me to break this down in the natural. Personally, I crave the presence of my significant other. To crave means to have a feeling or a powerful desire for something or someone.

There is not a day that I do want to see, talk, or be with my fiancé. I used to wonder why, but through my spiritual pregnancy I quickly learned. The reason why I crave my fiancé is because Jesus lives through her. So, essentially, I have a craving for Jesus. During your spiritual pregnancy, I dare you to crave Jesus. I promise you that when you start craving for Jesus, craving for your greatness will be easy.

There will be a day that you will wake up and not want to strive to be great. However, before you can crave greatness or even your significant other, you must first crave for Jesus. And did I mention that the craving must be organic? As you know we have to pay a pretty penny for any organic thing that we consume. That is why Jesus paid a pretty penny for His organic love by dying on the cross. Your organic love for Jesus will cost you sleepless nights along with other uncomfortable symptoms as you go through this spiritual pregnancy.

I cannot stress enough that your heart has to crave more of God. You cannot feed your greatness the right nutrients if you are weak from hunger. Spiritually speaking, you cannot feed anyone or anything, especially not your greatness, if you have not been already filled up. I dare you to indulge in Jesus. It is acceptable for you to crave for Jesus every day. According to the Amplified Bible, which breaks down the King James Version to a simple read. It says in Psalms 105:4, "Seek, inquire of and for the Lord, and crave Him and His strength. His might and inflexibility to temptation; seek and require His face and His presence continually evermore."

The success and health of your greatness correlate with your appetite or craving for Jesus. I need you to do a few things for yourself. I need you to crave Jesus by *giving thanks.* Earlier in the book, I addressed the benefits of giving thanks. While spiritually pregnant, giving thanks is vital., especially as it relates to your quest for more of Jesus. Even in my relationship with my fiancé, I learned that the more I thanked her, the more she was willing to do. Although the revelation may seem simple, I missed this revelation early in my relationship.

Never forget that one of the key ingredients to receive more blessings is to give more praise and thanksgiving; however, it must be organic. I found out quickly that if I did not thank my fiancé for cooking dinner, then I would not receive dinner for the rest of the week. The Bible says in Psalm 100:4, "Enter into the His gates with thanksgiving, and into his courts with praise; be thankful unto him and bless his name." I do not know about you, but I was and am so thankful that Jesus chose to impregnate me with these gifts, wisdom, and most importantly, this greatness. In fact, I am most grateful that He allowed me to wake up every day, to strive, to carry and to birth my greatness.

Craving for Jesus also requires *calling upon his name.* It is amazing how Jesus gives me life lessons through my fiancé. In my relationship, my fiancé loves when I address her as beautiful. Her name is Briana and I sometimes call her bae, but I mostly address her as beautiful. More than just hearing beautiful, she loves when I call her because she internalizes that I need her; she also loves assisting me. In this same way, Jesus loves for you to call on His name.

Most men believe that they need to do everything and that they need to be the provider. Listen up men, your lady loves feeling as if she is needed, especially when you are on a quest to birth your greatness. The same thing applies to Jesus; call on Him. Do not be intimidated or shy, call upon Jesus' name. When I was younger my mother's favorite show is "I Love Lucy", and every time Lucy's husband, Ricky came in, he shouted, "Lucy, I'm home!" My mother watched that show so much that I internalized it. Anytime I came home from a hard day of work, I addressed my fiancé in a similar manner. I entered the house, shouting "Beautiful, I'm home." Jesus loves when you acknowledge Him. He loves to hear the sound of your voice. Do not hesitate to call on Jesus.

Again, I learned from my relationship with my fiancé the importance of "*making her doing known.*" Keep in mind that I did not blast all of her doings on the internet. However, if expressing "her doing" on the internet is what you like to do, go right ahead, but I made known of her doings through my examples in my talks, in my one-on-one conversations, in this book, and to her. Through my relationship, with my fiancé' God taught me many things, both grooming me for marriage and for birthing greatness.

While craving for Jesus you have to make it known that the Lord is good. One of the ways people learn is with their eyes; it has also been proven that people shop with their eyes. By living through Christ, you are showing all of the wonderful blessings that God has given you. Your testimony gives people hope. When they see how Jesus brought you out of darkness, situations, and circumstances they will seek for Jesus as well. Someone may think craving for Jesus is hard. Seeking Jesus is not difficult if you start with a thankful heart; *give thanks*.

Then you will catch yourself singing praises to His name and *calling upon His name.* I promise you that the overflow will have you calling His name. Then it is your job to let the world know what Jesus has done for you, *making known of His doing.* If you are craving for the presence of Jesus, then you are in the perfect position for Him to feed you. Welcome Him in. Do not have Jesus waiting at the door. Do not allow the care of this life to distract you from opening the door for Jesus. Your greatness requires your craving for Jesus. Never think that you can do this alone. Your craving for Jesus is a crucial step in the journey of birthing greatness.

CHAPTER 5

5

DETOXING

With all of the attention on health today, healthy habits should take center stage. Around this time healthcare providers inform pregnant women to be aware of potential infection that can occur; everyone should want to avoid germs at any time. Wash your hands regularly and thoroughly after touching items and shaking hands; you know that germs are everywhere. It is no different concerning spiritual pregnancy. You still want to watch out for germs. In the spiritual sense, germs are filthy people, thoughts, words, negativity, wrong opinions, etc.

During this time there is also a particular symptom that

starts to creep in called diarrhea. I know you what you are thinking. DIARRHEA? Yes, diarrhea; women who have been physically pregnant know what I am talking about. Between six to eight weeks, some women start to take trip after trip to the bathroom. Diarrhea is usually nothing to worry about. Even when it comes to your spiritual pregnancy, there is nothing to worry about. However, spiritually speaking you will not have to run to the bathroom. During this time your body is doing what I like to call "a spiritual detoxing process." When I was spiritually pregnant, I had nights where I could not sleep and times where I woke up early. I did not know what was wrong with me but soon I learned that I was in need of a spiritual detox.

But what does that mean?

Just like your body, your spirit needs to detox. I believe that every human should go through a cleaning or detoxing. During the duration of a women's pregnancy the baby is eliminating waste. This is one of the reasons why women frequently go to the bathroom. Mothers know this to be true and you will quickly learn what your baby likes or dislikes because you will find yourself in a bathroom eliminating what the baby does not like. The same thing goes for your greatness. Your greatness will let you know what it does and do not like. You will start witnessing your greatness, eliminating some of the waste that is transpiring in your life that is hindering both you and your greatness. My question to you is, "Are you even aware of when you might need a spiritual detox?" Are you aware when you are feeding your spirit and greatness with unnecessary junk? If you are not aware, there are many spiritual junk food items that you can become addicted to; this is a sign that you need to detox.

Spirit Junk Food:

- Endless engagement on Social Media.
- Hours of Gaming.
- Too much Netflix & Chill time.
- Partying like there is no tomorrow.
- Endless eating.
- Being a couch potato.
- Hanging out with toxic people.
- Etc.

Now I am not saying that consuming any of these items is bad. However, it becomes bad when it is not done in moderation. When you are on a quest of birthing greatness you have to be mindful of what you consume in your body and in your life. Too many of us find ourselves-scrolling through our social media feed, reading posts instead of reading books such as the Bible and other books that can help us with our vision.

People spend too many hours playing video games, partying, or watching Netflix, or even chilling more than putting those hours into learning. Your greatness is trying to do you a favor by eliminating those negative cravings out of your system. You must be committed to not putting your hand back in the cookie jar of "junk food". It was hard for me in the beginning. I knew that I consumed too much "junk food", but it was so good.

Yet, I knew it was too much because I started to feel a bit off and wanted to pull the covers over my head and not get up on most days. I started to feel like I was all over the place during my spiritual pregnancy which often made me feel tired. Whenever times became rough, it was easy for me to lose focus. Trials and tribulations will come in your life during your spiritual pregnancy.

There will also be distractions such as games, people, partying, social media, and more but you cannot allow storms to consume and/or distract you. There were many things that I allowed to take my focus; this is why it is important to have people with their hands reaching up instead of reaching out. I had people seeing how sick I looked, realizing that I needed a spiritual detox, who started to pray over me. I seriously needed a cleansing, a recalibration, and an invigorating soul treatment.

SOUL DETOXING

To detox the soul, you must start with detoxing your heart. The heart is always the first thing that needs the most care. Without the heart nothing else flows. Spiritually speaking, it is the hub that pumps blood between you, your greatness, and God. I have learned that we cannot carry nor birth greatness without a healthy heart. Jesus will put you in position to test your heart. The Bible says in Psalms 26:2, "Prove me, O Lord, and try me; test my heart and my mind." I encourage you to ask Jesus to examine and try your heart. You always want to be aligned with God especially when you are carrying greatness. When a car wheel is out of alignment, your car is shaky. I learned the hard way that you never want a shaky relationship with Jesus.

Next, you want to detox your eyes. Remember your sight or vision lenses are one of the spiritual senses that we talked about earlier. Your vision lenses are an important key to birthing greatness. You do not want to sit online all day because you are bound to see something that knocks your vision off course. For me I was seeing people that appear to be living in their gift and I either started wanting to have their gift, or I started questioning my own gift.

Psalms 119:37 says, "Turn my eyes from looking at worthless things; and give me life in your ways." We consume with our eyes and on this spiritual journey we have to be careful what enters in our vision lenses. Our view of what God has shown us can be easily blocked. So, you have to do what the Bible says in Psalms 16:8, "Set the Lord always before me; because he is at my right hand, I shall not be shaken." I dare you to ask God to show you the road you must travel so you can see. And invite him to take a ride with you.

After you detox your heart and eyes you must detox your words. There is power in your words. As a matter of fact, there is life and death in the power of your tongue. In other words, we have the power to build or break so choose your words wisely. With all thy wisdom get understanding the Bible says. Your words flow from your heart which is why it is important that the first thing you do is get your heart together. In Psalm 19:14 it written, "Let the words of my mouth and the meditation my heart be acceptable in your sight, O Lord, my rock and my redeemer."

The world in which we live has a lot of unhealthy aspects to it; we have to discern what is good. The only way we do that is to detox our soul. This leads me to the last of your soul detoxing and that is the detox of your actions. The truth is that Jesus is our rock and our strength to fight problems. When I was struggling through my spiritual pregnancy, I wanted to retreat and hide. I did not know why God wanted to use me because I was living a life that was not designed for me. My actions did not line up with God's word and His plan. But Jesus still wanted to use me as an example. The Bible says in Psalm 34:14, "Turn away from evil and do good; seek peace and pursue it."

Finally, when my actions were aligned with God, the pregnancy was not that bad. Of course, I still had my challenges but as a result of the detox of my actions, it became somewhat easier. Did you know that certain physical actions that you participate in are neither healthy for you nor your greatness? Psalms 119:133 says, "Keep steady my steps according to your promise, and let no iniquity get dominion over me." This is what I repeated to myself when I felt as if I was getting off course.

Spiritual detox leads to life for you and your greatness. Although spiritual detox can sometimes be difficult, it enables us to think and function much clearer. If you ever have the opportunity to experience a natural detox, you will feel much lighter, more vibrant, and healthier. No matter the circumstance or situation that is happening in your life, Jesus is by your side. Although you are on a journey of birthing something greater than yourself, sometimes it is necessary to pull over on your journey in order to detox. I promise that you will feel much lighter, more vibrant, and healthier.

LIFE DETOXING

What you just read is the detoxing of your soul, essentially detoxing the place where your greatness lives. However, you need to also detox the place you live and that is your life. The reason why I started on the inside first is because your life cannot function correctly if your insides are messed up. When your soul is detoxed you are now able to listen to your voice of inner wisdom and know that you are guided well.

That means if your heart tells you to turn off the TV and go for a walk in the park, then go. If your heart is telling you to stop reading social media posts and start reading the Word of God, then listen. If your heart is telling you to do something that seems uncommon in your daily routine, then I dare you to tryout that change. Some of you need to detoxify your life pronto. Some of you are overworking, overscheduled, and overwhelmed. Life has somehow convinced you to define that as being productive, when in reality you are you are just a "busy body". Being a busy body is neither good for your life nor your health. It is time for you to detox your life.

First, you have to start with cleaning your mind. You need to have the right mindset in order for you to tackle this thing called life. When you make up your mind that you are going to have a healthy body, healthy soul, and a healthy life, then half of the battle is won. After I aligned my mind with the Word of God, I had to detox myself from certain relationships; I like to call this cleaning your space. Just like in a physical house, you have to take out the trash.

Well in your spiritual life, the trash can be negative or stagnant people who are just taking up space and not adding any value to your life. I promise that your greatness will do half the work of identifying people in your life that are no good, but you have to do your part in eliminating them from your life. I need you to write out all of the people that you talk to in life, regardless of what title they hold. Then write next to their name whether they add value or not; if the answer is yes, then under their name list what type of value they add.

This is something that must be done after your mind is correctly aligned with the mind of Christ and after you have taken control over your emotions. I learned the hard way that I was keeping people in my life because I did not want to be alone or because I had known them for years. I kept them whether they were good for me or not. Yet, my greatness was informing me that I had outgrown certain people because I had vision, goals, desire, and they were still living in darkness, taking life as it comes, day by day. Being healthy takes commitment and dedication. Are you dedicated and committed enough to eliminate waste and people that do you no good?

Your mind and the people in your life are important things to detox, but you also have to detox your schedule. Trust me you can be productive without working from sunup to sundown. You need a plan and a schedule when birthing greatness. Clear your schedule and then reschedule, but make sure that your schedule is well planned out and productive. Last, but not least I need you to do a little spring cleaning or detoxing in the finances department.

Now you are probably asking how can I detox my finances? What I mean by detoxing your finances is cleaning or getting rid of bad spending habits. Just like the spiritual pregnancy journal that you will soon possess; I need you to keep a daily spending journal. I need you to document what you spend every day. I mean everything, from what you spend on gas, food, and even a cup of coffee; this also includes bills.

When you begin to jot down everything you spend, I also need you to highlight everything that is not an essential expense. For example, your mortgage or rent, car payments, groceries and your utilities bill etc. are essential expenses. Now you will have a list on what you spend that are not necessities such as coffee, movies, etc. After you have a list, your next step is to make changes slowly to what you spend that is not essential.

In order to detox finances, it takes will. You must be serious about this assignment. You are probably asking what does this have to do with birthing greatness? Well just like a baby, you need money to feed it, to clothe it, and to house it. It is no different with your greatness. You need financial assistance to expand your greatness. My greatness was tied into me becoming a public speaker; therefore, I needed money for travel, lodging, eating, etc. That does not even account for writing a book, editing, photography, social media, and the list goes on.

Yes, I leaned on Jesus to help me, but He also created me to be self-sufficient as well. I had to get up and grind, but also sacrifice. Overall, I had to detox my finance. So, start making changes to your spending habits, reducing, or eliminating what you can live without. For one day try to not spend that money that you usually spend on that coffee or in the vending machine. Not one dollar. That means bye-bye morning coffee. Bye-bye newspaper and whatever else you buy that you can live without. I trust that you can do it. I promise that you can make it through the day. For some this may be more of a sacrifice than for others, but I trust that "you got this."

Then try one week of eating at home. No going out to eat no matter what. Even when it is late, or you are tired, or when the kids are getting on your nerves, do not spend that money in a restaurant or fast-food establishment. Make a lunch, cook dinner when you get home, carry a lunch to work with you; remember that you are dedicated and committed. This process is crucial to your growth because this shows how much discipline you have, but more importantly it creates a healthier diet, and cuts back on unnecessary spending. Every dollar counts when you are saving for your greatness. Now you will make it harder on yourself if you do no eliminate temptation which is your next step.

First get a journal. Second, start making changes slowly. In other words, cut back. Now you want to eliminate temptation. It will be hard for you to stop spending money on coffee in the morning if you are still passing by Starbucks or Dunk Donuts every morning on your way to work. Perhaps, you can resist temptation by taking another route. One way that way that I eliminated temptation was by not carrying my debit or credit cards in my wallet; that forced me set a cash budget for how much money I needed to carry for the whole week. This allowed me to have just enough money for gas and not much else, so I learned to adapt to the budget.

Inevitably, there was no temptation to spend extra money on unnecessary items or snacks throughout the day. This slows down and, in some cases, stops impulse shopping altogether. Now I suggest that you get an accountability partner to help you along your journey. Mine was my fiancé; we held each other accountable to not spending unnecessary money. Now it worked better for me than for her but do not tell her that I told you that. So, she set herself an allowance for the month, so she would not impulse shop. This made her angry but mindful of what she could and could not spend. When you have a budget buddy, it helps the process go by a little easier.

Lastly, you must know your budget breakdown which is vital to birthing your greatness. A healthy budget breakdown is simple, and you do not have to be a math whiz or a businessperson to construct one. You will want your budget to consist of the following: 50% fixed costs, meaning your rent, mortgage, bills, and transportation should take no more than 50% of your income. You also want 30% of flexible spending which means your shopping, entertainment, and groceries.

These things should only take up 30% or less of your income. The last 20% of your budget should be your savings. You need to dive in and find different ways in which you can save for your financial goals.

You want to work smarter, not harder. Make sure your greatness has financial support when your greatness arrives. When you follow these steps, you will not only increase in health, but also in finances.

CHAPTER 6

6

HEART OF A CHAMPION

Do not be surprise if you spiritual symptoms are not in full effect right about now. During natural pregnancy women usually start purchasing garments in bigger sizes because of the baby growth. Spiritually speaking, you do not need bigger clothes, but you should suspect bigger responsibility, bigger workload, and bigger trials and tribulation, as well as bigger blessings. One of the biggest blessings is the improvement of your spiritual sense of hearing. Around eight weeks of a woman's pregnancy they are now able to hear the baby's heartbeat. For you with the improvement of your spiritual hearing, you are now able to hear the heartbeat of your greatness for the first time. Yes, your greatness has a heartbeat.

You are probably wondering how. Just as during pregnancy a baby continues to develop, so does your greatness. By eight weeks a baby's hands and feet are developing fingers and toes. The arms are able to move around at the elbow and wrist. For you, during your spiritual pregnancy, similar things are taking place.

Your greatness is developing your gift, talent, passion and the list goes on. The heartbeat of your greatness is essentially your passion. When I birthed my greatness, it was public speaking; naturally speaking that was my "gender." However, during this time I did not know the "gender", I was only able to hear its heartbeat. The heartbeat of my greatness was my passion for helping people. I heard and felt my passion growing daily. I began to feel my gift developing on the inside.

At this time, I still did not know what God had brewing up on inside, but it felt good. Although it felt wonderful, knowing that God had something amazing growing on the inside. Now it still did not stop the symptoms. During pregnancy, whatever you are carrying develops a backbone and that is great, but that also means that there is room for you to start having back pain. My development got the attention of the devil; yours will to if it has not already. I need you to understand that the devil will attack the very thing you enjoy and use it against you. I was excited to hear the heartbeat of my greatness. I was glad to know I was able to identify my passion.

But I was not the only one that identified my passion, the devil did also. He started to play mind games with me. He started convincing me that I can help everyone. So, what did I do? I attempted to do just that, help everyone. The responsibilities began to weigh heavily on my emotions, body, and spirit. I start trying to put the weight of people's problems on my shoulders. I am here to tell you that you are not God. I learned that the hard way. I was trying to help everyone because I had a deep passion, and I did not realize that I was hurting myself through the process.

Essentially, these were spiritual back pains because I was trying to carry my greatness and carry people's problems at the same time. This had a trickle-down effect to other symptoms. That pain caused me to feel fatigue. I start to become sick and nauseous, because I did not know what I was really doing. I also began to get off track with my diet and began to accept spiritual junk food that was clearly not good for me. The devil was busy, and I must admit that at times I felt like he was winning.

But one day I remembered what my father told me before his passing, that pressure creates diamonds. It took me awhile to realize this, but I am stronger than anything the devil can throw at me. I started developing the heart of a champion. I started speaking over my life and started to seek guidance. I accepted that I could not help everyone and that it is ok. My joy started to come back, and my passion became reignited. I was well energized. You also have a heart of a champion. Your passion is going to take you places that you did not know you could go. You got this!

SLEEP DEPRIVED

Do not be alarmed because this is not necessarily a bad thing. When you have a passion, it often wakes you up and keeps you up. Successful people are usually the first to get up in some cases, they are last ones to go to sleep. There was many of nights when I was sleep deprived. The symptom is common during natural pregnancy. Women carrying a baby will try to get some sleep, while finding out that the baby is on a different sleep schedule than the mother. Carrying a baby is hard and carrying greatness is not any better.

Spiritually speaking, your greatness is an ongoing alarm clock. It will not let you sleep knowing that you could be doing something productive for yourself now and for your future. Being sleep deprived does come with side effects. Naturally speaking one of the reasons

why women cannot go to sleep is because of frequent

urination.

As the baby continues to grow the women uterus continues to expand, both of which put pressure on your bladder. Well in your spiritual case, it is a little different. You will have sleepless nights, but not because you have to continue to run to the bathroom. However, you will be up because during this process you will have frequent tears. People will not understand why you are so emotional, so you feel expressing this will not necessarily do you any favors.

Crying will have you talking to God even when you feel ashamed, embarrassed, or nervous. I cried out so many nights and most of the time it was not for a favor, but to say thank you to God for keeping me. Most of the time there were tears of joy. Yes, I had times where I wanted to give up, so it caused tears. Most of the time though I was thanking Him in advance for what he was going to do in my life. Do not be alarmed when the goodness of God makes you cry. I was a crybaby, but I was not ashamed. Fellas "men do not cry" is a lie. It is ok for me to cry.

Now there is another reason why women awaken during natural pregnancy and that is because the baby is moving on the inside all night. For me, my greatness was moving on the inside of me constantly. My greatness was telling me that we were going to change the world. When your greatness never stops moving, that is an awesome sign. I am here to tell you that certain signs are going have you up at all times of the nights which will frustrate you.

However, I need you to remember that this is a marathon and not a sprint. Trust me when I say that your greatness is what the world needs and it will change not only your life, but it will change the world.

By the way, spiritually speaking you have now reached your two-month mark meaning that you are eight weeks pregnant. Doctors suggest that you schedule an appointment with them once a month for the first two months of your pregnancy. Well since you are spiritually pregnant you have the luxury of visiting your doctor, which is God, every day, all day, at any time, and anyplace.

Your visits are by prayer. If your visits are not frequent now, I guarantee that they will be more frequent as you get closer to the birth. Now I do not suggest that you only visit him only when it closer to your pregnancy. I do recommend that you schedule your checkups sooner than later. Matter of fact I recommend that you visit him all the time. Frequent conversations, visits, and checkups with God give you the best opportunity to talk to God about any concerns you might have during this spiritual pregnancy. Your checkups allow you to ask questions, but you have to sit there long enough to receive an answer. I made it a priority to give Him all the praise and all the honor during my checkups. If you have not already visited your healthcare provider, God, then I believe that now is the perfect time to visit.

GROWING FAITH-LINE

We are now a few weeks(pages) away from completing your first trimester. It is important for me to take this time to inform you that I will not necessarily breakdown every week of the second and third trimester. It was, however, important for me to break down every week of the first trimester because I believe that the first trimester is the most important trimester of them all. Do not worry; I will not hold back in teaching everything you need to know to birth greatness. With that being said, in the words of the great Nipsey Hussle, "The marathon continues."

You are now nine weeks pregnant and as I told you earlier your symptoms are not going to slow down any time soon. In fact, around this time during a natural pregnancy, a woman still goes through morning sickness, fatigue, cravings, moodiness, and cramping. Also, during this time there is no hiding the fact that you are pregnant. When it comes to a natural pregnancy I am talking about your shape.

It may not be a round stomach being showcased, but you

can notice more than a baby bump. At nine weeks a new development or symptom as the doctors call it will be a growing waistline. In the time of spiritual pregnancy your stomach does not get round, however your greatness does start to make you look fuller. Allow me to explain. Remember, the foundation of your greatness starts with faith as small as a mustard seed.

Your greatness will push you to become a person who is full of faith, walking in the confidence of who you are and what you are carrying, but more importantly the confidence of who God is. Being full of faith is completely trusting in your greatness and in God's power and ability. When you are full of faith, your waistline or what I like to call your faith-line begins to grow.

During her nine weeks, a woman's symptoms include changes to her breasts as well; her chest will become fuller, heavier and more tender. However, spiritually speaking it is a little different. Your breasts or spiritual case, your heart will feel a little heavier, fuller, and more tender. Your heart is filled with love and faith and your faith indicates to you that you can make it to end of this pregnancy.

Your heart is also heavy because you are starting to love the fact that you are pregnant, but it is also tender because carrying greatness and birthing greatness, which is new for concept for you to digest. All of this is testing your faith; every assignment, every test that you pass, your "faith-line" starts expanding. You are full of emotions, questions, and concerns, but you are also full of faith. When you allow your faith to direct your journey, then you will not be led astray.

PICK YOUR SPOTS

Some women during their first trimester see some spotting. Spiritually speaking, you will not physically bleed, however you will go through spiritual warfare and in this war you will bleed spiritually. Spiritual warfare is a concept of fighting against the work of Satan forces. However, I have great news, I decree and declare that the devil has already lost every war he is trying to start with you. He knows that he has nothing to lose in trying to take you out and defeat you.

Being a soldier for God you are bound to bleed, but some battles are not meant for you to fight so "pick your spots." Spiritual warfare is real and there are battles that make up smaller components of the bigger picture. However, the devil tries to trick us into making certain situations bigger than they actually are. Every situation and circumstance do not need a battle. Doctors suggest that if there are more a few drops of blood, you must go to your healthcare provider. Spiritually speaking, if it is a battle that is going to have a lot of scars and make you bleed spiritually, then go to your healthcare provider and that is Jesus.

I need you to understand that we are in the world - not of the world. You are going to experience conflicts, situations, and circumstances and those are sometimes a part of spiritual warfare. That is the devil's way of distracting you, getting you off the course of birthing your greatness. Pick your spots or you will get picked to pieces. God will fight your battles. Now it is important for you to know that God did not create us to be punks. He has equipped up to war and win, but just know that you do not have to go to war alone nor fight it alone.

FIT IS EVERYTHING

Trust me when I say that those battles you will endure will someday whip you out. At times battles discouraged me to the point of wanting to throw in the towel and give up. I know that we touched on this earlier but during this time is when you must have the right support system around you. During a natural pregnancy, it is also suggested that a woman get fitted regularly for the correct bra size to keep themselves comfortable. The reason for this is to make sure that the chest and back are supported.

Well during your spiritual pregnancy, especially during war time you will need a great support system or what I like to call a

Spiritual B.R.A. Which stands for "Battle Ready Alliance." However, your Spiritual

B.R.A can only work if your B.R.A fits. You must surround yourself with people or an alliance that will life you higher. It is important for you to have the right people around that will both pray you out of a situation as well as lift you up when you are down. You must have the right people that will pull you out of darkness and more importantly, that will be battle ready. Jim Rohn once said, "we are the average of the five people we spend the most time with." Now some people do not agree with this statement.

However, research shows that we are much more affected by our environment and those around us. Your Battle. Ready. Alliance matters. One of my favorite old proverbs says, "Show me your friends and I'll tell you who you are." Well spiritually speaking, show me your alliance and I will tell how many battles you will lose. Your Spiritual B.R.A. will either have you remain the same or push you to another level. Your alliance should be able to help you birth your greatness.

Surround yourself with winners. Surround yourself with people that birth greatness and I promise you that you will be the next one to also birth greatness. Do not be the smartest in your alliance. You want people around you to help you grow. If you are not growing, you are dying. The world cannot afford for you to die, because you have something inside of you that the word needs to have.

You will know if the right people fit what you are trying to accomplish because they will push you forward and towards your goal. The only way your alliance can lift you higher is if they are already elevated. Get people around you that are living life at a higher level, because if you can look up, you can go up. Winners do not like hanging around with losers. You have to be on a high level of thinking to play with high tier people. They say if you surround yourself with nine losers, you will be the tenth.

My Spiritual B.R.A fits me well. In other words, my Battle-Ready-

Alliance fits me and my life well. They are hungry for success, God, and birthing their greatness. Get around hungry people, the people that are hungry to make a difference with what they have brewing on the inside of them. Great people love great people. Jesus is great and seems to think that you are great also; that is why He impregnated you. So, make sure that you get around great people because people will either inspire you to be great and birth your greatness or drain the life or greatness out of you. Choose carefully.

You will never be successful if you hang around greatness killers. Those type of people clock in for the devil and their 9 to

5 is to find reasons to convince you that birthing your greatness cannot be done. Do not allow a negative virus to come into the hard drive of your greatness and destroy your present and future. Stay ready. Make sure that you have the right Spiritual B.R.A, battle ready alliance, to prepare yourself to birth greatness.

CHAPTER 7

7

NOT QUITE TIME YET

Most people love to hear the news that someone is expecting, it is no difference when it come to your spiritual pregnancy. Some people excited for those they love to birth what's inside of you. Just like you their excitement continues to rise and the number one question that get asked throughout a pregnancy is, what is the gender. Well, it is not quite time yet for the gender reveal, so I hope you and others can stay patient for a few more weeks.

Around nine weeks for most women, their abdomen feels a bit firmer; this is the uterus. Also, during this stage for women, it is a strong possibility that she will not be showing during this time. Usually, women began developing a baby bump between 12 and 16 weeks. So, I hope that you have not yet spilled the beans that you are pregnant yet.

A study was done by *Science Alert* and it found out that the average person can only keep thirteen secrets, five of which they have never told another soul. This means that those five secrets will be taken to the grave. Do yourself a favor and do not tell or show your next move. Yes, I am talking about not telling anyone that you are pregnant with greatness right now. Remember that there is a time and place for everything. Currently, there is a massive change occurring in your life and that is wonderful news, but sometimes it is best for you not to share what is transpiring in your life.

Instead, it is best for you to show the world the finished product. Ironically, I am about to let a big secret out of the bag: Not everyone is rooting for you to succeed, nor is everyone rooting for you to birth your greatness. I learned this the hard way. I was announcing just about every move that I was about to make in my business and in my life. I always wondered why none of what I was trying to accomplish was coming to pass. I soon found out that certain people were praying on my downfall. They were praying that what I was working towards would not prevail; I was being sabotaged.

As I grew into adulthood, I realized that nobody is perfect. I made a lot of mistakes in my life, that in hindsight, were all learning experiences. Yet, one of my biggest mistakes or should I say lessons, was the fact that I was so public about everything that I was trying to do. I just could not shut up. I say this respectfully, "SHUT UP!" I am here to stop you from making the same mistake that I did. We will talk about this shortly but telling my next move caused me to have many miscarriages. I know that you are happy about what God is doing or is about to do in your life, however, sometimes your talkative self leads to you miscarrying your greatness.

DREAM SNATCHER

It is important that I take the time to differentiate between your next moves and your dreams. Just to make this clear, in some cases it is okay to share your dreams with other people. I only shared my dreams with my alliance, my circle, the people that were going to help launch me and my dreams to a higher place. On occasion, I have also shared my dreams outside of my circle with people that I aspired to be like.

I guess what I am trying to say is that it is okay to share your dreams with people I like to call "dream-catchers." Those are the people who will take your dreams and connect it to the right person or place in the right situation. The people who you want to prevent telling your dreams to are what I like to call "Dream Snatchers." These are the people who prey on innocent dreamers like you and convince you that you cannot accomplish those dreams. You want to get the right people around your dream, ones who will uplift.

Regardless of whether or not you are sharing your dreams with a dream catcher who can help to propel you to the next level, do not share the specifics of your vision. Jesus gave that dream and more importantly that greatness to you. Although no one can duplicate what Jesus have given you on the inside, there will always be someone who will try to copycat your dreams and greatness. It is incredible that God made twins. Although twins look alike, they are still different people.

No two people were made the same. The same thing applies to your greatness; there are no two human beings whose greatness is the same. However, there is a myriad of greatness that may seem to look alike on the outside. For example, I am not the only motivational speaker, but there is no motivational speaker like me.

If I would have given out all of the details about how I do what I do, then you would probably see another version of me on a stage. I learned to allow my greatness to talk for me and not for me to talk for my greatness. It is hard for people to respect, let alone be surprised about you or your greatness when you have spilled all the beans. As the saying goes, "You are all talk and no bite."

SILENT KILLER

When I decided to shut up and go silent it changed my life. It was very easy to take away the suspense of what I was about to do next when I was telling all of my next moves. Once I silenced myself, I took the expectations off of my shoulders. When I was overly talkative, I started to be inconsistent, and I also started to be fake; I created a façade about myself and my greatness. My soul was taking a dramatic hit and I started to lose myself. You will start losing your identity as soon as you start telling people what your plan is for your greatness.

The reason why God is so talkative is because He believes He can trust you to keep a secret. He does not give you plans for your life so that you can tell the world. My mother used to tell me, "Son you never want to be predictable." I know that we live in the days of social media where content seems extremely important. You may drop hints of what you are working on, but by no means should you tell everything to the world. Giving just a sample leaves people wanting more and creates an excitement that you are working on something that they

want and possibly need.

My life changed once I made the decision to not tell everyone about my spiritual pregnancy or my plans. As soon as I stopped sharing all of my business, my life began to improve. My life would not have done a 180 degree turn if I had not made the conscious decision to stop talking and start acting. Consider being quiet. Being like a silent killer is necessary because your time for public revealing is sooner than you think.

You may or may not see it, but your greatness has come a long way. For some, time flies by when you are carrying greatness. During my spiritual pregnancy there was a period when I felt like time was not moving fast enough. Although I wanted success instantaneously, I soon learned that good things come to those who wait. During the ten-week time period of a natural pregnancy, the baby's head shape takes on more of a human form.

Likewise, the baby's fingers and toes are growing longer, as well as organs are starting to work together. Now certain parts such as the baby's eyes, eyelids and ears are continuing to develop. Just like the natural one, your spiritual baby still has some growing to do before it is fully formed. I found some cool information that says at ten weeks the average fetus is about the size of a strawberry; yes, a strawberry.

Now remember when I told you that your symptoms would be neither stopping, nor slowing down any time soon. During this time, you will still experience "morning sickness, exhaustion, and mood swings. But there are a few symptoms outside of the ones that I have listed that can be added to the list. I told you that all are given greatness, but much is required to access it. You have to grow threw to get to.

SPIRITUAL HEADACHES

Occasionally, some moms experience headaches during pregnancy. For some they are more frequent than others and are usually caused by a lack of eating, stress, or menstruation. When it comes to a spiritual pregnancy, there will be times that you will experience headaches. Nevertheless, it is important to understand the reason for the headaches during a spiritual pregnancy, the type of headaches, and how to get rid of the headaches.

Sleep-Related Headaches:

Your greatness will have you staying up. The passion that is boiling on the inside of you will wake you up and keep you up. It is good that you have that much excitement about your greatness. However, your passion can contribute to head throbbing headaches, which will contribute to the lack of sleep.

Doctors will often tell a pregnant woman to take some over the counter drugs; this may offer temporary relief from headaches. However, for your spiritual situation I would prescribe you with some over the counter advice and that is prayer. In my case, prayer is equivalent to NyQuil. After a good dose of prayer, it gets rid of those throbbing headaches and I am off to sleep like baby.

Cluster Headaches:

For me cluster headaches are the worst. They occur suddenly and come in spurts, hence the reasoning behind labeling them "cluster headaches." The reason why I had cluster headaches is because I was allowing negative thoughts to creep in my mind as well as over thinking. It is normal for spiritual pregnant person to over think. For some people birthing greatness is a new experience.

However, spiritually speaking most cluster headaches start with what you consume with your eyes. You have to make sure that nothing blocks or interrupts your vision. Make sure that you keep your eyes on the prize because when you do, you can now say bye-bye to cluster headaches. If that does not work, see your healthcare provider, Jesus, and He will work it out.

Tension Headaches:

Try not to allow the everyday stress of life to get the best of you during your time of carrying greatness. Tension headaches are known to be the most frequently reported types of headaches for adults. During your spiritual pregnancy, birthing greatness can sometimes be stressful. Symptoms of tension headaches can be hunger pains, tiredness and low tolerance for various types of fumes. Do those sound familiar? Spiritually speaking, tension headaches can come for the lack of eating. When you do not consume the right nutrients, headaches will occur.

During this delicate time, fatigue will also cause headaches. Similarly, if you do breathe in the wrong scent your head will hurt as well; we have all experienced smelling a particular scent of perfume or cologne and instantly getting a headache. Well during spiritual pregnancy headaches come in a variety of forms and the worst part is that they sometimes come without any warning.

You have to pay attention to the signs your mind, body, and soul are telling you because if you ignore them, headaches of any kind will occur. The next time you feel an unusual headache coming on, take action, go see your Doctor G-O-D to pinpoint the correct diagnosis and treatment. If you have not noticed, I want you to stay on your knees, on your face, and pray continually.

ROUND LIGAMENT PAIN

You are probably wondering what round ligament pain is. Well, this is a term that some women, if not most women, do not hear during their pregnancy, nevertheless round ligament pain still occurs. Round ligaments are two of the ligaments in a woman's pelvis that help support the uterus, and as the baby grows during pregnancy they stretch and soften. Bear with me, this is going to make sense to you in a minute.

Now when these ligaments tighten, there is a strong possibility that a woman may start to feel pain on one or both sides of the abdomen. I need you to catch this spiritual revelation and how this applies to you during your spiritual pregnancy. Your two spiritual ligaments are called, grace and mercy, which support your greatness. Just a second ago you read that as the baby grows during pregnancy, they stretch and soften. As it pertains to your greatness, it does not stretch and soften, but it will start to stretch and to get powerful.

Your greatness will start to throw its weight around because it knows it is great. During this time of pregnancy life is going to throw curves ball at you which is going to tighten your relationship with not only greatness but more importantly Jesus. The devil does not realize that the more he tries to hurt you the closer you can get to Jesus. Your greatness is ready to come out and show the devil that you are not a punk.

Although it is not time, it will cause you some discomfort. This symptom does not go away on its own. The devil will continue to fight until you miscarry. I need you to tell the devil that you have two ligaments call grace and mercy and that they are more than enough to defeat the devil. The ligament means, a short band of tough, flexible fibrous connective tissue which connects tow bones or cartilage or holds together a joint. What Satan does not quite understand is that your spiritual ligaments; grace and mercy, connect and hold you together with God and that no weapon, nor devil formed against it shall prosper.

Allow me to inform you of the difference between grace and mercy. We often hear these two words used together, but most people never explain what they each mean. First, grace and mercy are not the same. Mercy is God not punishing us for our sins. However, grace is God blessing us despite the fact that we do not deserve it. That is why your spiritual ligaments, grace and mercy connect you to God. God knows that you are not perfect, and He does not expect us to be. He knows that sometimes the devil will get your attention. During your spiritual pregnancy, you are not going to do everything right.

That is when God shows mercy and during this journey you are also going to experience His grace.

Grace is God extending kindness to the unworthiness. God could have allowed you to miscarry your greatness a long time ago but He, instead, showed mercy. Mercy is deliverance from judgment. God does not owe us anything. Hold on to God through it all; your alignment with God will strengthen your ligaments. With a pure heart, He will rain down grace and mercy.

CHAPTER 8

8

KEEP PRESSING

I m excited for you and the growth of your greatness. I am equally excited about the changes that have already taken place in your life. Since the marathon is coming to an end it makes the completion that much more difficult. During a normal pregnancy leg cramps occurs. As a runner in this marathon, you have to make sure that you are trained to finish and win the race.

During any race, there are obstacles such as a leg cramp. Usually when a runner gets a leg cramp it is because of dehydration, muscle strain, or low potassium. We talked earlier in the book about thirsting for God. Well sometimes during a race you will lose focus on what or who got in position to win. We stop being thirsty for God and when we stop thirsting, dehydration sets in; this causes leg cramps. Dehydration is caused by not drinking enough fluids while working out.

Honestly, there is no difference when you are spiritually pregnant. Carrying a baby, or in your case carrying greatness, is and will be a workout. The Bible says in the New Living Translation in 1 Timothy 4:8, "Physical training is good, but training for godliness is much better, promising benefits in this life and in the life to come."

If the devil cannot attack your thirst for God, he will attack your muscle and create muscle strain. A muscle strain is the tearing of a muscle or a tissue connecting muscle to the bone. Spiritually speaking, the devil attempts to tear the relationship with you and your greatness. He will attempt to convince you to abort your greatness or worse, attempt to tear the relationship between you and God. You are probably wondering if you thirst for God, how can you have a muscle strain during this marathon?

It is quite simple, and again the devil uses what is *good* against you. You can have a thirst for God and when He does not seem to come when you want Him to, the devil convinces you to believe that God does not hear you. This can possibly make you tear your relationship with God. The marathon runner's best method of getting rid of muscle strains is by applying heat, exercising, as well as stretching. Allow me to explain.

The stretching you want to do that is very important and the stretching I am referring to is your faith. Do not make up your own stretching exercises because you are liable to pull something. Not only is God a licensed and proven Doctor, but He is also an awesome coach and trainer. If you have done physical activity you know that coaches express the importance of regularly stretching.

You can increase your efficiency, strength, and you can give your muscle the ability to grow. Be careful because the devil is going to attempt to stretch you while God is stretching you. The devil will try to have you stretch away from God. Meanwhile, God will ask you to do somethings which will require you to stretch in faith.

In Exodus 7:19 the Lord said to Moses, "Tell Aaron, take your staff and stretch out your hand over the water of Egypt, over the streams and canals, over the ponds and all the reservoirs and they will turn to blood. Blood will be everywhere in Egypt, even in the wood buckets and stone jars." Now Moses was not supposed to perform a physical stretch, but it was a stretch of faith in response to God's word. Moses did realize that God was having him stretch his faith so that Moses could be in the best shape for the toughest battles.

Moses was essentially a mayor over a city. He was responsible for millions of Israelites and God trusted Moses with this huge assignment. Likewise, He is trusting you with your greatness. In Exodus 14:15-16 it says, "Then the Lord said to Moses, why are you crying out to me? Tell the Israelites to move on. Raise your staff and stretch out your hand over the sea to divide the water so that the Israelites can go through the sea on dry ground."

God understands that the devil is attacking you and that your journey to birthing greatness is challenging. However, God is wondering why you are crying out to Him. He worked you out for this moment; you just have to stretch your faith so that you can defeat the devil and get you and your greatness safe to the other side.

STRETCH YOUR FAITH TO FIT GOD'S PLAN

The job and goal for a coach and trainer is to push you even if it is uncomfortable for you. The plan, job, and goal of a coach and trainer are no different from God. Your coach is very strategic, God puts you in situations to shake you up, to move you from your comfort zone, to grow your faith. On this journey to birthing your greatness it will often require you to take some risk. The great news is that every risk that you take will stretch your faith closer to God.

Every risk you take will lead you to lean more on your faith. One of the best news that I can give you is that you will know when your faith is driving your spiritual pregnancy journey; you will be stretched to what will appear to feel like your limit. God wants you to stretch beyond your understanding and to lean on His power. With God's power, you will not only accomplish all of God's plans for your greatness, but more importantly, you will accomplish all of God's plans for your life.

I cannot stress enough the fact that this marathon of birthing your greatness is not an easy run. You will go through battles and all battles create scars. Do the world a favor by not hiding those scars. I am talking about your emotional and spiritual scars; don't hide them. This is going to sound crazy but celebrate and show those scares. Your scars remind you and show others that you have stretched your faith to overcome situations and circumstances that transpired through your journey. In the natural, these are called stretch marks. Scars tells you where you have been. It tells the beautiful story that when you stretch your faith to fit God's plan for your greatness and your life, victory is inevitable.

THE CYLCE IS BROKEN

I believe that some of you are still in disbelief that you are pregnant with something great on inside. Well, I am here to tell you that greatness is upon you. Your spiritual pregnancy was not and is not an accident. One of the indications that you are indeed pregnant and carrying greatness is when your *cycle* is broken. Now I am aware that we spoke on "cycle" earlier in the book and I know that the word "cycle" still maybe shocking to most of you, especially for my fellas.

To be honest, I was in shock as well. This "cycle" word and experience was a lot to take in. I remember when Jesus came into my life uninvited and manage to disrupt some cycles that were happening in my life. And I can honestly say that it was the most nerve wrecking, but the greatest time in my life. I believe that this is the time where God is going to come into your life and break the cycles that are transpiring in your life. From the generational curses, the lack of graduates in your life, from not having a business owner in your family, and much more.

Get ready for the first in many areas of your life. Get ready to be the trailblazer for things to come in your life. The generational curses and cycles in your life are about to be, if not already, broken. I decree and declare that your cycle is being broken and is going to change you and your family's life from this day forward.

Speaking of change, there is a natural change that occurs in a female reproductive system that makes pregnancy possible, and that change is called, the menstrual cycle. This particular cycle is required for the preparation of pregnancy. However, some of you are trying to prevent the birth of greatness. That particular action in the natural is called birth control. Can I tell you a secret? You cannot control what God has set for your life. You cannot control what God has placed on the inside of you. The only thing you can do is accept what He has called over your life or deny it.

Let's be honest, some of us are on birth control because we allowed people to convince us that we are too young or too old to carry greatness, too young or old to birth greatness, too inexperienced to access success or too poor to become wealthy. Some of us are taking birth control because we believe that if we give birth to what God has placed on the inside of us, we will be made fun of, be talked about, or be judged. We would rather think about how it feels to have success on the inside of us instead of going through the process of what it actually takes to become successful.

We cannot control the birth. Trust me, I knew that God had placed something on the inside me at a young age, but I was too afraid to birth what was given to me; I did not want to be looked at differently. I knew that I wanted to birth what He had placed on the inside me, but I wanted to do it on my time and not His time. That is what you call *birth control.*

Now I must warn you that taking birth control comes with side effects. One of those effects is the change of your body shape. A birth control pill causes the fat to be stored in surprising ways and in surprising places in your body. Hint: Why do some women gain

weight when they are on a birth control pill? Spiritually speaking, your attempt to control your birth will take your gift and greatness hostage, storing it in places where it will be hard to find to set free. When it comes to your spiritual pregnancy, the devil loves to see that you are trying to take control of your birth. The reason for this is because attempting to control your birth is a battle.

Yes, birth control in the spirit is a battle and it can cause you to lose strength which will eventually cause you to become weak. In the natural, women who are on the pill gain 40% less muscle than those who were not on the pill. You are probably saying, "What about exercise?" Birth control affects the ability to grow a women's muscle even through exercise. Early in the book we talked about the importance of exercising. Trying to control your birth puts a strain on your exercising.

You start to have a hard time stretching your faith. All of a sudden you will start resisting training from your trainer which is *God.* Trying to control your birth leads to stress, which leads you to stop being intimate with God. Slowly but surely, you begin to stop laying before God. If you have not caught on yet, trying to control your birth; *birth control* does not lead to anything great.

Being on birth control sometimes delays cycles or sometimes stops cycles completely. However, God is in the business of breaking cycles and when we interrupt or stop His process, life changes for the worse. We sometimes try to do God's work for Him. When we submit, we put our self in position to succeed. However, when we allow anything and anyone to convince us that we can control our birth we miss the opportunity to impact change.

When God breaks cycles that haves transpired in our lives, we take a shift from having a testimony to becoming a testimony. Change is essential for success. God knows that when He breaks the cycles in your life, change will come. We become a walking testimony. True change requires leadership. Change has a look. That is the reason that when you see pregnant women in the natural, their faces, their bodies and their feet starts to take shape and change. And as long as you continue to try to control what God as place for your life, you will never experience a Godly change.

Now I am not here to judge you; again, I was once trying to control my birth. I remember when I met someone that introduced me to something that changed my life at that particular time. I must admit that I was vulnerable; they came into my life when I was weak from trying to control my birth. The devil witnessed me in battle and took advantage. The devil with his tricks sent someone my way to inform me of an alternative to birth control.

In my vulnerable state, I was all ears. It was told that I could experience my gift and whenever I did not like the results that it produced or if I was scared or nervous about the results, I could take this particular substance and essentially "kill" the dream or passion. Now this did not mean that I could not get pregnant with greatness in the future; at least that was what they told me. And they were really adamant about informing me that this substance could only be consumed via mouth and that it must be taken within seventy-two hours (three days) after intercourse to prevent pregnancy; in my case, it would be after spiritual intimacy. They told me that the sooner I took this, the greater would be the chance of it working. Ok, no more being around the bush. Yes, you guessed right, they gave me a Plan B pill.

PLAN B

Will Smith once said, "There is no reason to have a plan B because it distracts from plan A." This could not be truer. I allowed that person to come into my life and provide me with an unprescribed drug called, Plan B. However, I cannot place all of the blame at their feet. I got hooked and started to think I needed a plan B just in case my plan A did not work. My addiction was so bad that I started to focus more on the plan B and it quickly became my plan A.

God had a plan for my life, but I had to have options just in case His plan did not work. Ok, I must be completely honest, I created a plan B just in case I did not like His plan. Some of us go for a plan B because it is what our parents want us to go for or if we are honest, it is because we fear God's plan. We are scared to go after the plan that was set for our lives because we do not want to go through the process to birth greatness.

Spiritually speaking, taking a plan B pill is equivalent to you giving yourself permission not to succeed. I learned during my time of being spiritually pregnant that when you are planning for failure it gives you permission to fail. Trust me when I say that successful outcomes manifest when you plan for success. That requires you to go after your plan A and throw out your plan B.

On your journey to birth greatness, you will become moody. You will be on an emotional rollercoaster. However, a Plan B is an emotional safety net. When striving to reach a goal, but you fail, it brings some level of emotional pain. I understand; after all who likes pain? Needless to say, there is no greater motivator or tool for achieving success than failure. What if I told you that failure is one of the main ingredients to success? Birthing greatness is not easy. There are tasks and goals throughout this process that God will place in front of you and trust me you will fail. But if you do experience failure, what most people do is have a Plan B to fall back on.

This backup plan prevents failure from becoming an essential learning tool that will not only help you to succeed, but to ultimately birth greatness. My question to you is, how bad do you want to birth the greatness that is on the inside of you? If you answered that you want it, "really bad" in any form, then you must be committed to success; this means that you have to accept the process it takes to get there. Plan B's are not part of the journey. God says in Jeremiah 29:11, "For I know the plans I have for you," declares the Lord, "plans to prosper you and not to harm you, plans to give you hope and a future." Get rid of plan B's, because having a plan B is indicating that you are planning to fail.

CHAPTER 9

9

MISCARRIAGE'S

Forget what you heard; the devil is far from stupid. He knows that your faith is the key for you to birth greatness. He realizes that he brings static to your communication with God than it is a possibility you will lose faith in the process. A miscarriage often happens before a woman is aware that she is pregnant. Regardless of whether or not you know that you are pregnant or not, a miscarriage can occur. It usually takes place during the first three months of pregnancy, specifically before the 12th week.

Doctors believes it is imperative to inform women and I want to echo the statement, that miscarriages are not caused by anything that you or your partner have or have not done. I am not going to pretend that I understand but I can only assume that losing a baby must be emotionally devastating, especially if you were not aware that you were pregnant to begin with. So, if you are reading this, and you have experienced a miscarriage, I want to say that I am deeply sorry for your loss.

I have to be honest about how difficult it is for me to transition to my next point because I cannot fathom how my own mom would have responded if she had lost me. Nevertheless, what I can tell you is that my mother did have a miscarriage with my sister. Of course, I was too young to understand the thought process of miscarriages. When I got older, however, I began to understand the reason for not only natural miscarriages, but as well as spiritual miscarriages.

God sometimes will allow a miscarriage take place in the natural and the spiritual, because this is not the correct timing for you to birth something great. I wanted to write a book for years, but then was not the time; now is the time. I had great ideas just like you had and or have great ideas, but a miscarriage will occur if now is not the time for that idea to manifest. Just like I did when I miscarried, you probably thought that you missed your window of opportunity, when in reality God's true timing will come. I hope that this correlation between natural pregnancy and spiritual pregnancy that you are about to read will bless you.

MESSAGES GOD TEACHES US THROUGH MISCARRIAGES

When I got older, I had a conversation with my mom about her miscarriage with my sister. I was nervous because I could not imagine how it felt so I did not want to strike a nerve and bring back memories for my mom. Nevertheless, with hesitation I called her and asked her to talk about that moment when the doctor told her that she had a miscarriage. She told me that the news came as a complete surprise. She even asked the doctor if he was certain because she could not believe the news.

My mother proceeded to tell me that riding home with my dad after the doctor's appointment was so silent that you could hear a pin drop. Every time she wanted to break the tension in the car, she could not fix her lips to say a word. She informed me that the only thing that she could think of was how she was going to break the sad news to me; I was excited about having a little sister. When they arrived at home my mother rushed to the bathroom and locked the door behind her. With love, she questioned God asking, "Why me?"

As my father and I continued to check in on her it made us nervous because we were not getting much of a response. My mother eventually told me that she was sitting in the bathroom grieving. She snapped out of it and prayed, "God, I trust you, and I know you will provide me and my family with understanding and reveal what plans you have over our lives." As she wiped her eyes at that moment, God started to reveal Himself to her through his Word. All of a sudden, we heard a loud outburst come from the bathroom, screaming, "Lord you are good!"

A few minutes later after she gotten herself together, she called me into the bathroom. The funny thing is, up until this day, the bathroom is our talking room. She sat me down on the edge of the tub and she began to first explain to me what a miscarriage was. She felt that even though I was young, she would still "keep it real" with me. She told me that a miscarriage is simply the passing of a baby that is on the inside of a women. She then proceeded to talk to me about three lessons that God taught her during this miscarriage.

"All things work together for good."

This is a scripture in Romans 8:28. This was the first thing my mother said to me after she told me what a miscarriage was. I asked her, "What is good about losing my sister?" "What we believe is good is not always good for our future and growth," she said. And in your case while carrying and birthing greatness, everything is not always good. God teaches us to trust Him and to have faith that He would never lead us astray.

God is good all the time and all the time God is good.

My mother stressed to me that even though God took my baby sister from me, He was still good. She felt that it was important to teach me, as she always had, that taking things that do not belong to you is a sin and that sin is not good. She explained to me that even though this circumstance was difficult to understand, my sister's life belonged to God and that no matter how short my baby sister's life was, it was a blessing. I agreed with my mom that God is good. She shook her head and said, "Yes, baby God is good."

Now as an adult, I still believe that God is good all of the time- no matter what the circumstances are. For example, in Job 1-3 and 38-42, Job lost his children, his health, his wealth, and his friends; his wife said, "Curse God!" However, because God was and is good all the time, Job experienced a deeper relationship with God. Job was blessed by God and restored by God as well. The miscarriage that my mother experienced was the beginning of a new relationship with God. Our family was restored, and our relationship with each other became closer because of that situation. Nevertheless, in the back of my mind I still asked the question, "Why?

The secret things belong to God.

Just like anyone who has experienced a miscarriage has wondered, why. I had many questions, but the question "why?" was the main question that I wanted to be answered. All of my questions included why this had happened which would only lead to anxiety, dead ends, and frustration. Gods says in Deuteronomy 29:29, "The secret things belong unto the Lord our God: but those things which are revealed belong unto us and to our children forever, that we may do all the words of this law." So do not worry about the why, seek the revelation that God gives from your experiences in life. You are probably wondering what impact does this have on birthing greatness? In spiritual pregnancy you can also have a miscarriage, but I like to call it "*miscarried*" instead.

MISCARRIED THE GIFT

Have you ever met talented people that were not successful? Have you ever met someone who was and still is gifted, but has not used their gift to the best of their ability? Can you honestly say that you know someone whose expectations for their life were high, yet that person never lived up to it? If you do not know of a person, hi my name is Christopher Williams and I miscarried my gift or rather, I had many spiritual miscarriages in my life.

According to the 1 Peter 4:10 it says, "Each of you should use whatever gift you have received to serve others, as faithful stewards of God's grace in its various forms." The important message from this verse was to use your God given gift to help each other. For the longest of time, I did not use my God given gift, especially not for others. When you do not use your God given gift(s), then the world suffers. I want you to realize that God did not give you a gift to only benefit you. He gave you a gift to benefit other people. Gift stands for **Giving. Internally. For. Those.**

I am so glad that people gave and utilized their God given gifts to help me. God knew that I was not good at fixing on cars. He knew that I just wanted to buy cars and drive them. So glad God gave mechanics the gift to change oil, rotate tires, and fix a wheel alignment because He knew that the only thing I could do was to put gas in the tank. I am thankful that people identified their gifts and shared it with the world. God has given us all gifts, but some of us mishandle and miscarry the gift. One of my gifts is the ability to connect real life, such as a women's pregnancy and match it to the Word of God in order to make it clear.

For so long I miscarried my gifts. I had the ability to use my words cleverly, but instead of doing the Will of God, I did it for personal gain; I *miscarried the gift*. My gift was given for you first, not for my personal gain first. When I realized that and accepted that, I started to become a blessing. I pray you have learned something or have been blessed from one of my gifts, which is this book so far. If you have been blessed so far, please send me a Tweet @Chris_Empowers or message Instagram @Chris_Empowers. Now if you have learned or have been blessed by this book that is wonderful, but what if I did not identify my gift? What if I continued to use my gift for personal gain? The world or specifically you, would not have been blessed.

My mother loves to see the fruit of her labor. She loves to see me succeed in life. You bring joy to God by using your gifts to impact the world. Your responsibility is to identify that gift; your greatness depends on it. God loves to see the fruit of His labor change and impact the world.

GIFTS, USE THEM OR LOOSE THEM

I was being easy on myself earlier when I said I mishandled my gift. To be honest I was reckless, careless, and probably extremely selfish with my gift. My mother was big on manners, never wanting me to be selfish, and always expecting me to be thankful for any and everything I have been given. My favorite holiday was Christmas when I was a child. I could not wait to open the gifts my parents had purchased for me. I would sit on the floor to embrace all of the gifts. Some gifts I would look at the box and then toss them to the side. Sometimes I would open a gift, look at it and put it down to go to next gift without even saying thank you.

There would also be times where I opened a gift and my eyes lit up with joy; I would scream out thank you! My question to you is which person are you when God gave you your gifts? Are the one who just tosses your gift around? Are you the person who accepted the gift, opened it, and quickly moved on without saying thank you? Or are you the person who opened their gift with joy and screamed out thank you? You want to birth your greatness, right? You want God to use you, but in order for that to happen, you must first unwrap your gift. Many of us do not value gifts because we do now what is in the "box." We never get past the wrapping paper.

Unfortunately, I was the person who saw the gift, looked at the box, then tossed it to the side. I never open it because I was trying to open the best-looking, wrapped gift. God sometimes does not wrap your gift in the best wrapping. He does not always unleash your gift at the best times, in best situations, or circumstances you will like. But if you only look at the exterior of it, there is a great chance that you will miss your blessing.

I know that you have not opened up your gifts because you are fearful of what is in it. You fear that what is inside will make you look stupid or different in people's eyes. You are afraid of what they are going to say or are fearful of getting hurt. We talked about risk earlier; you have to be a risk taker. I promise you that the day you decide to open your gift, it will be uncomfortable.

When I was younger, I shook gifts before I opened them. Some of you are scared because the gift sounds like one thing, but the gift does not match how the wrapping looks or what you expect. Some of you are very creative with your words. You may love how the wrapping paper looks, but your gift may reveal to you that you will be a poet or a pastor, but that is far what you expect. People are afraid to open their gifts because they believe that what is inside of it may not be what they desired or expected.

The unwrapping of the gift is a process; it does not happen overnight. God believes and trusts that we will do well with the gifts that He has given us. But I must keep it real with you, I'm not to scare you but to light a fire under you. If you do not use your God given gift, two things will happen. First you will never be truly happy. You can make all of the money in the world, but if you are not utilizing your gift you will not be happy.

Secondly, you could end up like some people in the world, full of potential, talents, and gifts, but are so miserable because you know there is something inside of you that needs to come out. I say when it comes to your gift, if you do not use them you will lose them. And I am not talking about physically losing the ability to unwrap your gift. I am talking about the desire to unwrap your gift. Some people know that they have a gift, but after so long, after so many situations and circumstances have transpired in their life, they give up completely on unwrapping their gift. I know that you have something great on the inside of you that the world needs; do not miscarry your God given gift.

I THOUGHT ABOUT ABORTING

Can you imagine going to the doctor's office, sitting on the examining table telling Doctor G-O-D that you want to abort your gift, your dream or more importantly your greatness? Well, essentially that is what I did at one point of my life. According to doctors, 39% of girls under the age of 18 who have gotten pregnant, have had an abortion. Spiritually speaking, at an early age in my life, I knew deep down inside that I had a gift and a dream, but I thought that I was going to get made fun of, talked down to, and would receive no support. This led to the thoughts of me not going through the process of birthing greatness. Similarly, things happen in a woman's mind that make her consider aborting her baby. They believe they not ready, that someone will mock them, judge them, or not support them. In this same way, I remember like it was yesterday, wanting to abort my dreams and gifts.

During my process of birthing greatness, I attended this conference to help improve my chances to birth a healthy greatness. During one of the breaks, I walked up to the speaker and asked him, "What advice would you give someone like me who is trying to speak to the world about identifying, living out, and unleashing their purpose." He looked at me and said, "Nobody is going to want to hear about purpose. No one is going to pay a motivational speaker to talk about purpose."

Let's just say after the conference, I essentially went to the abortion clinic in my mind. I allowed him to convince me to kill my dreams, but more importantly, to kill my assignment sent by God. All of the dreams I had about traveling across the world teaching people how to unwrap their gifts, ignite their passion, unleash their purpose, but more importantly, to birth their greatness just died inside of me after hearing his comments.

I remember the night after the conference I had a dream. And I love how God speaks to me through dreams and He probably speak to you and your dreams as well. In my dream, I was walking into another doctor's office. However, this doctor's office was different. In my first dream I spoke earlier about the doctor's office, but I never told you that it was cold, just like the doctor's office we go to today. However, this doctor's office was warm and cozy, I know you are probably saying, "What's wrong with that?" The problem was that I knew this was not just a regular dream. This was a dream that God was trying to speak to me. Yes, it was warm and cozy, but there was nothing warm and cozy about me entering a room, sitting on the examining table and telling my God that I wanted to abort the greatness that He trusted me with.

Sadly, this was one of the most uncomfortable times in my life, but as the great doctor that God is, He said something to me that made me fall on my knees and cry my eyes out. He looked at me as I was sitting on that examination table and told me that He loves me. At that moment He taught me that human love could not match up with God's love, which is unconditional. Jesus was dying on the cross and was praying for His killers (Luke 23:24); that is unconditional love. God did not love us because we loved Him first; rather, "We love because He first loved us", 1 John 4:19.

Love is a verb; it is what you do, not just what you say. That moment in my dream not only made me wake up in tears, but also at that moment changed my thought process. The revelation I received was that not everyone was going to understand and love your greatness. People that do not understand or talk down about your dreams do not necessarily mean for you must abort it. Trust God: He got your back.

DISCLAIMER

I mean this will all my heart. If you are reading this part of the book and you went through an abortion, I am neither here to judge you, nor judge your reasons for getting an abortion. I did not write this piece to make you feel bad; that was certainly not my attention. Nevertheless, I apologize if I did. As well as I am fully aware that I will never understand a woman's pain and process when making decision or going through with an abortion. I am speaking through my experience of aborting my greatness. I hope that you understand. Again, I am sorry.

DO NOT ABORT YOUR DREAMS

Abortions is the ending of a pregnancy by removal or expulsion of an embryo or fetus before it can survive outside the uterus. Never and I do mean never abort your dreams. You are never too young or too old to get impregnated with a dream or greatness. Sarah, the wife of Abraham, was 90 years of age when God blessed her to carry and birth a child. There is no age requirement to birth what God as given you. I realize that there are really no words to fully describe living out your dreams; it is something you can only experience.

If you abort your dreams you will block the fulfillment that your dreams could have given you. The joy that you receive when you live out your dreams the way God intended is unexplainable. God gave you a dream to show you a movie trailer of your greatness. When you do not abort your dreams, but live out your dreams, you enter into a world of possibilities. You begin to develop a superpower like no other. You start to believe that nothing can stop you. By having that attitude and living out your dreams, you will be able to change the circumstances and situations that are transpiring in your life, more importantly change the world.

Living out your dreams helps you to develop a spirit of gratitude. I started to be more grateful when I did not abort my dreams because when I started living out my dreams, I knew that all things were possible. I could not stop telling God thank you for allowing my dreams to live. Allow your dreams to live and I promise you that your life will change for the better.

Aborting your gift nor your greatness is an option. Steve Harvey says, "A gift is not a gift until it is shared." The reason why aborting your gift is not open for discussion is because other people can benefit from your gift. Our gifts were purposely created not just for ourselves but to help those around us. Not only do other people benefit from you and your gift, but you benefit from the gifts of others.

We benefit from Steve Job's Apple creation, Howard Schultz's Starbucks Coffee, and even your grandmother's cooking. The world does turn without the sharing of gifts. So, the question is how can others benefit from your gifts if you are attempting to abort them? When a person aborts their gift, you essentially have slowed the world down from turning. Your gift is a game changer and world changer; we need your gift.

Now do not think that you do not benefit from sharing your gift. It is a win-win situation. When sharing your gift, you get to not only exercise our gift, but you also get to please God. When we please God, He pours down blessings from heaven. I have witnessed my gift change the lives of people. I promise you that you have something inside of you that is life changing for someone, do not abort it.

YOUR GREATNESS NEEDS YOUR PASSION

Your passion is important, not only to your greatness, but also to your happiness. I am convinced that one of the biggest cheerleaders to a person's happiness is passion. All passionate individuals know that it is not easy to suppress one's passion. Your passion pushes you to keep learning and working towards your gift. Passion does not just bring happiness to the person who ignites it, but it also brings joy to those who are witnessing the passion.

Every successful person has witnessed someone following his or her passion, whether the successful person has been watching up close or from far away; usually passion drives a person to follow his or her own dreams. Personally, I witnessed Steve Harvey, Kevin Hart, T. D. Jakes and Will Smith from afar; I watched them follow their passion. Additionally, I had the privilege of having a close-up view of my mother following her passion; this taught me to allow my passion to fuel me and push me.

My passion to help people birth their greatness gave me the drive to finish this book. Without passion you will always wait until the perfect time. Well, I am sorry to tell you there is no perfect timing. The most important thing to remember about passion is that it does not wait for anyone. You cannot be passionate about something for ever with no action attached to it. If you do not ignite your passion you will live an unfulfilled life. At the same time, having a strong passion to birth greatness is kind of risky. My question to you is, "Are you willing to risk it all to birth your greatness?"

I do not know about you, but I am willing to risk it all in order to birth greatness. I know that some women in my life have had the doctor tell them that their pregnancy is high risk and that there is a high possibility that the mother and/or the baby will not make it. However, some of those women who go to that particular information leaned on their faith, believing that God was going to make a way out of no way.

These powerful women reshaped my thinking. I changed my mindset, deciding that I will birth my greatness even if my life depends on it. I do not care if my greatness comes out looking weird to people; I am still birthing it. I also have family and friends who have given birth to a child with special needs. I always tell them that the reason why a child has special needs is because God knew the world would need something different or special. I do not expect my greatness to come out looking like everyone else. I expect my greatness to be something special needed by others.

Yes, risk taking is scary, but the reward is amazing. There are people in the world that do not like taking risks but remaining in your comfort zone is a risk in and of itself. There will come a point of time in your spiritual pregnancy journey when your only option is to risk it all. Hopefully, you already understand that accepting the gift that Jesus has placed inside of you is a risk. It is not because it is something bad but because you do not know what to expect, nor what will come from birthing greatness. It might require you to quit you job; therefore, the risk is not knowing how you are going to pay bills and rent for months to come. Where there is a risk, there is a high reward. Let yourself fall into life's challenges without controlling them. Lean on God and soon enough, you will find yourself flying.

CHAPTER 10

10

FEELING LIGHTHEADED?

During a woman's pregnancy, their body produces more blood vessels, and their hormone levels start to change. This can leave you feeling dizzy or lightheaded from time to time. It is not called a bun in the oven for no reason. A woman's body is generating plenty of heat during her pregnancy, which means spending too much time in a hot or stuffy room can contribute to feelings of lightheadedness. Also, during this time, progesterone increases the flow of blood to the baby, resulting in lower blood pressure and reduced blood flow to your brain giving you that dizzy feeling.

Dizziness means the loss of one's balance, feeling unsteady or confused. During your spiritual pregnancy, there is a period when time weighs on you. Since it took a while for me to birth my greatness, the time I spent carrying it took a toll on me. I was trying to control everything around me, while trying to avoid seeing uncomfortable truths, and trying to hide from certain circumstances and situations.

This can cause you to be lightheaded or dizzy. Remember, the devil loves to attack the mind. Just like any boxer who takes enough hits to the head, you will feel lightheaded. When your opponent sees a window to attack, he does not hesitate. Satan only attacks when he sees that you are physically vulnerable. Satan loves to come around when he sees us in a weak position, either physically or emotionally.

When a fighter is lightheaded in the ring after getting hit, his trainers would advise him to keep his hands up, so he would not get knocked down. When you have your hands up it reminds you that it is safe for you to move forward at this time. This birthing of greatness is a new spiritual endeavor you are on. Usually when you are a new boxer you do not know the importance of keeping your hands up. Satan finds comfort in attacking someone in the beginning of any new spiritual journey.

I want you to know that the devil is a real risk taker and if he believes he can get in a really good punch, he will. The devil is very smart, and just like a skilled boxer he will attack, then leave and return again. However, having God as your trainer, you can never lose. God does not prevent you from being hurt, but He gives you the necessary tools to win. You have to remember that you are victorious. Yes, I understand Satan does attack, and sometimes we fall into sin. But the Bible says in Roman 3:23, "All have sinned, and come short of the glory of God."

A fighter may either forget or not listen to the trainer in the corner until that fighter gets that devastating right hook which makes him or her lightheaded. The great thing is that our trainer will never leave our corner. We are victorious through Christ; this is what God has promised us. In 2 Timothy 4:18 it says, "The Lord will rescue me from every evil attack and save me for His heavenly kingdom. To Him be the glory forever and ever. Amen." I know that you might feel alone in the boxing ring called life, but you are not. God is in your corner. You just have to have your hands up and always be on guard on the journey to birthing greatness.

I LOVE HIM. I LOVE HIM NOT

Let's be honest, we all want great things to happen to us in our lives, but we often want it immediately. We may not want to work or wait for it. If you are anything like me then when those great things are not happening how or when we expect it, then we proceed to question God's timing. This can translate to the lack of intimacy time with Him. You are currently reading what takes place in the 12th week of a spiritual pregnancy. In the natural it is normal for a woman or for her partner to feel an increase or decrease in sexual desire at various times during the pregnancy.

Doctors say enjoy intimacy with your partner and do not worry; the baby will be safe. Likewise, during your spiritual pregnancy, your drive to be intimate with Jesus will increase and decrease. I am not going to lie; most of us need to learn how to trust God in all areas of our life, especially when it comes to birthing greatness. Your trust will grow when you start being intimate with God.

Intimate: *closely acquainted; familiar, close, private and personal. A very close friend.*

Most women when carrying a child cannot wait to birth that child. However, women rarely enjoy the entire process. Although, I do not know how it feels to carry a child, I know that it is important for you to learn how to trust the process of the spiritual journey. When I was pregnant with greatness, I lost both joy and peace because I was not trusting God. God did not allow Jesus to impregnate us so that we would be miserable. Just like you, I wanted to know about everything that was going on inside of me.

Knowing everything can be detrimental, not only to your mind, body, and spirit, but also to your greatness. I am young but I spent most of my life being impatient; the spiritual pregnancy only increased my lack of patient. Women usually lack patients when it comes to learning the gender, for the most part because they are excited. I have a friend named D. Miles who taught me many things over the years, but there was one thing that he taught me that was extremely mind blowing.

When he found out that he was expecting a child, he and his other half chose not to know what the gender was until the baby was born. Now for you that might not surprise you at all, for me, I never heard that before. And because of that, from that moment I realized that what was inside of me was in God's hand; whatever He had for me, I would accept. You must learn, like I did, that you truly have trust God, because when you do you will worry no more.

My mother used to tell me that God may not come when you want Him, but He will always come on time. This is very true because God is never late and to be honest, He is never early either. This brings us back to what you read earlier; He is waiting for you to stretch our faith in Him. If you knew what was about to happen next, then you would not need for God. I know that this stretch of faith is not easy to do but trust me, it is necessary. I spent many of nights saying that I love Him; I love Him not. Why? Because I was truly impatient.

During a natural pregnancy neither a woman nor a doctor can change the process that happens during pregnancy. Ironically, we spend a lot of time wanting to change the process to fit our current situation, circumstance, and lifestyle because we do not want to go through the process. Little do you know that we have to go through to get to the other side. In order for a child to be birthed it has to go through a process and no part of this process can be skipped or ignored.

Yes, waiting on anybody is hard and waiting on God may be especially difficult because we cannot always see what He is doing. However, God is with you and will never leave you. God allows things to transpire in your life to see if you will trust Him and is willing to be patient. In Roman 12:12, it says, "Be joyful in hope, patient in affliction, faithful in prayer." Affliction means, something causing pain or suffering. God wants to see and know that even through affliction, you are patient that God will bring you through.

ACCEPT GOD'S TIMING

A few of the greatest gifts that God gives us are dreams, passions, and gifts; however, the most frustrating issue is that He does not give us a timetable for his plan. Yes, I know that a pregnancy takes nine months, but sometimes babies come earlier or in a few cases later than when the doctors say the baby will be due. Consequently, it is frustrating not knowing God's timing because time is how we stay on schedule in our life. It is also important because we cannot control time. We need time to know when to wake up, when to eat our favorite meals, when it is time to get off from work.

Yet, I challenge you to trust Him and the process. God has our back. He knows that if we knew the timetable of his process then we might give up, not only on the process, but on Him. God is the ultimate trainer and when you have a trainer you do what he says, how he says, and when he says. Listen to God and trust Him and do what He says, how He says and when He says; I dare you to do it without any hesitation or questions. It took me awhile, but it is important to learn how to rely on God.

Your first trimester is almost over. You have come too far not to continue to rely on God. This pregnancy was unexpected to most and sometimes it does not make sense where He is trying to lead us. You never want to be pregnant and confused.

The Bible says in Proverbs 3:5-6, "Trust in the Lord with all your heart, and lean not on your own understanding; In all your ways acknowledge Him, and he shall direct your paths." Some would say that this is easier said than done and I agree.

I was one of those people who was pregnant with greatness but was trying to figure out everything on my own. The transformation occurred when I confessed to God that I did not know what I was doing, but that I trusted that He would lead me to where I need to be. In this book I figuratively speak on greatness being birthed in nine months. However, for some of us it can take nine weeks, ninety days or even ninety months. For me it took me most of my life to birth greatness. I miscarried it; I aborted it, but finally I took it seriously, trusting God and allowing my relationship with Jesus to be unbreakable. That was when I finally birthed my greatness.

HE'S WAITING

Waiting on God is very important. It is essential that we who are spiritually pregnant wait and not make moves without God's guidance and instruction. But it just as important, if not more important, to not wait passively for God to something supernatural in your life because that is not how God works. It is really satisfying to know that God was waiting on me; trust me when I say that God is waiting on you.

He is waiting for you to take a faith step. The results of you taking a faith step are mind blowing, because when you take a faith step, then that is when you will see God at work in our lives. The Bible says in Isaiah 30:18, "The Lord waits for you to come to him so he can show you his love and compassion. For the Lord is a faithful God. Blessed are those who wait for him to help him." God wants us to step out in faith. He wants us to take a faith step and trust Him with our lives. Most people wait for God to snap His finger to make their situations and circumstances better, while listing all of the details on how we want Him to do it. But God is waiting on you to trust Him with all of the details. He is waiting on you to trust Him that things will work out in your favor.

I know sometimes because of our past and for some of us present that we believe that God would not welcome us. But I am here to tell you that God always welcomes us. I know that you not perfect and that sometimes you probably do not think you are not worthy of all the things God has done for you in your life. I am here to tell you that God loves you as you are and all of us are God's children. We are always welcome even when we are a mess. Usually, we have to ring a bell or knock on the door for someone to open the door to welcome us in. God neither has a bell nor a door to be knocked on. Just like I do, you have direct access to God. The Bible says in Hebrews 4:16, "Let us therefore come boldly unto the throne of grace, that we may obtain mercy, and find grace to help in time of need.

This is not Allstate, but you are safe in God's hands. When I was a child my favorite place to be was in my grandmother's welcoming and loving arms. When you are in someone's loving arms, you feel as if nothing or no one can hurt you. No matter what age you are, we always need reassurance and love; we need someone who can embrace us, love us, and accept us with welcoming arms, reassuring us that everything will be simply fine. This is what God can do for you. Through your spiritual pregnancy you will face many storms, situations and circumstance that will hit you left and right, but you have incredible life insurance called "God arms." He will wrap you in love, understanding and peace. I promise you that God is not waiting on you on a high throne, He is waiting on you with open arms.

Before we move on to the final part of this book or should I say first trimester, I have a challenge for you. In your spiritual pregnancy journal, I need you write down several of your fears about being spiritual pregnant, if you have not already. Afterwards, talk to God about them. Sitting in His presence is equivalent to sitting in your grandmother's loving arms. I want you bask in His love.

CHAPTER 11

11

HANG IN THERE

You have just about made it to your second trimester. I have read that moms-to-be describe the second trimester as the honeymoon period of pregnancy. Spiritually speaking, I would not say that your second trimester is your honeymoon period because this makes or breaks certain people. The devil is angry that he could not kill you or convince you to abort your greatness. By this stage, your blood supply and flow from God to you will continue to grow as your spiritual pregnancy progresses. The devil knows this; he is strategizing how he can stop you from entering into your second trimester.

Yes, I know that you have fallen short in your life. The

Bible says in Roman 3:23, "For all have sinned and fall sort of the glory of God." I trust that your issues have not stopped you from still loving God; it is your love and commitment towards this process and towards Jesus that drives the devil mad the most. During many times in your life, especially in this part of your spiritual pregnancy, the devil will use one of his favorite weapons to knock you off of your quest of birthing greatness, discouragement.

The first story I learned in the Bible is the story of Adam and Eve. You heard of the Adam and Eve story, right? Discouragement was the sin that caused both of them to lose their confidence and instead of boldly going before God with the problem they were facing. Discouragement filled their hearts which causes them to run away from God. One of Satan's objectives is to knock you off your focus, your dominance, and your confidence to birth greatness. The devil does not stop there. There are three tricks that the enemy sends to discourage you.

Discouragement From People:

The devil knows the importance of your support B.R.A; Battle Ready Alliance. He knows if he attacks the ones that support you, then you have no support system when you need one. At that point you begin to question their lack of support because you do not know why they are not available when you need them to be. You start to lose confidence in people; these feelings may also crush your hope in God because you will feel alone, and the devil knows that thus is the perfect time to attack you.

Since the devil is a coward, he sends people to do the dirty work for him. He convinces you to be discouraged by the words of people. Remember you need people around you to tell you things that you need to hear, not those things you want to hear. The devil will have you interpret those things as bad or hating, when in fact, they may have good intentions. Most of the time God is trying to send people into your life to communicate something in order to get your attention. But the devil wants you to receive those words as being negative and not helpful.

Discouragement With Self:

Now that he has you questioning and losing confidence in people, you are starting to separate yourself; sadly, this is a time in your last week of the first trimester when you need your support B.R.A the most. When he has you discouraged with yourself, you are building confidence in the devil. The devil loves whispering to you that you are worthless, that God does not love you, and that you cannot birth greatness.

If you allow him to convince you that God does not really love you, then you are starting to believe that you are not really worth carrying and birthing greatness. Do not worry; you are not alone. I was also one of those people that fell for the devil's tactics. He attempts to use various issues and events that have transpired in your life to make you blame yourself such as, "I am not pretty so that is why I have not found anyone;" "I did not get a promotion, so I must not be any good;" or my favorite line when I was discouraged, "God does not love me because I am a sinner." Remember that God gives tough battles to tough soldiers, so a discouraged solider is a dead solider already.

Discouragement With God:

Any battle that you are in requires help. Ideally, you need people who are like minded, but with different strengths in order for you to win the battle. During my battles, I called on God. However, He does not always answer when you call on Him. The devil knows that and will try to use God's silence or what I like to call, God's peace against you. Sometimes you are calling for help, but He has already equipped you with the tools to defeat the enemy.

We sometimes become shocked when God says no to us.

The devil creeps in and tries to use God's "no" as a source of discouragement. No one likes getting turned down or ignored when they ask for something, especially as a child. When I was a child and I was told "no", or could not get what I wanted, I immediately felt unloved.

As God's child, the devil makes us feel as if God does not love us when He does not give us what we want, nor an answer. The word "No" is not an evil thing. When we were children, we can remember a few times that we begged for a "yes"; however, as a child of God we cry out to God and when we hear "no" it can still discourage us. I am here to tell you, "God says no because He always has something better in mind." [tweet this] @Chris_Empowers

HEARTBURN

Entering the tail-end of your trimester can be a challenging process. Why? Because it is you will now have to go through a crucial stage in this spiritual pregnancy. When I was spiritually pregnant, I was nervous about what to expect in the second trimester because I had gone through so much in only the first trimester. While in the 13th week of pregnancy, some women will experience heartburn. The cause of heart burn during pregnancy is when the baby moves from one position to the next, and as her growing uterus puts pressure onto a woman's stomach. Heartburn also presents itself by the intake of certain foods such as chocolate, citrus fruits, and fried or spicy foods. Ironically, there is a difference when it comes to a spiritual pregnancy.

To your surprise spiritual heartburn is when your heart burns within you because the presence of God, with the addition of your greatness, is on the rise. Unlike physical heartburn which brings discomforts, spiritual heartburn is attended to bring a breathtaking of joy. However, if we go against what God wants from us and we know we are straying away from Him are spiritual heartburn can bring discomforts. Now I can say that there are two similarities that a woman experiences during her pregnancy and what we experience during spiritual pregnancy. Sometimes when the baby moves from one position to the next, it may cause heartburn. Well, when your gift and greatness is moving and growing sometimes you experience a heartburn or what I like to call joy. When God shows up and shows out in your life, displaying how awesome He is, you get this unexplainable joy.

Honestly, I only have experienced one heartburn in my life, and it was not pleasant. However, I have experience multitudes of my heart burning for God that were joyful. Throughout my spiritual pregnancy I desired God but at the tail end of my trimester God's presence was a must. I love how God set my heart on fire; it is just like any relationship you are in or have experienced. When you put your significant other first, you will reap the benefits and that also shows that he or she is the center of your joy. Thankfully, my significant other is Jesus, and He is the center of my life, and one of the benefits I have reaped is this book. My heart for Jesus burns with love and joy. In your spiritual pregnancy journal, I need you to write down a few things that you are grateful for and how your heart burns for God.

Now be aware that just like natural pregnancy if you are intaking certain foods you can get an uncomfortable heartburn. You will have heart pain if you are intaking the wrong things during your spiritual pregnancy. There are a few things that can cause heart pain. When you intake fear, not only will you struggle in your walk with God, you will also risk the chance of miscarriages during your spiritual pregnancy. When you have a fearful heart, it exposes your hearts. Now fear can create stress and since your heart is exposed, the devil can put the spirit of anger in your heart.

In much the same way that a wounded animal becomes angry, trying to defend its brokenness, and trying to keep away any potential threats. When you are wounded and have scared off everyone, you will start to realize that you are alone. That causes your heart to transition from fearful to angry, and finally, to hopelessness. You can only be angry for so long until you realize you really need some help. Unfortunately, by that time no one is around because you have chased everyone of value away. Depression and irritation set in while your energy level becomes lower than ever.

Now your faith is starting to take a drastic hit in terms of your relationship with Jesus; whenever the devil can make the foundation of this relationship rocky, your heart begins to burn. If this continues to happen, you are in the perfect position for a heart attack. And when your heart is in attack, your greatness is in attack. Allow your heart to burn for God but do not intake things that will cause disease and damage to your heart.

SPIRITUALLY CONSTIPATED

Just imagine eating your favorite meal but your body never digests it. That means that your favorite meal is just sitting in you. This will lead to you being sick because your food is made to consume, to enjoy, to digest, and to release. If you do not have the opportunity to released what you ingest, then you are subject to constipation. In terms of birthing greatness, at some point you will have to digest your gift or simply accept your gift, but more importantly release your gift. The reason why people are not living out their purpose and unwrapping their gift is not what you would expect.

One of the main obstacles that keeps people like you from birthing their greatness is what I like to call spiritual constipation. Earlier in the book I told you that I had so much inside of me, but I did not know how to get it out; essentially, I was constipated. The reason why I could not release what was inside of me because I was not yet who God created me to be. In reality, I was like a liter bottle with soda in it, but my faith was shaky, and we all know when you shake a bottle enough times, you lose the taste or the value.

Eventually, the pressure starts building up and explode, but what comes out is not your authentic gift. Jesus allowed me to stay constipated and when I was truly ready, He allowed me to be to release what He placed in me. Being spiritually constipation does not seem like a big topic to talk about. We kind of brush it off like it is not a big deal. We do not talk about it but most of us, especially we that are in the process of birthing greatness, need advice on this more than ever.

God has put dreams, gifts, passion, purpose and so much more in us. If we just trust Him and His word, we will find ourselves in the third trimester, ready to birth your greatness. However, this journey to birth greatness comes with obstacles. We both know constipation is not a good feeling. God allows us to go through this because His intention is to refine us and prepare us to release what He has placed in us. A pregnancy belly indicates to others that a woman is pregnant. The great thing about a spiritual pregnancy is that no one can see your greatness. God does not like to promote us before we are ready.

ARE YOU READY?

Speaking of being ready, I think that you are ready. Not only are you ready to release what Jesus has put in you, but you are ready to move on to the second trimester as well. In fact, I do not think you are ready, I know that you are ready. You must continue to have strong faith along with the hunger to carry, and more importantly the hunger to birth your greatness. Failure is not an option. Aborting your gift, passion, purpose, or your greatness is not an option. If you were going to abort your greatness your chance to do that was before you picked up this book.

The possibility that I could have missed out on what God had in store for me was a huge deterrent for me slacking off; I had to stay on track to birth greatness. Yes, it was hard and at times it is still hard. I had many motivations from making my mother proud, and changing my fiancé life for the better, but my top motivation was the desire to grow into God's purpose and assignment for my life.

I understand that you are not perfect; neither of us is perfect. We have both made mistakes. I have certainly made plenty of them when I was also spiritually pregnant. Just like you, I questioned what God was doing, not only inside of me, but in my life. I resisted because I was fearful. Just like you, I went through confusion and misery. But through it all, He kept me close to His arms and I see you was wrap in His arms as well because you are still here. On your journey to birth greatness, I need you to trust God and to have faith. I cannot wait to see what you will birth.

My prayer is that you have enjoyed reading the furst part of "Birth Your Greatness." Before you move on to the second part of this book, I want to leave you with some words of encouragement. Great things are going to transpire in your life while you are carrying your greatness. Better yet, great things are already here! Your greatness will open doors that you never knew existed. Just believe in God as He believes in you. Stay focus! Keep God first! Don't give up! Keep Push'n.

CHAPTER 12

12

THE TIME HAS COME

Congratulations and welcome to the second part of this book, or should I say the second trimester of "The Birth of Greatness." If you cannot tell by now, I am so excited for you. Let me tell you why I am ecstatic, and why you should be excited too. I found a statistic that was very interesting and that is that 63% of people do not finish books and over half of those people do not finish the first part of a book. Well guess what? You have achieved what most people do not and that is surpassing the first part of a book. I believe that is something to be excited about.

Now you should also be excited because your passion and

thirst for greatness is growing. In the natural, a woman's belly expands around fourteen weeks which is the beginning of the second trimester. The growth of a woman's belly indicates that her baby is developing. The idea of her baby growing on the inside of her brings another level of exuberance and joy for a mother. The anticipation during this time translates to energy. You will think going through the natural process of carrying a baby can be tiring and at some points it is. However, during this time a woman's energy level increases tremendously. Well, there is no difference in your experience of carrying greatness.

Your energy or passion level will, if it has not already, increase. Your passion to finish that book, to start that business, to finish school, or even to carry and birth greatness at this time is on another level. In the natural it is called increased energy. Now that women have found an unexpected burst of energy, this is the time when they prepare the baby's nursery. Spiritually speaking there is no such thing as a baby nursery. However, this is time for you to prepare your mind, body, and soul, not in your baby nursery, but in your "prayer closet."

Now a baby nursery is clearly for the baby, hint BABY nursery. But in the spiritual sense there is no such thing as a baby nursery. Spiritually speaking your "baby nursery" is your prayer closet. Your prayer closet is not only a place for your ideas, goals, passion, and greatness, but more importantly it is a place where you can go before God in worship and prayer.

A baby nursery has multiple purposes; one of them is sleep. Sleep is crucial for a baby's health and development. What is crucial for your baby's health and development or should I say for your greatness' health and development, is prayer. And with the right surroundings, it can help you pay attention and focus on your greatness.

It is very important that parents pay close attention to their baby. In a baby nursery, babies need a temperature that is ideal for the most comfortable sleep. A room that is too warm is not a good sleep environment for a baby, and although I personally prefer a room that is cool when I sleep, unfortunately that is not the best temperature for a baby. Well, your greatness is no different.

However, it is not about the temperature that is set in the room. It has more to do with whether or not the spiritual atmosphere is in the room. *Atmosphere* is defined as a pervading tone or mood. So, when some individuals talk about spiritual atmosphere, they are referring to the invisible tones or moods hovering over the particular room you are in. To simplify that definition, those who speak on atmosphere are referring to the *Holy Spirit.*

Let's dive into this a little deeper. Prayer is an important part to anybody's life, no matter what walk of life you come from and no matter what you believe in. Prayer opens the door for the opportunity to enter the presence of God, to talk to God, and to hear His voice. When you are spiritually pregnant, prayer as well as the presence of God is vital throughout this process; this allows you to talk to and hear from God. I spoke on prayer earlier in the book and informed you that prayer can and should take place anytime and anywhere. However, sometimes it can be more effective when it occurs in a designated time and place. Yes, that designated place is your prayer closet. When your attention is given to the spiritual atmosphere, your prayer and conversation becomes more intimate and intentional with God.

Ok, I know that you probably have a few, if not a ton of questions. I hope these five tips not only help you to create a spiritual atmosphere of prayer but also help you to understand what to do while in you are in your prayer closet.

Remove Distractions:

I know some of you are probably asking, "Do you want me to actually pray in a closet?" Listen, do not be ashamed nor feel like that is a silly question; to be honest that is a great question. When it comes to my mother's prayer closet, she goes into her room, closes the door, cuts the television off, and begins to pray.

However, my mother-in-law actually goes inside of her bedroom closet before she begins to talk to God. It is not important that you pray in a closet or in a specific room, but it is important that you find quiet location.

The common denominator in the two examples that I used is that both women utilized quiet places to pray; they both want to be intimate with God, without distractions. You should put your phone on silent, do not disturb, or simply turn it off. You also should inform anyone that is in your house that you are unavailable for whatever time period because you are about to enter your prayer closet. Last but not least, you should get comfortable and set the atmosphere to spend intimate time with Jesus.

Get Comfortable:

This comes from experience; it is very difficult to direct your attention to Jesus when you are uncomfortable in any fashion. Your uncomfortable state can stem from the smallest things such as your clothing, noise, light, or what we spoke on earlier in the book, your position. For any first timers, entering your prayer closet can easily get uncomfortable just because this is a new experience. Make sure that you are relaxed. Remember that prayer is just a conversation between you and God. In order to hear what the Holy Spirit is revealing, you must not only be comfortable, but more importantly, you must be focused.

"But Chris what do I say and where do I start?" you may ask.

Prepare Your Heart with Praise & Worship:

I embrace the phrase, "The apple does not fall far from the tree" because just like my mother my prayer closet is in my room. I pray with the television off and with the doors closed. However, the difference in my prayer routine is that I begin my prayer time with praise and worship. There is no Golden Rule on how to start and what to say. I set the atmosphere by softly playing praise and worship music; it is a way to get my mind off of what is or what is not going on around me. I do not know about you but sitting in a quiet room and talking out loud, although I am talking to God, seem weird at first.

The praise and worship music distract me from my thoughts and helps me to focus on the time spent with God. More importantly, it is a way for me to usher God into my prayer closet. I use my time in God's presence, not to merely ask for personal favors, but to acknowledge His presence as well as to offer thanksgiving. Psalms 100:4 says, "Enter his gates with thanksgiving and into his courts with praise. Be thankful to Him and bless His name." Your prayer time in your prayer closet is one of the best times to just lay on your face and thank God for all of the things that He has done and that He will do in your life.

Listen to the Holy Spirit:

Your praise and worship will get the attention of God and throughout your time in your prayer closet, you will witness a shift in the atmosphere. This shift is the indication that God has showed up. In my own experience, once I sensed that God had shown up, I began to be quiet. I knew that God had something to say, but in order for me to hear from God I had to be still. In your journey to birthing your greatness silence is key. If you have a trouble hearing from God, it is because you are either not quite enough or you are not in position long enough to hear Him.

When was the last time the Holy Spirit spoke to you? What has the Holy Spirit spoken to you in your last conversation? Am I saying that God only speaks to you in your prayer closet? Of course not. However, it is important for you to take advantage of your intimate time with God in your prayer closet. It is equally significant not to allow anything to distract you or to interrupt your time with God. Trust that God is yearning for you to talk to Him, but He is also looking forward to talking to you; He wants conversation. The question is, "Are you ready to listen and receive what He has to say?"

Open Up Your Heart:

Now that you have removed distractions, have become comfortable inside of the room or closet, have prepared your heart with praise and worship, and have begun to listen to the Holy Spirit, now it is time to open your heart. During my first time going through this experience. I began asking God for what I wanted. In any case, you should open your heart and speak from your heart when talking to God. Give the Holy Spirit the opportunity to speak through you.

This is a judge free zone, where you can communicate while your emotional guard is down. Eventually, your prayer language will begin to change and your conversation with God will become so different that it might scare you. When you learn how to talk to God without always asking Him for something, then you have taken your prayer life to another level. But first you must open your heart, to these intimate moments that you will share with God.

The Bible says in Matthew 6:6, "But when you pray, go into your room, close the door and pray to your Father, who is unseen. Then your Father, who sees what is done in secret, will reward you." Dedicate your time to setting the atmosphere so that God is welcome in your prayer closet; likewise let the time that you spend with the Holy Spirit be fulfilling and life changing for you and your greatness. Whether this process will be new for you or whether you are experienced with a prayer closet, I would like to hear from you about your last experience; Tweet me @Chris_Empowers.

LEAKY HEART

Allow me to educate you on why a prayer closet and continual prayer to God is important, especially on this journey to birth your greatness. Once a year I go to the doctor and get a check-up. Now I know what you are saying, "just once a year?" Yes, once a year, do not judge me. I promise I am trying to do better. And as you know the doctor will do a checkup regardless of whatever reason brought you in.

My last experience at the doctor went well. The doctor performed a thorough checkup which revealed that there were no problems with me or my heart. When it comes to being spiritually pregnant, we need to go see our spiritual doctor which is God, more often; He must consistently check our hearts. The truth is that all of our hearts are in some type of condition that needs checking. Usually in the second trimester women experience what is called a leaky breast. Spiritually speaking, you will experience a leaky heart. Through your journey of being spiritually pregnant, your heart will be challenged.

When you start to get closer to birthing your greatness and closer to conversing with Jesus, certain people will not understand. This may cause you to feel isolated which will challenge your heart or what I refer to as a leaky heart. If you have not already noticed the difference in some of your friendships and relationships since coming closer to birthing your greatness. I must warn you that drawing closer to God on your journey can be challenging to you on so many levels: physically, mentally, emotionally, and spiritually. But it is all worth it.

I know that your heart will hurt at certain moments and that you will start looking for support from the people you thought were your friends or loved ones. Unfortunately, you will look up and they will be nowhere to be found; that will hurt your heart. Since everyone will not be on the same page as you, people will judge and condemn you because of your quest for birthing greatness. The Bible says, "If you are insulted for the name of Christ, you are blessed, because the Spirit of glory and God rests upon you", 1 Peter 4:14. Remember this, hurt people, will hurt people.

Trust me, I understand that it is not a good feeling to lose friends and relationships. However, during the tough times, which you will experience tough times when you are on the quest of birthing greatness, you will discover what you are made of but as well as what your relationships are made of. So, when you experience a leaky heart do not be alarm. I know it is going to be tough, but sometimes God will isolate you in order to elevate you. When you are elevated in Christ it is a sign of spiritual maturity. While I was attending college, I learned that not everyone is meant to be your friend forever. Also, during that time, I learned that the term "unequally yoked" is not just associated with dating or marriage, but that it also includes any form of relationship.

You must reevaluate your BFF, boyfriend/girlfriend or any relationships if they do not see eye to eye with your core values, with your goals, with your relationship with Jesus, or with your quest to carry and birth your greatness. I know that this may be a hard pill to swallow because it was for me. Yet, you really have to ask yourself, especially while you are carrying greatness, "Why do you spend most of your quality time with someone who does not spend their quality time with Jesus?" In 2 Corinthians 6:14 says, "Do not be yoked together with unbelievers. For what do righteousness and wickedness have in common? Or what fellowship can light have with darkness?" When your faith grows some of your relationships will die.

I learned from my fiancé that her hair cannot grow to its potential if her hair ends are not clipped. In other words, if you do not clip some of your friends, family, and other relationships out your life, neither your faith, your relationship with God, nor your greatness will be able to grow to its potential. This process will cause a spiritual leaky heart; it is better to have a leaky heart than to have people in your life who are trying to stop you from birthing your greatness. A real friend is one who walks into your life when you have a leaky heart, when the rest of the world walks out.

If they cannot grow with you in Christ, they cannot go with you. As the great Ciara says, "Level up... Level up, Level up, Level up!" At some point in your life during your journey to birth greatness you must come to grips that everyone cannot level up with you. Here is why:

Seasonal(ships):

Some relationships and people are only designed to be in your life for a season. People are like leaves on a tree. When it is warm or when things are going well, they like to blossom with you. However, when things get windy or get cold, they tend to fly away or disappear. You do not want leaf friends and relationships. You want rooted friends, the ones who have been holding and who will continue holding you down until the wheels fall off. But hear this, you cannot be upset with them, or with yourself if they fly away when times get rough.

It makes sense if those relationship fly away with the wind because they were only designed to be in your life for a season. Your heart will hurt because you may lose friends and relationships that you believed would stay in your life forever. As long as you have friends that produce something on your tree then they are useful; if they do not produce on your tree, they are wasteful.

"You Changed" - Friends:

Earlier in my spiritual pregnancy the two words I kept hearing were, "you changed." Do not allow those words to affect your growth. We all have friends who only remember us from our past. Many times, we will find it fascinating to look back into the past, to discuss all of the memorable moments with those people.

However, when you are on the journey of birthing your greatness, unfortunately, you cannot afford to spend time looking back into your past life. Looking into the past will stunt your growth. People who are so fixated on reminiscing on their or your past will either consciously or subconsciously stagnate your growth. Seek to be around people who propel you to your future and not people who will make you stuck in your past. I am not saying that it will be easy but dry up your tears and stitch up your leaky heart. You have greatness to birth.

Some People Can't Handle Where You're Going:

As usual, I must be honest with you. Not everyone can handle you carrying something great. When that digests in your spirit and you stop allowing your heart to leak over losing unnecessary people who have left your life, then your spiritual pregnancy will be much easier to handle. Trust me when I say that not everyone is not intended to go with you. God places people in your life for a test, a lesson, or to help you get to your destiny that God has set for your life. Everyone cannot go with you because everyone will not grow with you. FACTS!

HUNGRY!?

Now that you have trimmed some unnecessary friend from your life, I bet you feel a little lighter in weight. When I allowed people to walk out of my life, but also took the responsibility to eliminate people out on my life. I started to develop a different type of hunger for greatness. In a natural pregnancy a woman in the second trimester has an increased appetite. Being spiritually pregnant, your hungry should never stop.

It is not uncommon for the appetite to increase. A tree grows when it has the right nutrients. Your greatness is screaming on the inside, "Feed me!" Hunger leads to action; and action leads you to success. And I do not know anyone who does not want a successful life, because I keep hungry folks around me. You do not realize how much energy bad relationships take out of you until they are gone.

When bad relationships are gone your hunger to birth greatness will be increased. When you are starving you will find food because your life depends on it. If you really want to be great and birth greatness, you will be willing to do anything that it takes to access greatness. Let your hunger for success push the greatness out of you. You cannot dream big but snack on little goals. Always have the hunger and desire to carry and birth your greatness and to become great. I learned that you must have your mind and attention set on the future in order to create one.

During a natural pregnancy, it is common that your appetite will increase, and interestingly enough, it is no different in a spiritual pregnancy. During the second trimester those cravings for God increase. You will start desiring more calories, or in your case more of God. A mother's increased appetite is very important to the baby. Your appetite for success, and more importantly, your appetite for God will increase rapidly. An increased appetite tells God that not only are you grateful, but also you are hungry for more. Your hunger says to God that you are not complacent with where you are in life. Your greatness needs your hunger for Christ. In 1 Peter 2:2 it says, "like newborn babies, long for the pure milk of the word, so that by it you may grow in respect to salvation."

Now I understand that you are hungry for success, hungry for God, and hungry, not only to be great, but hungry to birth your greatness. However, I must ask a question that can be very controversial in relationships; in fact, this may actually be one of the top three questions that incite arguments. And that is, "What do you want to eat?" In John 1:38 Jesus asks, "What do you want?" We state that we are hungry, but most of the time we do not know what we want to eat. Spiritually speaking, we have a hungry heart, but do not know what we want. This is probably one of the most important questions that you must answer on your journey of birthing greatness. What do you want? You must be intentional about what you want from God. Jesus loves when we bring a hungry heart to Him.

It says to Him that we still want Him and need Him

regardless of what reality tells us. I would like for you to read all of Psalms 27; it is important to know that in Psalms 27, David knew what he wanted. In Psalm 27:4 David says, "One thing I ask from the Lord, this only do I seek: that I may dwell in the house of the Lord all the days of my life, to gaze on the beauty of the Lord and to seek him in his temple." We must have a David mindset and not only cultivate a hunger for God, but also know what we want. You will recognize when your spirit takes a hit because you will lose your appetite for Christ. When we do not continuously hunger for the presence of God, it is a clear indication that something is spiritually wrong with us.

When you look somewhere else or someplace else to fulfill your appetite you will never be fulfilled. I was one of those people who searched for "food" in other places than God Himself. Some of us become satisfied with mere church or the religious activities themselves. Now I am not saying that there is anything wrong with church or religion, however it is no replacement for God's glory and the Holy Spirit. What do you want? Tell God and watch Him fill you so that you are no longer hungry.

THE QUESTION & THE VISIT

During a woman's second trimester it is suggested that she does a few prenatal visits, specifically every four weeks. Throughout this book I have and will continue to tell you to visit your healthcare provider and doctor which is God. However, God will sometimes have someone visit your life to do the work of God in your life; this is what I like to call "The Question & The Visit." Here is how: In 1 Samuel 16:1-13.

God is attending to anoint David. However, God knows because of David's environment that he may not be able to clearly hear from God. So, God sends Samuel to anoint David. God sees your pain as well as He sees your faithfulness.

Remember that God's timing is always the right time. God does not always come when you want him, but He will always come on time. When you clear people out of your life you will have room to receive God blessings. And on some occasions, God's blessings are delivered by a person that you will never expect. Now when God sends someone to transform or redirect your life, He always gives that person specific instructions. God told Samuel, "Do not consider his appearance or his height for I have rejected him." The Lord does not look at the things people look at.

People look at the outward appearance, but the Lord looks

at the heart." I understand that you may not look like the Next Top Model, or you may not be most popular, or you may not have the biggest house, fanciest car, or greatest living environment. You may not be the most educated or talented as the next person. Do you want to know something? All of those things are nice, but God does not put a lot of stock in those things; instead, He cares about your heart. In 1 Samuel 16:6-8, when Samuel arrived, he made it known that he had come in peace but that he had also come to anoint one of Jesse's sons as king. When Samuel arrived, and saw Eliab, he thought that Eliab looked like a King, but he remembered what God told him. God does not care about looks. Jesse was shocked that Samuel did not pick his most attractive son, so he decided to call on the rest of his sons. Ironically, Jesse had seven sons who had an equal opportunity to pitch themselves and show off their talents, but Samuel told Jesse that the Lord had not chosen any of them.

Samuel then asked Jesse, "Do you have any other sons?" Jesse had one more son by the name of David. This son was in the back attending to the sheep. Jesse and his sons treated David like a maid more than a son. Now it is important for you to know that God will make your enemy your foot stool. Sometimes your family can hold you back. You might feel down and out, like no one is there or like no one cares, but God will send someone into your life that will change your life forever.

Although Jesse saw David's messed up hair, dirty and smelly, ripped clothes, his modest build, Samuel did not hesitate in knowing that God wanted David to be King. Jesse saw a dirty boy, but Samuel, through God, saw a glow on David like no other. Throughout your life God has sent people to get your attention. You have either denied them or thought that you were not worthy of Gods elevation in your life. David never thought he was "not worthy." He knew that he was gifted, and that he was not defined by his environment. This section in this book is called, "The Question & Visit", because David never questioned his ability nor questioned his relationship with God; he just waited for God's visit. A woman during pregnancy has to wait nine months in other to see what God has blessed her with. The biggest and perhaps the hardest question for some is, "How long are willing to wait to deliver what God has implanted in you?"

CHAPTER 13

13

THE JOURNEY

As I mentioned earlier, soon to be mothers usually have more energy during their second trimester of pregnancy. Well spiritually speaking you will also gain an abundance of energy throughout your journey. The energy that you will gain is well needed because birthing greatness is a journey. Any journey that you take on will not only take a toll on you mentally, and spiritually, but physically also. That applies to a mom-to-be as well. During their pregnancy, women develop swollen feet and legs.

In your case, on your journey to birthing greatness, you will not develop swollen feet and legs, but you will develop some level of fear. In hindsight, this may make your feet and legs feel swollen. That fear will put a constraint on you so that you will either want to move nor continue on the journey to birth greatness. I understand that you fear throughout this journey; likewise, I had some level of fear through mine. We all have fears and sometimes we allow those fears to take over our lives and to prevent us from taking a step. Even if we have the tools, talent, wisdom, and gifts on the inside of us, because of the unknown, we can still become paralyzed by fear.

Moses knew that he was gifted and chosen by God. He had the confidence to tell the people in Israel not to be afraid, God has your life in His hands, and He will fight your battles. However, just like us, Moses could not speak that confidence in his own life. In Exodus 14:15, "And the Lord said to Moses, "Why do you cry to Me?" God knew Moses' ability; He placed a gifted on the inside of Moses. God's assignment to Moses was to go on this journey to and bring the children of Israel out of Egypt. The only way Moses was able to do that was to activate his faith. However, the journey was hard for Moses at first.

When fear creeps in, it will have you second guessing yourself and the process. Pastor Rick Warren says, "God won't part the water in front of you until you take your first step in faith." We may need to take one more step in our journey of birthing greatness in order for our life to change. Moses took one step and lifted his rod and stretched his hand over the sea and it divided. I dare you to take a step forward in faith and lift your hands to God and watch how He changes your life. It is important to know that the key is taking that step. Faith does not work if every day you are sitting and waiting for an answer from God or for change to occur.

FAITH WITHOUT WORKS IS DEAD

It is important to know that faith follows the work. You must understand that you have to put in the work. God gave you the tools of wisdom and gifts and those tools when connected to your faith will cause the reaping of benefits. It is always interesting when people ask me how I got to where I am today. When I tell them that, I put in the work, they usually look stunned. They probably expected an elaborate answer. Every bit of wisdom and gifts that God gives you, requires your commitment. In order to get the life that you want, you have to put in the work.

This book took years to write and it is not because I did not know what to write, but it was because I did not put in the work. It is probably safe to say that at some point in your life, you were unhappy with your job, relationship, current lifestyle, or even your body. Trust that you are not alone; I believe many of us have felt down at some point. However, the only way to profoundly change your reality is to put in work. Now do not forget to add the faith because that is a key element. But it is important for you to know that you cannot, and I repeat cannot sit back and expect wonderful things to fall into your lap. In order to shake up your world, you unequivocally must put in the work.

If you are tired of the same old things happening in your life, the change that you desire requires you to put in the work. If you dislike your boss and your job, you have to put in the work to either get a new one or to go after your passion or purpose in life. This is the only life that God has given you. Take control of the wheel and drive. With God's help you are the only one who can change and rebuild your life. The truth is, if you want to birth your greatness badly enough, you will go after it no matter how what life throws at you on your journey. Do not hold back or doubt what God has placed on the inside of you. Live your best life, be committed to the process, and the work.

SPIRITUALLY BLOCKED

It is common during a women pregnancy that they may get sinus and nasal congestion. They both may result from having allergies or a cold. In most cases, this will cause your nose to be constantly stuff or worse yet, to bleed. Well spiritually speaking you can become congested or what I like to call spiritually blocked. But what does be spiritually blocked feel or look like? Well, have you ever felt like you were taking action and putting in the work, but yet you kept getting the same adverse results over and over? Then guess what? It is a strong possibility that you are spiritually blocked.

A spiritual block allows us to realize that we need spiritual help. Sometimes we must fall to the very bottom, losing everything in other to know that we need spiritual healing. Some blocks are bigger than others and some people handle their spiritual block differently than others. Spiritual blockage is common. For instance, the sign of experiencing a spiritual block is saying or feeling things like, "Am I unworthy? Am I capable? Am I smart?" I am here to tell you that whatever blockage you are feeling right now in your life, you can get through it.

You can overcome whatever trials and tribulations that are transpiring in your life. To be honest, sometimes opposition, obstacles, and blockages can be caused by the man in the mirror, ourselves. Sometimes spiritual blockage stems from our own iniquities that we still hold onto; we may have a lack of confidence that is within.

We all have faced and engaged in spiritual blockage. The enemy loves playing games with our minds in the hope that those blockages will permanently hold you back. In the natural when you have a blockage it is important that you go to your doctor and get it "drained." If our spiritual arteries are clogged, Christ cannot flow within us freely. Clogged arteries slow the pumping of the heart. Spiritually speaking, when your spiritual arteries are clogged, it slows the blood flow between you, Jesus, and your greatness. I believe that it is important to tell you that I sometimes still feel spiritually blocked. So, what you are going through is not abnormal; we all go through this from time to time. Here are a few places that you can start to unclog your arteries.

Be Honest with Yourself

It sounds obvious, but sometimes being honest with your self is the hardest person to be honest with. Honesty translates to clarity. When you are honest, you become clear and that is when you can identify what you need. I am one of those people who need something catastrophic to happen in order to change or to seek help. And honestly, a spiritual blockage is catastrophic.

However, identifying that you need help, and an honest understanding is clear. When you identify that you need help it is easier for you to get help. You have got this. You were born to carry and birth greatness. You are not on this journey alone. Remember that those people that have been around you should have similar faith and those people are vital to helping you get over this hurdle. You need to trust and utilize support systems around you. And remember that through it all you can trust God will all of your heart. Proverbs 3:5-6 says, "Trust in the Lord with all your heart and lean not on your own understanding; in all your ways acknowledge him and he shall direct your path."

Trusting God gives you all that you need to unclog your arteries, enabling you to take the next step on your journey to birth greatness. No matter what is blocking you or slowing you down, God knows how to heal your pain. He knows when you are spiritually congested and what you need to be healed. Trust the process and trust Him.

BEAUTY IS PAIN

It is safe to say that all of us have heard this phrase before, "Beauty is pain." This quote paints the picture of what mom's-to-be go through. Women go through nine months of different levels of pain in order to give birth to something beautiful at the end. This applies to people like you that are spiritual pregnant. Carrying greatness is painful at times. Many people start the journey to birth their greatness, but not everyone finishes the journey.

If you truly want to birth your greatness you must have the resilience and confidence to go through the pain in order to access the beauty. Everyone on their journey to birth greatness will experience pain. Nothing about birthing greatness is easy, but every painful story has a beautiful ending. I am telling you now that you might as well accept pain now, because pain will not leave. But you want to know something amusing?

Pain does not know that by showing up it is helping you it does not know that it is strengthening the growth and development of your greatness. I need you to thank God every day that you wake up and look at yourself in the mirror. Realize that you have greatness inside of you that is ready to come out and change the world. Today is a new day. This is the day you have the chance to not only succeed but to also kick pain's butt.

Now I do not know anyone except the great Floyd Mayweather that is undefeated so that means there is a great chance that you will lose some fights with pain. Through your journey of birthing greatness, you will fail. In the natural some women go through a pregnancy risk. Through a spiritual pregnancy there are also risks. You are the one taking the risks. Saying yes to God's will is a risk.

The question is are you willing to risk it all to birth what God has placed on the inside of you? Taking a risk to birth greatness can cause criticism and humiliation. It can also cause you to lose friends, family, and relationships. On your journey to birth greatness, I suggest that you give up what you know for who you could be in Christ. Embrace the pain. Pain's purpose is to fine tune your efforts in the birthing process to birth greatness.

Trust me, it will be all worth it at the end; regardless of what people think or say, carrying greatness is the right thing. You have to believe that you will birth greatness and that your greatness will change lives. You must trust the journey and the pain that comes with it. God will not let your efforts go in vain. The grass is always greener on the other side, but God's plan for your life is greater. Seeing your greatness change your life and others makes the struggle and pain well worth it. I believe in you; the question is do you believe in yourself?

PREGNANCY BRAIN

Pregnancy brain is a term used during a woman pregnancy that indicates that a woman can become more forgetful, especially during the second trimester. Usually, it occurs because of the lack of sleep or even an amount of stress a woman receives. Although beauty is pain no one like to endure or go through pain. Going through the process to birth greatness can produce pain, stress, and a lack of sleep. And it does not help that when you are going through a spiritual pregnancy that it is possible that you can forget things merely because of what is going on around you. And unfortunately, the devil knows that this whole process can be painful.

The devil prides himself on striking when you are in a confused state, and especially when you are accomplishing goals. You must remember what and who can bring you out of what you are going through. If that does not work, he will continue to attack as you forget who brought you this far and out of bondage. Deuteronomy 6:12 says, "Then beware, lest you forget the Lord who brought you out of the land of Egypt, from the house of bondage." Do not forget where you came from. But more importantly do not forget that it is God who can or did bring you out.

During my time reading the word of God I found it amazing

that God was not born in the nicest neighborhood. God was essentially born in poverty. It is even more amazing that all of the stories that I study in the Bible are about Jesus returning to His community to bless those in need. For believers, once we finally put our past behind us, we tend to never want to go back and make a difference. Well God blessed you to have a testimony and to become a testimony. He blessed you to be a blessing. When you forget that God brought you out, you cannot become a testimony to lead people to Christ. Honestly, we did not deserve the grace of the cross, but God loved us so much that He made a way. Sometimes we tend to forget how much we need grace throughout the journey to birth greatness. This is forgetfulness is "Pregnancy Brain."

This might sound simple, but we have to remember who God is. We sometimes may not know why He does what He does. And sometimes we wonder when and what He is going to do in our life. Although we might have many questions, we should not have to worry about whether God is with us, because He is with us all of the time. *I love me some God.* Hope is dope. When it felt impossible for us to reach up to God, He came down to us.

I know that the devil wants us to have pregnancy brain or spiritual amnesia, but we cannot forget what God has done in and for our lives. When the devil is trying to attack your mental state, go inside of your prayer closet. Go in there and remember the countless times that He has saved you and answered all of your prayers.

Remember that in 1 Peter 2:9 God says, "But you are a chosen race, a royal priesthood, a holy nation, a people for his own possession, that you may proclaim the excellencies of him who called you out of darkness into his marvelous light." And through it all remember what God will do in your life. God promised you milk and honey and nothing less. God is good all of the time and all of the time God is good. He lives for us and died for us to that we can live. Do not allow the devil to take your memory away. Hold on to hope because hope is dope.

BE INFECTIOUS

During pregnancy, the last thing that a woman wants is to be infected with anything harmful because she knows that if she is infected then her baby can also be infected. However, it is quite the opposite in your case. Surprisingly, you want to infect others. You never want to be silent throughout your journey of birthing greatness. People need to see your passion for your greatness, but more importantly people need to see your passion for Christ. Passion is one of the tools to help you push pass the trials and tribulations that is happening in your life.

Passion is contagious and it spreads like a virus. Do not worry that it is a positive infection you are spreading. For some of us we unconsciously become role models to those who may be watching us. It took me a long time to realize that people were not only following me but were also becoming infected by my words and actions. But it is important for you to never ask those who follow you do things you are not willing to do yourself. I must admit that I lost motivation throughout the process and was not infecting those who were looking for hope, motivation, and inspiration. Many of us lose motivation because we forget about the purpose. I lost my sense of purpose or the "why" as well the "what" that God promised me. In your journal, I need you to write the purpose of you birthing greatness.

Why do you need to birth the greatness that is on the inside of you? I pray that this book is a great virus in your life that you cannot shake off. I want you to birth the greatness that is inside of you. Through this process, I need you to set smart goals; **S**pecific, **M**easurable, **A**ttainable, **R**elevant and **T**ime-bound goals. Do me one more favor; celebrate all of your wins no matter how small or large they are. Broadcast your passion for Christ, and for your great accomplishments, but ignore those who do not celebrate with you.

Now I need you to be careful. Yes, you may be infectious,

but you may also be infected as well. Although everyone is not natural attentive, you must be careful who you allow to speak in and over your life. Be careful who you let into your life; their words and energy can spread an infection that can be hard to get rid of. Everything around us is energy; we are energy. We must be mindful about the energy we put out and the energy we take in. The devil will use certain individuals in your environment to you suck the energy right out of you.

Satan knows that if he can get your mind, he has a great chance of getting to your blood. When the devil gets to your blood, he can interrupt the blood flow between you, God, and your greatness. You are born with something the devil is intending to kill, steal, and destroy. God loves a cheerful giver, but the devil loves it also, and he will try to take what you have started with your passion. Remember to protect your body live.

CHAPTER 14

14

GREATNESS GLOW

You might have heard about "pregnancy glow," at some point, in your life. During your spiritual pregnancy, you will experience a "pregnancy glow". In the natural, a pregnancy glow affects your skin, but spiritually it affects the presence and grace of God shinning on you. All are giving greatness, but much is required to access it. This journey will have challenging moments but remember that God has given us the victory. It is God who puts joy in our hearts so that it may show on our faces.

If we genuinely love God, then we should have a heavenly glow so that others are convinced not only there is a God, but that we have encountered God. They will also be able to see from your appearance that your experience with God produces a great feeling. During your conception, people will start to ask you, in some shape of form, "What's happening to you lately?" Do not be alarmed when you get those type of questions, because that is just your greatness glowing and shining through you. Matthew 5:14 says, "You are the light of the world, like a city on a hilltop that cannot be hidden."

I pray that you dedicate more time living in the presence of God. And watch how your glow will be so bright that some may think you are using some facial or other treatments to enhance your skin. In your journey to birth greatness, you will need the Holy Spirit to come and reside on you and in you. You need God to shine on you in order to make it through this spiritual pregnancy.

You may not know this, but you are incredible. God created you to be a light that the world needs, and you were created to glow in the darkest of places. Get your shine on! In the natural a pregnancy glow comes from the increased blood flow. Spiritually speaking, blood has numerous meanings, but the one that I believe is the most important is love. When Jesus died on the cross, the shedding of His blood did something for us that should have us praying and giving thanks continuously.

The shedding of blood redeemed us from sin, purified our

hearts and minds, giving us eternal life with Christ. It allowed us to be forgiven for our sins; it brings us peace that passes all of our understanding, cleanses us of all our sins, but more importantly, it brings us closer to God. A pregnancy glow is a good thing. A greatness glow is an incredible thing. God is incredible. While you are trying to make sure that your life is together, God is doing an incredible thing on the inside of you. Naturally speaking, there are a couple of things that happen when a woman is rocking that baby bump.

In the natural, a glow comes in different ways such as the breaking out of the skin. Some women are blessed with flawless skin during their pregnancy. Unfortunately for you, when you are spiritually pregnant, it does not matter what you do, you are bound to "break out". Now I am not talking about bumps, I am talking about breaking out in a praise. When I sit and think about all of the wonderful things that God has done for me, I could not sit back in silence. God kept me when I did not want to be kept.

I do not know about you, but I did not have a flawless life. God brought me out, so I broke out in praise. Doctors tell moms not to-be alarmed if acne breaks out during their time of pregnancy. Likewise, I need you to not be alarmed or nervous when you break out in a praise.

Praise changes things. When praises go up, blessings come

down.

Now another issue that occurs during this time of pregnancy glow is sensitive skin. Some moms-to-be are dealing with this acne related inconvenience. Well spiritually speaking, not everyone is going to break out in a loud praise. Some might praise God for everyone to witness; yet some may be like I was and do it internally. I was sensitive about expressing what God has done for me. No, I was not ashamed, but I did not know to express my praise to God out loud.

I was also sensitive about sharing my dedication to God's plan for my life. Just like new parents, it was difficult for me to adjust to having people coming around me and my newborn greatness. I had the same level of uncertainty before my greatness was born. Similar to how moms to be experience changes in their skin, the miracle that is on the inside of you will bring changes in your life. Nevertheless, no matter how you may glow, just know that greatness looks incredible on you!

NO CAP!

You are moving along in your pregnancy which means that it is necessary to take the cap off. Yes, no cap! What I mean is that you have to take off and let go what is restricting you from birthing and being great. Some of you are letting your age, race, sex, friends, family, background, or living environment stopping your growth and development to birth greatness, NO CAP! I was one of those kids who had a cloud of expectation over his life. As a result of the high standards that my mother set for her own life, perhaps subconsciously, a similar standard was expected of me.

People who knew of her greatness expected that or greater of her offspring. Although it took me quite a long time, at the right time, I took the cap off of those expectations. I started to live for me. You must take the cap off of other people's expectations for your life even if that includes your parents; you must eventually learn to live for you. Do not limit yourself; live for yourself. God created you with no limits and no cap. He created you to be free, to be great, to fly amongst the stars, and to ultimately, birth your greatness. However, sometimes we allow people to stunt our growth, to redirect the path that God has set for us, to determine our ability and to limit how far we can fly. Now I cannot put all of the blame on others because, we also play a part in stunting our own growth and development, NO CAP!

Your gifts are great, and your potential is limitless, NO CAP! Dream big! The bigger you dream, the bigger your greatness can be come. We were created to live beyond that cap. We were created to fly amongst the stars, NO CAP! I mentioned this a little earlier in the book, but I would like to remind you of a time I attended a conference down South. During this conference break time, I walked up to the well accomplished motivational speaker and asked him, "Is it possible to talk about purpose and if so how?" He responded by telling me that no one is going to pay for purpose, and that I must come up with something else.

At that moment I allowed those words to put a limit or a cap on what God placed on the inside of me. I allowed that particular speaker's opinion to reshape my thinking as well as to direct my path. I was down and out for weeks, feeling like I had to go back to the drawing board. However, I later realized that God sent this guy into my life so that I could remove the cap of limitations that I placed on myself. I need you take off the cap that is over you, start living your life to the fullest. No cap!

YOU ARE AWESOME

Now that you are in the process of removing the cap off of your life. One of the tools you need to birth greatness is accepting not only who you are but whose you are. You are the vehicle that your greatness drives in. In order for you to get to the promise land, you must know that you are capable and that you are great. A natural pregnancy takes nine months; that is forty weeks. During the second trimester, it is a thirteen duration until you the next trimester. Spiritually speaking, you must not worry about how much time it takes for God to elevate you to the next level or to the next trimester.

You are great and it takes a process to birth greatness. This part of the book is to simply remind you that you are enough. Sometimes we focus entirely too much on looking for answers and clarity from others. To be honest some of the answers that you are looking for are already inside of you. You must sit back and look in the mirror and recognize that the person you are looking at is awesome, with something great on the inside of him or her. One of the reasons why you have not received another blessing is because you have not taken care of the blessing that God has given you. You are probably wondering what blessing I am referring to. The blessing that I am referring to is you.

You must take care of the temple that He has given you and watch how He will open the windows of heaven and pour blessings down. You are better than what your bank account shows. You are better than what people say. You are better than your living environment. However, you cannot change anything if you do not start with uplifting and believing in yourself. You are awesome! You are gifted, talented, brilliant, and so much more. Do me this favor; I need you to get some

Post-It notes, different colors preferably. I need you to write affirmations on each card. I want you to describe yourself in a few words on each one of them and place them in a place where you can see it every day, maybe your bathroom mirror door. Whenever, you do this task, please take a picture, or send me a short video on Twitter or Instagram @Chris_Empowers, showing off your affirmation. I believe in you; you are enough, and you are awesome.

WATCH OUT!

When you start affirming your existence and start to grow confidence within yourself the devil gets scared. And just like a dog, when the devil gets scared, it starts to growl, bark, and attack. Getting attacked is inevitable for anyone that is on the journey to birth greatness. A mom-to-be during her second trimester may have symptoms of dizziness. In you case during your spiritually pregnancy, you will also experience some dizziness. Doctors tell mothers-to-be not to stand too long because there is a strong possibility that they will get dizzy.

Well, the devil will see that you are standing with God throughout this process and consequently, will attack you. He will try to convince you to sit down on God. The devil will try to creep into your mind in order to make you feel spiritually imbalanced. As I told you before and will continue to tell you throughout this book, this journey to birth greatness is a battle. Sometimes you will experience if you have not already experienced, a deep inner sadness for no apparent reason. You may even start crying for no apparent reason. Although it is good and healthy to allow the tears to flow, the devil likes to come in and persuade you that those tears are an indication of a lack of accomplishment but that is far from the truth. It will seem convincing because this a marathon not a race so sometimes we forget. Being spiritually off-balance can be dangerous. It can lead to you not feeling excited or passionate about anything.

Unfortunately, one of those areas you may not be passionate about is birthing your greatness; since we get tired over the long haul, you may not feel excited anymore. The loss of family, friends, and relationships that you thought were forever can be tough and can also create negative emotions or a state of dizziness. These things usually disrupt sleep patterns. And when the devil gets you to this stage the only remedy that can get you out is the Holy Spirit and the grace of God. Enter your prayer closet and talk to God and ask for a game plan on how you can get through another hurdle in your life. You are capable of winning any battle that the devil throws your way. You got this!

I know that carrying greatness can be bothersome, but who

said that the road to success is easy? If birthing greatness was easy, then everybody would have accomplished birthing greatness. When a woman feels uncomfortable around this time, she is given few options to ease the pregnancy. Spiritually speaking, being uncomfortable is a stimulus to get you closer to God. I know that sounds strange but trust me. He will provide the necessary support that will ease the pain of carry greatness. You cannot grow if you are not uncomfortable. A special pregnancy requires a special process by a special person, and that special person is you.

ITCH'N

During the 17 weeks of a natural pregnancy, a woman's belly continuous to grow and with growth, the skin on the belly begins to stretch. Ultimately, this will lead to stretch marks and itching. I do not know about you, but any and every itch bothers me. When you are pregnant with greatness, being patient is an itch that bothered me during my time of being spiritually pregnant; I could not seem to get rid of it. However, if you want something in life that you have never had before, you will have to do some things that you have never done before. I never was one to have patience; instead, I always wanted things to happen instantaneously.

Well birthing greatness is not magic; you cannot make it appear when you want it to. Well, my itch for success was uncomfortable but an uncomfortable feeling should not stop you during your journey to birth greatness. And to be honest it will not get any easier from here. Listen, I know that the comfort zone is a beautiful place to be, but nothing ever grows there and that is where the itch will begin to occur.

It is suggested for women that are pregnant to drink lots of water and to apply moisturizer to the skin throughout the day in order to reduce itching. In your case, there is no remedy. The devil tries to convince you to get rid of your itch by giving up but giving up is not in your DNA; you are a fighter. Through your journey to birth greatness, you must start to get comfortable with the uncomfortable feeling of an itch. Embrace it and be thankful for the itch because that itch will propel you to another level.

Do not stop having an itch for success and greatness. Life and time do not stop for anyone. Life does not guarantee you anything. You have to live your best life. I know that life may suck sometimes. I also know that you will get knocked down and become tired in life. Nevertheless, if you continue to have an itch to be great, to get over the hurdle, to change not only your life but to change the life of your family, then the only way you can truly do any of those things you must go through the process. You must birth what God has placed on the inside of you. The great news is that you can handle it. It is up to you to navigate through the trials and tribulations.

You must live with and for a purpose. All are given greatness, but much is required to access it. I know that this may sound random and quite weird, but you must come to grips with death. You have an expiration date and what God has placed inside of you was placed in you to be lived out before you expire. That itch is much required in your journey to birth greatness. Regardless of what life means to you, it still does not wait for anyone; your itch should be an alarming reminder of that. However, it requires for you not give up.

Now this does not mean that you rush success. Shortcuts do not exist while trying to birth greatness. When you rush the development process of your greatness, you miss the opportunity to allow your character and greatness to develop. It does not matter how life changing your greatness is, if you do not have yourself together, you will neither know how to manage success nor greatness.

When you get something too soon, you will not know how to value it or how to maintain it. That is why you see athletes go broke in their first few years. They are gifted but they do not know how to maintain what their greatness has produced. Go through the development process during your journey of birthing your greatness, as difficult as that may be, all things will work for your good. God's plans are much greater than any rushed plans that you or anyone else may have for your life. Author and Director DeVon Franklin says, "Commit to the process of success, no matter how long it takes." Stay itchy. There are going to be a lot of temptations to try to convince you to take a quick and easy path to success, but there is no such thing when trying to birth greatness. Again, all are given greatness, but much is required to access it. The bottom line is many of us are rushing for success but rushing causes unhappiness.

Stay itchy to get one step closer to birthing greatness, not rushing to go from point A to point B in 0.2 seconds. Trust me, when you rush what God has planned for you, it can potentially cause you to be unhealthy. It can also start to affect your decision-making skills.

When you start rushing your thoughts and process nothing great will come out of you. Rushing through life will cause you to struggle. I know this may sound strange but admire yourself and all that is going on around you even if it does not paint a pretty picture. Please do me a favor and do not rush. I know we live in a time where people are afraid to miss anything, but your season is approaching. Your time is near. Remember, Ecclesiastes 3:1 says, "For everything there is a season, a time for every activity under heaven."

HE HAS HIS HANDS ON YOU

God hands are always on you. His hands are always moving because He is always at work. Proverbs 16:9 says, "The heart of man plans his way, but the Lord establishes his steps." God sees when you cry. He understands your pain, even when nobody can quite understand what you are going through. I know sometimes you wonder why He allows you to go through the trials and tribulations that you endure. But as the song writer says, "He has His hands on you." God has your back. I do not have all the answers, but I pray that this book encourages you to keep pushing. When you stop pushing, it becomes kind of disparaging to those who believe in you and especially to God. When God is for you, who can be against you? I know you are probably going through some things in your life that are challenging.

From dealing with the loss of love ones, your job undervaluing you, your financial issues, relationships drama, etc.… but regardless of what it is I need you to know that God has you covered. God's purpose over your life is bigger than what you can see with your natural eyes. God designed the greatness that is inside of you to be fruitful and multiply. You never know you may have a double blessing inside of you. Yes, that means you may birth TWINS! Can someone say #DoubleBlessings? I need you to know whose you are, because being a child of God come with perks. A child of God gets covered, protected, loved, and favored. You will be blessed beyond your understanding.

The awesome thing about God is that when life takes unexpected turns, you can expect God to always show up on time. The feeling being covered in God arms is an unexplainable feeling, but a feeling that you cannot live without. His arms bring us rest from not only our reality but also from our soul battle. In Matthew 11:28-30 it says, "Come to me, all who labor and are heavy laden, and I will give you rest. Take my yoke upon you, and learn from me, for I am gentle and lowly in heart, and you will find rest for your souls. For my yoke is easy, and my burden is light."

Life and birthing greatness can be exhausting, but we are safe in His arms. Your day to birth greatness is near and on that day, your suffering will end. Our tears will dry up and life will be changed the day we put our trust in God's plan. I promise you, the greatness that is on the inside of you is a plan that God had for your life before you were born. God's got you, trust me. You are safe in God's hands.

I know this may sound strange, but when you accept God's

plan for your life you encounter a spiritual heartburn. This is when your heart burns with joy because of what God is doing in your life or for your life even if cannot see it. Now spiritual heartburn is different than the regular heartburn that the average person goes through or that a mom-to-be goes through. Physical heartburns bring misery and pain, spiritual heartburns bring unspeakable joy. In a natural pregnancy it is suggested to stay away from spicy food and eat small meals throughout the day. Well during a spiritual pregnancy, you want to stay away from not spicy food but "spicy" toxic people and situations. Another difference is that you actually want to consume more food. In this case, I am referring to consuming more of the word of God. In the Message Bible in Romans 12:11 says, "Don't burn out: keep yourself fueled and aflame. Be alert servants of the Mater."

You never want to allow the fire in your heart to burn out. You want to stay on fire for God. Now some people will take you having a spiritual heartburn as weak, but do not mind those people. Having a fire for God is an indication that you are with Jesus. I do not know about you, but I will fight for the ones I love. God loves firefighters and I love me some God. Now we know that a firefighter job is to put out fire, but you are not in the business of putting out fire, you are fighting with fire. You have heard the term, "fight fire with fire" right? This means to retaliate and to match aggression with aggression. Now I am not talking about getting physical or being aggressive with a person. No, that is far from what I am saying. It is time for you to start fighting the devil back.

You have to fight fire with fire. In the Romans 12:20 Paul says that godly response toward your enemy "will heap colas of fire of his head." We that are carrying greatness must fight fire with fire because the devil and certainly people will try us. However, our fire is different from the fire that is used by our enemies. This may catch you off guard, but our fire is goodness. Now I am not saying if you get hit upside your head you have to just take it. However, in Roman 12:20-21 it says, "If your enemy is hungry, feed him; if he is thirsty, give him a drink; for in so doing you will heap coals of FIRE on his head. Do not be overcome by evil but overcome evil with good."

This might be hard to digest, but your goodness cuts our enemy to the core. Surprisingly, it will hurt more with goodness then if you were retaliating with the same aggressiveness, anger, or ill-mannered behavior. When a woman is pregnant, doctors prefer that they make their lives as stress-free as possible, as stress can complicates the pregnancy. When you are carrying greatness, you have enough on your plate and the last thing you want is stress to take you or your greatness out. Stay on fire for God through it all because the power of goodness changes people; from your enemies to even your love ones. Allow me to explain how goodness will change people. In 1 Peter 3:1-2 it says, "Wives, in the same way submit yourselves to your own husband so that, if any of them do not believe the word, they may be won over without words by the behavior of their wives, when they see the purity and reverence of your lives." Most people get stuck on, "submit to your husband." However, this passage was not about submission, it was about how the wife fought fire with fire. What is her fire you might ask? Her fire with her husband was goodness, which was a bridge for him to Christ. Goodness can lead those who do not believe to Christ; it can change person's perspective on life.

When you experience spiritual heartburn, it is a good thing. Fire changes things in our lives. It changes people and their lives, but more importantly it enhances your greatness. Now when I say fight fire with fire it does not just applies to goodness. Fire also represents prayer; yes, you can fight with prayer. The scriptures states in Matthew 5:43-44 "you have heard that it was said, "love your neighbor and hate your enemy." But I tell you, love your enemies and pray for those who persecute you..."

I understand what you must be thinking: who thinks about praying for your enemy? There were definitely, times I did not, especially when I was pregnant with greatness. However, practice making praying for you enemies a habit because during your spiritual pregnancy you will develop many "haters". During your prayer time, ask God to help and restore your enemies' hearts. When you cannot pray for your enemy, your heart cannot fully flow in Christ.

Now throughout the duration of this book I have quoted many scriptures and this not only to provide context, but also encourage you to pick up the bible and read for yourself. Why is stating that important? Fight fire with fire also means fight with the Gospel. In other words, fight the word of God or what we talked about earlier in the book the sword of the Spirit. In Romans 1:16 it says, "For I am not ashamed of the gospel, because it is the power of God that brings salvation..." Regardless of if you a believer or non-believer we all need salvation, including our enemies. Having a spiritual heartburn for Christ is vital not only for you but for others as well. God is fighting battles and that not only mean Him taking action, but it also means to you do your part. Fight fire with fire and never let your fire die.

YOU HAVE TO SEE IT TO BELIEVE IT

Do you see it? Can you see it? Albert Einstein once said, "Imagination is everything." The bible says in Proverbs 29:18,

"Where there is no vision, the people perish." You have to be crystal clear about your vison because it will drive everything else you do during your spiritual pregnancy. I know you have a fire but where is that fire going to take you? Do you know where you want to go? For a long time, my attention, energy, and focus were solely on my present. When you only focus on what is going around you, such as your environment and your finances, it will quickly become your forever. I know you have a fire under you, I understand you are passionate, but you must clear your vision lenses. I need you to upgrade your imagination. Put this in your journal or on one of those Post-It notes, "my present situation will not define me." I believe that is tweet worthy, tag me @Chris_Empowers. How you look at yourself and your future is everything. When I am feeling down and out, I remind myself of the vision that God gave me. The phrase "a land flowing with milk and honey appears 20 times in the King James Bible. Milk and honey are what God promised us.

Set your mind on the version of milk and honey that God promised you and go after it, no matter where you are in life. I do not care if you have reached a level of success in your career or as an entrepreneur, or if you are struggling in life in whatever capacity, I need you to push your imagination. Where do you want to go? What do you want to accomplish? How does this place look? This is your vision, there are no limitations to it.

The problem with most of us is that we cannot see past our reality. You must condition your mind that you are better and will achieve greater in life and you will settle for nothing less than greater. My mother use to tell me that I must see it in order to *see* it. She informed me that I must see it in my mind before I can see it in reality. First, you must believe what you see in your mind.

Allow not only your faith but your imagination take over your reality and your thoughts. Sometimes we get in our own way, which stops our growth and development because we over thinking. When I was a kid, I allowed my imagination to run wild and the world quickly became my playground. This is going to sound strange to most, but I need you to go back to when you were a kid and allow your imagination run wild. Trust me during your time of being spiritually pregnant it will be a multitude of situations where you will have to think and use logic and reasoning. But do not use logic and reasoning with your imagination. It is also important for you to remember that faith without work is dead. Your vision needs some of that fire that you possess, but it also needs you to put in work. With that being said, your vision will need to be connected to your gift.

Look at your life as if God were ComEd, He provides your energy.

Now imagine if you are a surge protector; you are plugged into what He promised you which is your greatness and the vison He has given you. Now that you are connected, He is providing energy, grace, mercy, and abundance of more. Now one of the outlets that is connected to you is your gift. Your gift needs everything that God is providing in order to have you one step closer to your vison. If your vision and gift are not connected then you are not putting in any work, which mean you are just dreaming. It does not matter what is connected to the outlet, what matters it that is turned on. Put the work in.

Believe me when I say that you just cannot sit there and wait for whatever you want to fall into your life. I also want you to stop believing that you are not capable of accomplishing greatness. Leave your history of mistakes, downfalls, trials, and tribulations behind you. History just stands for His-Story or Her-Story. Allow what has happened to you, to push you to the vision that God has given you. Your vision is ready for you to land and takeover.

I have some homework for you. I need you to create a vision board. On your vision board I need you to put where you want to go and what you want to accomplish and possess. So, that mean if you want a mansion, you need to have a mansion picture on your board. If you want to start a business or have your dream car, then you need to have pictures of those things.

When you finish, I need you to take a picture and send me a tweet @Chris_Empowers or on Instagram at @Chris_Empowers of your board. A vision board will allow you to see it and prayerfully help you believe it. You can even do what my fiancé and her best friend did and have a vision board party. You can invite like-minded people to this vision board party and have a good time talking about dreams, goals aspirations and just imagining.

While you are at it, I suggest that you write your visions down in your spiritual journal before creating your vision board. I want you to hang this board somewhere in your house, somewhere where it can be is visible. Remember, if you can see it, you can believe it. Now I need you to spend the rest of your life trying to make those pictures go from that board to your reality. I would not get any sleep if I did not tell you that some of your visions will take longer than others. However, I do believe a clear vision board will help you one day live out your vision. But you have to promise me that you will not only stay focused and, have faith throughout the journey, but that you will put in the necessary work as well.

Writing a successful book was in my vision and look it came to pass; but it did not come to pass on accident. It took many long and sleepless nights, headaches, tears, and ultimately hard work in order for this vison to come to pass. Some things require your work, but it is other things that you have to leave in God's hands because God and only God can handle certain things in our lives.

CHAPTER 15

15

IDENTITY

Do you want to know something fascinating? During a woman's pregnancy at 18 weeks the baby is the size of a sweet potato. I do not know about you, but I find that amazing. Also, during that 18 weeks' timetable a unique characteristic is developing for the baby; fingerprints. I sit back in awe at with God sometimes, because during your spiritual pregnancy not only is your greatness growing but it is developing fingerprints. But your greatness is not alone, you as well are developing fingerprints. Spiritually speaking this is called an identity. Through your journey of birthing greatness, you have probably asked yourself such as I have "Why am I here? What have I been put on this earth to do?"

To be honest these were the questions I asked myself, but when I sit back, I realize I was really directing those questions at God. Every part of my spiritual pregnancy I started to retrieve more pieces to this spiritual pregnancy puzzle. Now do not get me wrong, I asked those questions before I found out that I was expecting. However, God always came on time with what I needed to know. He started to make it clear that I was uniquely made and that I was not and could not be duplicated. I was questioning God because I was not seeing someone different when I looked in the mirror. What I was seeing was other people appearing to be great and looking as if their life was good, while I was sitting back unimpressed with my life.

I still remember when at one point in my life, I was being desperate for what others had. But there came a point in my growth and maturity that, I had to give up trying to be anyone other than myself. I had to come to grips with what was said in Psalm 139:14 and that is that "I am fearfully and wonderfully made." As long as you continue to invest your time in trying to be something or someone that is not pleasing to God, you are pushing the timetable back on birthing your greatness. God did not create you to live out someone else's life or to be someone else. In your journey to birth greatness, I give you permission to stop looking at other people lives and possessions and live out the life God promised you.

It is important for you to invest the time to work on you and birth your greatness. Your identity is just what the world ordered. You have a purpose that is to unlock change in this world. You were created on purpose. I do not care what has happened or what people said, you are not an accident. There was a time in my life that I thought that my gift and even my existence was a mistake that God made. But I am here to tell you that you were not a mistake and what you are carrying was not mistakenly given to you. Your identity was purposeful. You have a divine purpose on your life. Out of millions of sperm cells God chose you. I do not know if you know this, but God does not make mistakes. He created you in the likeness of Him, trust me. In Genesis 1:26 God say, "Let us make man in our image, according to our likeness..." God created you uniquely. Do I really believe that? Yes, I do, will all my heart.

However, at one point in my life I thought God was punishing me because I was so different than the other students in my class and the kids in my neighborhood. But as I got older, I realize that I am not "different" as in strange, I am different as in unique. Once you realize and accept that you were created on purpose with a purpose, you will soon realize your uniqueness. Can I tell you a secret? What makes you unique is what is stored on the inside of you. My greatness makes me stick out like a sore thumb. My gifts, talents, and wisdom were strategically handcrafted for me and that caused me to not fit in. Have you ever put the wrong key in a door before?

Throughout my life, I tried putting my key in many wrong doors. I was constantly wondering why God was not opening doors in my life, but it was really me putting my key in the wrong doors: doors that were not designed for me. The answers to my problems were inside of me the whole time. God is not in the business of mistakes, duplicates, or plagiarism, He does not like copying work. I suggest you stop trying to copy somebody else's work and work on you and your greatness. You have a vision that is ready to come to past, right? I believe you do, and I believe that God did not just throw you together, He took years and years to craft you. Trust me, He took His time with me, so I know He took his time with you. Do not miss your blessing trying to be a copycat. You are a masterpiece literally. Listen, I know you want to succeed, and I know the journey is tough, but you have everything you need to do what it takes to birth greatness. I do not care what the devil says, the devil, is a lie and the truth is not in him. You are great and you have a purpose over your life.

God is not surprised by your shortcomings He knew you was not going to be perfect. The Bible says in Romans 3:23 "For all have sinned and come short of the glory of God." I love God because he is not caught by surprise at our problems. He is just sitting back waiting for you to dig down deep and use what He has given you. You cannot allow anything, or anyone to come between you and your purpose. God has already equipped you with greatness, now it is up you to use what He has given you to release your greatness.

WHO AM I?

It is important for you know that it is a gift to be yourself. However, there is a process to identifying who we are. We often become victims of identifying who we are through our job titles or financial statuses. We sometimes define who we are by how we look or what people say, however I am here to tell you that your identity is not defined by any of those things. A person once told me, "To know thyself is the beginning of wisdom." But what exactly does it mean to know yourself? Who am I? Is the most important question you have to answer before you leave this earth.

I am far from Jesus but what I can tell you is that in Jesus Christ, you are possible. You are powerful and mighty. You are strong and you are able. In Jeremiah 1:5 God says, "Before I formed you in the womb, I knew you, before you were born, I set you apart; I appointed you as a prophet to the nations." You are a child of God.

I had to understand that I am connected to the greatness powered by God. And that means that all things are possible, and those possibilities are for me. If you are wondering how I answer the question, who am I? I simply answer, I AM POSSIBLE. That is who I am. "I can do all things through Christ that strengthens me." Philippians 4:13. If you do not understand who you are, you will not understand where you are going.

"Who am I?" is the foundation for "Why am I here?" and "Where am I going." You will never be able to answer the question, "who am I?" outside of you. The answer to your question comes from within. Despite growing up in church, I could not fully grasp the concept that I was created in the image and likeness of God. However, as life continued to progress during my spiritual journey, I started to learn how factual that statement was. Your identity or purpose is solely dependent on your relationship with God. All my life my mother dared me to spend time alone with God.

When I got engaged, my fiancé kept it going to challenge me to spend time alone with God. When you do not spend alone time with God you will never learn how to leave a significant impacted on the world, which will hinder your experience with peace. In Philippians 4:7 it says, "And the peace of God, which surpasses all understanding..." If your experience with peace is hindered, you will never truly understand what God has placed on the inside of you. So, when you attempt to answer the question, "Who am I?" Remember, your answer is not measured by whether you are smart or not, or whether you are rich or poor, nor is it measured by what people say.

You were created in God's image, so you are possible. Matthew 19:26 says, "But Jesus looked at them and said, "With man this is impossible, but with God all things are possible." You are possible!

UNDERSTANDING YOUR IDENTITY

There is a certain beauty in understanding your identity. Once you recognize that God is the Master Carpenter of your life and that you are the perfect result from the perfect Craftsman, you will start living your life according to his plan. Now when I say perfect results, I am not stating that we will or have to be perfect. God does not make mistakes when creating His blueprints and in his blueprints, He did not require us to be perfect. Now it is important that you take care of God blueprints.

Growing up in the inner city of Chicago, I have witnessed individuals vandalize property all of the time; since you are technically God's property, there will inevitably be some people trying to vandalize you. We sometimes allow people and circumstances to damage God blueprints and if we are being completely honest, we are sometimes the ones doing the damage. The beauty of it all is that since God created us, He is able to fix the blueprint that we or others have vandalized or destroyed. Understanding your identity is a breakthrough. Now it is important for you to know that although this is a significant part of your journey to birth greatness, it is not the whole journey.

However, when it comes to you birthing your greatness, it is incredibly significant. Bask in this moment of not only finding your identity, but also *understanding* your identity. When you understand your purpose, it can take you to places no man can. Watch how understanding your identity will bring clarity and will show you that there are no limits to your life. Pastor T.D. Jakes once said, "We serve purpose, because we serve God. Remember, God is the God of purpose. We are here to serve His purpose, not that other way around." For this example, let us just say that purpose is a customer. We know that Customer Service is a very vital part to a business. Customers do not serve us; we as servants, serve the customer. We do not tell purpose what to do. Purpose dictates what we do, and the expectation is that we do it well.

Now we do not serve any purpose, we serve God's purpose.

It is amazing the way God thinks. Sometimes we do not understand it, but it is not for us to understand. God has a plan for our purpose, and although it may be uncomfortable to do, we must submit to His plan for us to unleash our purpose. It is crazy, because I thought when I submitted to His plan, I was supposed to start saving the world. I started to put other people problems on my shoulder and thought I was here to be a superhero in their lives. Well, if you are anything like I was you have to realize that your purpose is just a piece of a puzzle that will change the world.

Now you must know that your puzzle piece is a significant part to God's overall plan. We must always see ourselves in the greater picture of God's plan. Those of us who are in an identity crisis are a missing piece to God's puzzle. I was one of those missing pieces for a long time. It took me a while, but I started realizing how important birthing my greatness was not only for me but for God's plan. Birthing greatness is beyond you and do not be surprised if it is beyond your understanding. I need you to understand that you are one of a kind and you are fearfully and wonderfully made.

LET IT RAIN

I am excited that you are identifying who you are. Watch where understanding who you are will take you. I am happy that you are about to embark on a new chapter in your life. Now you are going to have to stay properly hydrated during this journey. In natural pregnancies, it is suggested that moms-to-be drink at least ten glasses of water daily. Why is that important? Water helps to transport nutrients to the baby during conception, but not just any water; it is important that the water that is consumed is purified water. This also even applies to you during your time of being spiritually pregnant.

However, you are not consuming water through a bottle, cup, or glass. When you are spiritually pregnant you need fluids, but it comes from above. You need rain that which will transport the right nutrients from you to your greatness. Spiritually speaking, rain is a blessing from the Lord, because rain symbolizes God's blessing. Song writer and Bishop Paul Morton wrote a song titled "Let it Rain." And one of the lines in the song that is important for you during your time of being spiritually pregnant and that is, "Open the flood gates of Heaven, let it rain…" During your journey of birthing your greatness you will need God to rain down on you and to unleash blessing and grace upon you and your greatness. This is the time for you to get the right nutrients transported from God to you and your greatness.

During this exchange, nothing else matters but being in the presence of God. Sometime in your prayer, I need you to ask God to open up the windows of Heaven and pour down a blessing. Now rain or, water, has another fascinating meaning. During baptisms, water symbolizes spiritual death and resurrection. In other words, it a symbol for spiritual birth and any form of birth is a blessing. Allow God to rain over your life. Asking God to open the window of heaven is an intercessory cry for God. I promise you God hears your cry. In Isaiah 45:8 it says, "Your heaven above, rain down my righteousness; let the clouds shower it down. Let the earth open wide, let salvation spring up, let righteousness flourish with it; I Lord, have created it." When you allow God to shower on your life, your life has no choice but to be changed.

During a natural pregnancy drinking water will decrease your risk for infections and discomfort. Your need for rain will do the same for you during your time of being spiritual pregnant with greatness. God's rain will decrease the risk of infections and discomfort in your life. His rain prevents dehydration and of course will make you feel renewed during your journey of birthing greatness. We talked earlier about the importance of staying hydrated and if you prioritize staying hydrated during your time being spiritually pregnant, you will be setting your little bundle of joy that is on the inside of you up for a healthy life outside of the womb.

ADVICE OVERLOAD

Have you experienced advice from your parents, friends, family, coworkers, and others about your spiritual pregnancy? They have made attempts to try to advice you of the do's and don'ts about your talent, gifts or about carrying and birthing your greatness. Now you do know that not everyone utilizes their gift or talents. You do know that not everyone has gone through what it takes to birth their greatness.

Remember, all are given greatness, but not everyone is willing to go through the necessary steps to birth greatness. There is a process to birth greatness, and you will go through a different type of experience when you carry and birth greatness. So, you have to be mindful of what you listen to during your journey. You can quickly experience advice overload during this process of birthing your greatness.

While some people mean the best, those persistent opinions can, delay your blessing or sabotage what God has promised you. Now is every person and every bit of advice that is being giving is bad? No! However, you have to discern what is good or bad, as well as to make sure that you are equipped with wisdom during your journey. The Bible says in James 1:5, "If any of you lacks wisdom, you should ask God, who gives generously to all without finding fault, and it will be given to you."

Ask God to equip you with wisdom. Some people mean well, and they are excited for you, but you must make sure the advice they are giving you has been sent and accepted by God. It is very easy for us to fall into the trap of believing everything we hear. There is a lot of things that sounds good but is not necessarily good for you. I was once told that I was going to be a pastor, and have I even heard I was going to be a comedian. Those titles sounded cool. I thought I was going to be famous and successful as the great Pastor T.D. Jakes or cool and talented as one of the greatness comedians of all time, Kevin Hart. Oh, how wrong I was in thinking that was what God had planned for my life. Now I do not blame them for speaking those things over my life.

However, if I never took what I heard and laid it upon the feet of God, I would have been led astray. Before I knew to bring what was told and advice to me to the feet of God, I actually believed some of it. For years, I believed that I was going to be a comedian; funny thing about this is that what had me believing I was going to be a comedian was the whooping's, detention, and failing the 8th grade. I thought since people thought it and said it that it would turn into my reality. Again, I am not saying that believing what you hear is always false. There are some people that will come into your life and confirm what the Holy Spirit laid upon your heart. However, for me I never been told by God that I was going to be a comedian; but I believed those who told me that throughout my early academic career. Belief in what was said did not put me any step closer to birth my greatness.

Listen to me and listen to me well, advice during your spiritual pregnancy is needed and I suggest you welcome it. Nevertheless, be careful, there are a lot of people who have delayed their greatness because they listen to people that either aborted their greatness or miscarried their greatness. And for those who are trying to inform you of their journey who carried and birth greatness, does not mean you will encounter those same experiences. Everyone's process and journey when carrying and birthing greatness is different. It is important to know that regardless of if you are carrying a child or carrying greatness that your life is about to change. Not only would the body change but as well as the mind, because you will soon realize that your life will never be the same.

Realizing that your life will not be the same leads to pushing the frantic button in your life. Most people speak and show emotion with their faces. This leads to well-intentioned, unsolicited pregnancy advice, that moms-to-be and mothers can attest too. During your spiritual pregnancy you will find yourself frequently in these weird and uninvited situations where unsolicited advice happens. Trust me when

I say that it will be hard for you to ignore some of the advice, especially if there is judgement or shaming involved. During my journey to birth my greatness I remember that my spiritual pregnancy put me in an isolated state. Well, it was advised that I need to stay around friends and family to make sure I get through this.

Now granted they did see greatness in me and wanted to make sure I stayed close so they can help me during this time. However, God placed me in isolation during certain seasons in my life to elevate me. God knew that I could and would be distracted easily, so even though isolation was uncomfortable He knew that it was the only place I would listen and grow in.

We can agree that a supportive community of family and friends are awesome because they will give advice on what to do and what not to do during any time of need. Just remember that you make sure that their advice is from and of God. Now it is equally important to be mindful of strangers giving advice. When getting advice from people you do not know can be interesting. We sometimes think it has to be confirmation because they spoke the same things your family, friends or pastor spoke into your life. That is not always the truth. Sometimes it is those who you do not know who see greatness in you more than your family and friends.

When receiving information about you and your greatness just simply reply with "Thank you" and then you move right along with your day. Do not touch and agree with that until you lay it in front of God. Most people who are giving you advice really believe that they are offering and adding value to you and your greatness. Then there are some people want to see you fail. You then have individuals who like to reminisce. In some case, there are people who just enjoy reliving their past experience.

Regardless of their reason, I never get angry. In the past, I have questioned it and even believed it. But wisdom, with the addition of communication with God allowed me to navigate through advice overload. I learned how to listen as well as how to block non-sense. Remember, everyone is going to have an opinion about your greatness, from what you should do as well as what you should not do. But it is important for you to remember that the only opinion that matters is the one from God. Yes, sometimes God sends people to deliver His message, but it is important for you to confirm with God whether it was sent by Him or man. Throughout your time of carrying and birthing greatness, make sure you do what is best for you. Be secure in what God has given you. Most of what you are going to hear during your journey is not important. Keep your eyes or in your case your vision on the prize and that is birthing your greatness.

DIZZY SPELLS

I know it was easier said than done to discern between good advice or bad advice, and the truth is that is not always clear. This time period in your life where people want to give their opinions can be called spiritual dizziness. They say women that is pregnant at some point will experience dizzy spells. The heart is working much harder that it did before conception. In other words, the heart is working overtime and it is suggested that women who are experiencing this should lie down on their side when they are feeling faint or dizzy. During your time you cannot allow the devil to knock you off your feet. You cannot allow the opinions of others to cause you to be dizzy or confused in

Christ.

So often we allow the opinions of others to overwhelm us. The opinions of others can take us off course when we are trying to birth greatness. The devil is slick. When everything seems to be going well in your life that is when he attacks. He sends people to drop opinions off at your footstep because he knows we will listen. Then in the snap of a finger, opinions start to get our attention and all of a sudden, the spirit of dizziness come upon you. In John 15:5 God says, "Yes, I am the vine; you are the branches. Those who remain in me, and I in them, will produce much fruit. For apart from me you do nothing." Staying connected with God gives you premier access to all updates in your life, especially during this time of birthing your greatness. When you are connected, it is hard for somebody to drop an opinion on you that will stick in your mind or in other words, connect. Because when you are plugged in to Christ, there is no room for non-sense.

In a natural pregnancy when a woman is dizzy it is also an indication that her blood sugar is low. If you are dizzy in the spirit, you are now questing if someone's opinion is right and God's word over your life is possibly not; then you are dizzy in Christ which means your blood level is low. To prevent dizziness for natural pregnancy, it is suggested that they eat fruit that will help boost blood sugar levels and settle dizzy spells. For you I recommend the fruit of the word regularly, not when you feel like it or when it is useful for you.

You should avoid being comfortable; ironically, it is suggested that women should wear loose, and comfortable clothing to avoid restring circulation of the blood. Well, you want the complete opposite. You want to be tight with God and

His word. Being tight with God actually circulates the blood from God to you and your greatness. God's plan for your life is set and stone. He makes no mistakes and there is no change in plans. Do not allow individuals to come in your life and cause you to be dizzy. Dizziness is a tactic that is sent by the devil for you to question and cause confusion in Christ Jesus. We all have had some level of confusion before, during, and after our time being spiritually pregnant. The question is which side are you going to be on? The side of other opinions or the side of Christ. The devil is persistent in trying to cause you to be dizzy. Life will test the blood to find out if your blood levels high or low. Shake the devil off and go get what God promised you.

DOUBLE PORTION

I am still amazed that you are at the halfway mark of this book and no, it is not because I did not think you could make it this far. No, it has all to do with the fact that I am happy that you found this book interesting, and I hope informative as well as transformational to continue to read. Your actions tell me that a lot of growth and development has transpired in your life, which needs to be celebrated.

You should be proud of yourself. If you take the time to see where you came from and who you use to be, then to fast forward to where you are now and who you are now, that should be more than enough to jump for joy. From going through seasons with no support and no backup and wondering why you had to go through those seasons alone. I know your journey have been rough with all the trial and tribulations with carrying greatness.

Dealing with loneliness and isolation because nobody sees the vision or no one believing your greatness is going to come to past. See, some of you have been going through what you have being going through because for you this not a regular pregnancy. Oh, no! For some of you that are reading this book are expecting twins. You better get ready for a double blessing. Everything in you is ready to come out and you have to go through pain in other to birth the greatness that is within you. Going through pregnancy carrying twins is different than carrying one baby.

Now, not everyone will be blessed with twins. My mother use to tell me and still tells me today that favor is not fair. For those mothers who received the great news that they are expecting twins, I imagine they might feel like they have just hit the jackpot. Spiritually speaking when you are expecting twins it means you are about to receive a double portion for all your troubles. Carrying twins takes a different toll on a woman's body then the mom-to-be who is carrying one. So, when you do not quite understand why you are going through what seems to be more than those who are around you, just know that you might be carrying a double portion of blessing.

When I am in stores and see mothers with twin babies, I sit back at aw because I think that is so cool. On the same hand when those twins begin crying and then the next day it seems like they are growing, I can see how stressful it can possibly be. Spiritually speaking there is no difference, when God blesses you with a double portion it can be somewhat overwhelming. Am I saying you can be overwhelmed by God blessing? Yes! Now is God ever wrong? No! God's timing is without a doubt perfect, even when we do not think so. I know this because when I laid all my burdens at his feet my prayers were heard and met. Not on my own timing but God's perfect timing. And not only did He meet my prayers, but He also doubled them and yes it was overwhelming.

An overwhelming blessing or a double portion is not a bad thing because God does not give us more than we can bear. Sometimes our prayers are too small and thus we limit ourselves because of the magnitude of God's ability. I do not know about you, but I believe God shows out because He want you to never forget who He is, but more importantly because He loves us.

Allow me to show you how although a double portion can be overwhelming it is still a blessing that you can be handle. In

John

21:5-6, "He called out to them, "Friends, haven't you any fish?" "No," they answered. He said, "Throw your net on the right side of the boat and you will find some." When they did, they were unable to haul the net because of the large number of fish." In John 21:10-12 Jesus said to them, "Bring some of the fish you have just caught." So, Simon Peter climbed back into the boat and dragged the net ashore. It was full of large fish, 153, but even with so many the net was not torn."

It is amazing how God can bless you with a double portion and it is not more than you can handle. God did not ask them why they have not caught any fish. He did not think less of them because they did not catch any fish. He simply gave them instructions on how to access their blessings that was already promised to them. You do not have to have the greatest talent. You do not have to be the smartest. You just have to be able to hear when God tells you to move. Just like Simon when he tried to lift the net out the sea, you will struggle carrying your greatness, but you can handle it. And when it is all said and done you will be able to enjoy the fruits of your labor. In verse 12 Jesus said to them, "Come and have breakfast." God has and will continue to bless you for you to not only be a blessing, but for you to enjoy your blessings well. #DoublePortion

WHAT'S REALLY INSIDE OF ME

What is really inside of me? This is a question I asked myself time and time again. I have been told I have something great on the inside of me more times than I can count. For so long I had a hard time believing something was great on the inside of me and when I did start to believe, I had tons of questions. One of the questions I asked God countless times was, "What does greatness look like?" You cannot tell me all of these wonderful things that are on the inside of me and what this *thing* called greatness is going to produce but do not tell me how it looks.

I know it sounds crazy me asking what greatness looks like, but I really wanted to know. To find out the sex of the baby it is suggested that the mom-to-be get an ultrasound. This is usually done in between the 16 and 20 weeks of a woman's pregnancy. The purpose of the ultrasound is not just to identify the baby's sex. It is also to provide important information about the baby, such as health, size and position the baby is in.

During your time of being spiritually pregnant it comes to a point where you want to know what your greatness looks like. The gender excites parents, especially in this day of age. One thing that might be equally as important as the gender is who the baby is going to look like. You are probably wondering what this has to do with being spiritually pregnant. Just like in the natural, spiritually speaking we have a hard time with making the decision of if we want what that mom-to-be is carrying to look like us or our significant other.

Well, if you need a reminder, Jesus is our partner and we also have to remember He is the one that put something amazing inside of us. However, because we our selfish and naive we rather have our greatness look and act how we want it to look and act. When we should actually want our greatness to reflect and resemble Jesus. If you really sit back and think, having your greatness reflecting you is not the wisest idea. Do I have to remind you of all the times we have aborted and miscarried our greatness? Did you forget that we are imperfect and that we sometimes make the wrong decisions? Having your greatness reflect God would result in your greatness taking you places that you yourself could not have gone if your greatness reflected you. I get when parents want their children to look like them because hearing your child look like the grand parents or worse the other parent makes your skin crawl.

Trust me, I get to see my mom's reaction when I am with my mom and people say I look like my dad. However, when someone see your greatness and they say they see Jesus, I promise you it is going to be an amazing feeling. When they say your greatness looks different, it is an indication that Jesus is living through you. Let go and let God. Remove yourself, your ego, your narrow understanding and preconceptions about you and your greatness. Let go of the fears of your greatness looking different than others. Let go of the distrust, misconceptions, and suspicion on what your greatness should look like and do for your life.

To "let God" starts from your heart. When you allow Jesus to go to work on your life and for your life then you will see the result of carrying greatness. Life is going to seem out of control and your trials and tribulations are going to be overwhelming. Sometimes you are going to want to give up. But if you stick with it and fight to the end and birth that which is on the inside of you, the only thing you will be able to see and say is, "God." Why, because He is the only one that got you through all the hell that as transpired in your life. So, you want to know what is really inside of you? Just take a look in the mirror and you will see your answer. GREATNESS!

INVOLVING YOUR PARTNER

There are things you can do to help your partner experience more of your spiritual pregnancy along with you. This is not up for debate; you need, and you must involve your partner throughout your journey to birth greatness. If you missed who your partner is, it is the one and only Jesus Christ. You do not have to go to the Maury show find out who your greatness's father is. Proverbs 3:6 says, "In all thy ways acknowledge him, and he shall direct thy paths."

During your journey to birth greatness acknowledge God. You have to involve Him in all that you do. You cannot birth your greatness alone. You are a dependent. Yes, everything you do depends on someone else and that someone is Jesus. Greatness was given to you by Jesus, so it is only right you depend on Him to give you instructions and guidance on how to birth greatness. Do me favor, ask any mother who gave birth to their first child if they know what they were doing when carrying their child. I promise you that none of them knew what they were was about to embark on. They had to learn and ask questions on how to properly carry and birth their child. It is no different when it comes to you birthing greatness.

You have to learn, go through and ask questions in order to successfully carry and birth greatness. And the only person with the blueprint to give birth to greatness is Jesus. Others and I can share experiences and tips but that only will get you so far. Involve your partner through your journey.

Rely on God's infinite knowledge. He is all knowing. He knows the end from the beginning. God knows what you been through and will go through. He knows things that you do not know. For so long I thought that was unfair, but I now realize that I would rather God know when something is about to transpire in my life because that is when I can begin to activate my faith. Everyone's greatness has different a timetable to enter the world. Natural pregnancy takes 40 weeks or 9 months. For you your greatness it may take 100 weeks or 48 months. God knows the best route for you and when is the right time for you to birth your greatness. God has a unique perspective on life that nobody will never understand.

Although you know greatness is upon you it still leaves questions. Just like a mom-to-be, it is human nature to have questions and concerns. There is no mom-to-be that never worried about the health and care of their unborn baby. I do not know about you but during my time of birthing greatness, I was concerned about how my greatness would impact others, and especially my own life. However, God will send you on the best path for you to travel even with that path does not seem like the best path toward your greatness in that moment.

Involving your partner comes with you being submissive and most of us do not like giving up control. Some parents believe their plans for their child would be more beneficial than what the other parent believes. However, during your spiritual pregnancy you have to defer to God's will. I promise, He has great plans for you. God's will for your life is a reflection of God's plan for your life. I know this may be hard for you to digest because of your reality at times but you will not go wrong or be led astray when you submit to His plans.

At one point in my relationship with my fiancé, my communication sucked. I wanted to do things my way and although I had great intentions that still was not a good enough reason to leave her out in the dark. And it is funny because every time I did not include her things did not go as planned. I not only failed, I failed miserably. You cannot leave God out as you go through your journey of birthing greatness, especially if He is the reason why you are pregnant. Leaving God in the dark will have you missing instructions and blessings to help you birth the ultimate prize and that is your greatness. As you know to birth greatness is a battle and if you leave your partner out of the mix it can lead to you being available for an attack from the devil.

If you leave God out of your journey you will not be able to receive what God is trying to give you and that is to know His will for your life. Just like any relationships you will go through growing pains, but where there is pain, there is progress. It is a never-ending process of learning about your significant other. One thing is for sure when you are dedicated to having a great relationship with Jesus, then your communication has no choice but to grow and develop. Even though God is all-knowing He still want you to talk to Him and inform Him what is going on with you and your life. Include Jesus throughout this journey and allow Him to guide your feet. You cannot do this alone and when you truly understand that your pregnancy will not feel as if you are alone during this journey. God has a lot in store for you and your life. He is just waiting for you to include Him through in journey.

TRAVELING WITH GOD

Speaking of journey, how far are you willing to travel with God? Better question, are you traveling with God? Some people call this walking with God but regardless of what you call it, it simply means communicate with Him throughout this journey. Traveling with your partner is important. They say during a woman's pregnancy, the second trimester it is a good time to travel. Fun fact: most airlines allow moms-to-be to fly up until about 36 weeks. Now it is also important for that mom-to-be to not travel along. Regardless of how independent she might be, traveling with someone preferably her significant other is suggested.

Traveling with whom helped you conceive will allow a bonding and learning experience you would not be able to get at home. This also applies to you and your significant other, Jesus. When you travel with God you are able to have life changing conversations. You will start learning things about your greatness that you never thought were imaginable. More importantly, traveling with God is about how deep and how far you are willing to go with God. We have all traveled with someone before, regardless of if it was on a plane, train, bus or even a car and we know how at moments it can be stressful and that person can be annoying at times. Well do not think it will be any less stressful when traveling with God.

Stress will be prevalent when traveling with God. He will be silent at times possibly for long stretches at a time. Which as we know silence can be awkward at times. God can also be talkative and tell you plans over your life that can be hard to believe. Nevertheless, traveling with God is a must, or a need in your journey to birth greatness.

Being well-traveled with God will order your steps, model your character and decisions as well as enhance your gifts. The process of traveling is never pretty. You have the long lines at the airport, the annoying people, long distances, uncomfortable rides, and the list goes on. Are you willing to travel with God? Traveling with God will tack on a tremendous amount of mileage but watch how much more impactful and meaningful walking or traveling with God can be for your greatness.

Your travel with God will help you leave a mark on this world that you never thought you could make. In order to birth your greatness, you have to believe that you only can go as far as you will let God take you in this spiritual pregnancy. You cannot travel far without God. In Philippians 4:13 it is said, "I can do all things through Christ which strengthens me." You cannot reach your destination without Christ Jesus. You must travel with God; when you allow God to lead your life, you will never get lost. God is bigger than your mistakes. Yes, you have made many of mistakes in your life, but God has not stopped guiding you. God is like a GPS; you know, like the one that is in your car or on your phone. The birth of greatness is your entry.

When you take a wrong turn, it reroutes us. Do not you think it is fascinating that the GPS never gives up on us until we reach out destination? I know a GPS can be annoying at times, we can ignore and even turn it off, but when you stay with it eventually, it will say "You have reached your destination." I know God is not a machine, but this is the clear example of how God works in our life during your journey to birth your greatness. Throughout your travel with God, He will lead you and guide you. During a natural woman's pregnancy, it is suggested that women who are planning to travel to stay hydrated, eat regularly to boost energy and eliminate anything or anyone that can cause stress.

During your time of being spiritually pregnant I need you to stay thirsty for God, eat regularly or should I say stay in God's word and make sure to eliminate people that cause stress but more importantly try not to stress yourself because that it is not beneficial for you nor your greatness. I know this journey is a process like no other but if you trust God and travel with Him instead of away from him, He will direct your path. Through your journey to birth greatness, I need you to pray this prayer, "Lord travel with me on this journey, calm me and cover me with your blood. Amen."

CHAPTER 16

16

GIFT REVEAL

I hope at this point you are excited about giving birth to your greatness, as well as the birthing process. And just like anything that is worth getting excited for it gives us butterflies. Many moms-to-be go through the same whirlwind of emotions as well. They get excited about knowing that they are expecting, their bodies get filled with excitement and they start planning how their baby's room will be as well as thinking of other great ideas and plans they have for the baby.

During the second trimester they are able to reveal the gender of their baby. So, you know what that means…GENDER REVEAL PARTY! Gender reveal can be so exciting, and they keep getting more creative by the day. The excitement is borderline mutual for those outside looking in. Those people have already built a tremendous amount of excitement because the people they love are expecting. Then when it is time for the reveal you are all sitting there will anticipation, ready for what color would reveal itself so you can know the gender of the baby. OMG, what an exciting moment in anyone's life that is expecting. You get people fellowshipping with you, loving on you and giving gifts to celebrate life with you.

However, birthing greatness is a different story. Gender reveals or in your case gift reveals, is something that is not recommended. Some people want you to do well but not better than them. Remember favor is not fair and sometimes God has different plans for you than other people. Some people's blessings will take them further than others and that is ok. But some people will not like that or understand that. They will be just ok with you making it but if you make it father then them, then it becomes a problem for them. I have come across people who were ok with my success as long as if it did not surpass their own. This is very common for people in any journey in their life especially for those who are on quest to birth greatness. Yes, this even applies to family, coworkers, friends and even relationships. Some people cannot stand the success of other people.

Everybody does not need to know what your greatness entail. A lot of us are not immune to social pressure and feels as though we need to broadcast our gift via social media. When you reveal your goals, ideas, plans, vision, or greatness you leave the window up for someone to pray on your downfall. Everyone is not going to understand your greatness. In a gender reveal, there are those who had children or want children. Everyone wants greatness but not everyone is willing to do what it takes to carry and birth greatness. So, when they see you are happy about what is to come in your life, it brings a level of jealousy.

Now am I saying everyone is out to destroy or wish bad on your greatness? No. But what I am saying is that there is a time and a place to reveal what God has done in your life. Haters are going to hate. I learned throughout my journey to birth greatness that certain people do not want to see you happy. I encourage you to have a private reveal and ignore what anyone else thinks. A baby is supposed to stay in a woman's body for 9 months. When a baby has come out before it is time problems can occur. I understand that there are people in this world that came out prematurely and are perfectly fine.

However, when it comes to greatness God has a time and place where your greatness will be born. I am not saying keep your relationship with God private, nor am I saying when you birth your greatness to keep it private. Because during your time of carrying greatness blessings will happen. God will show you your potential, but when we become quick to tell and reveal all of what God is planning to do prematurely, that is when complications start to happen.

Like I told you earlier, I was revealing all of my plans and blessings that were occurring in my life and the people that I was telling were informing me that those ideas did not make sense and to not attempt those plans. I was so happy to tell or reveal all the good news, good ideas and plans in hopes that they would agree and help, as well as encourage those ideas and plans. I ultimately had to come to grips that everyone does not want to see me happy. Everyone was not coming to my reveal with gifts. I spoke earlier about having people in your life with their hands up and not their hands out all the time. Well, when you come to a gender reveal it is appreciated if you come with a gift and not empty handed. You want to adopt that same mindset.

You want people to come to the table with a gift, their gift. People that have their own gifts to offer are usually too busy trying to help, encourage, and enhance you, rather than coming in your life to try to give fake love, bad advice, and negativity. I know you have great intention behind sharing your goals, but there is a gap between intention and results. And that gap is where haters live. They know that you have great goals and aspirations. They know you have great plans and a vision that sounds like it is going to change not only your life, but the world's. So, they sit in between your intention and the results and when you reveal to them your greatness, they attempt to slow you down and hinder you getting to your results, which is birthing your greatness.

Have people around you that want the best for you. Do not allow people in your life and in your circle that are destructive, create and have bad habits or just people with bad energy. Some people in this world do not want the best for you and your greatness because they have low opinion about their own worth or their own greatness that is within them. Having a baby is a blessing because not everyone can have one.

A spiritual baby is also sacred. Revealing to any and everyone puts is bullseye on you and your greatness that is not needed. Some people just do not want to see you do good. Those type of people are trapped with hatred and those type of people should not be close to you nor close to your greatness. You do not have to reveal and make an announcement that you are carrying greatness or that greatness is approaching.

People will notice something great on the inside of you because your life will change in front of their eyes. People will start seeing a glow on you like never before. Walk the walk and let God do all the talking. I learned over the years that we often need a spiritual insight, not a public website. You and everything you do does not always have to be public.

BALANCING ACT

I know you were excited to tell everyone about your greatness. I know I wanted everyone to know about what God as placed on the inside of me. However, it is important to know that you do not have to take the time to plan a gender reveal; God's got this. He knows when it will be the right time for that one person or that large body of people to see the full revelation of your greatness. I know you are wondering how you are going promote yourself and put yourself out there if you are hiding or being secretive about your greatness.

I know we live in a time where you must have social proof and we also live in the time where people want a sample before they buy the whole thing. Trust me I understand, and I am not saying promoting or providing samples is wrong. However, it is important to have balance. In Proverbs 13:3 says, "Whoever guards his mouth reserves his life; he who opens wide his lips come to ruin." Sometimes it is ok to just be quiet. We sometimes want to help as well as want to let everyone know what we are doing and where we are going before we accomplish and reach the destination.

We must make it to the top before we can pull someone up to the top. As I like to say, "We can drop a few *nuggets,* but not give a full course meal." In 1 Thessalonians 4:11 it says, "And to aspire to live quietly, and to mind your own affairs...". When you put in the work you do not have to reveal the work; your work will reveal itself. You must be mindful of the sincerity of your greatness. The importance of your greatness is not only for you but for the world. But you must be mindful that everyone's heart is not pure enough to receive what God has placed on the inside of you. I know you are excited and ready to reveal to the world what God has blessed you with. I know you see everyone on social media "living their best life." Birthing your greatness takes time.

Unfortunately, your greatness can not be birthed instantaneously; your greatness requires a slow cooker. You know the slow cooker that your grandmother cooks that pot roast in? You remember how delicious it was? Well, the reason it melted in your mouth is because it slow cooked for hours. Your greatness is like grandma post roast. It is incredible. but in order for it to be so incredible, it has to marinate for an extended period of time. You will mess the pot roast up if your time and seasoning is not balanced. You need the right amount of time and seasoning balanced in this slow cooker. If any seasoning is off, it does not matter how long it cooks, it will not turn out right. Make sure you have a balance in your life. P.S. do not let anyone stick their fingers in your slow cooker to get a taste before it is ready.

Women during pregnancy have a hard time balancing at times. It is suggested that they should wear flat shoes, as well as to be careful on stairs and to avoid slippery surfaces to reduce the chance of them falling. Now during your spiritual pregnancy, I do not want you to just focus on balancing what you share and what you keep, but I also want you to maintain balance in your life. Allow me to explain. All of us work long hours at work; those who have children have to drop them off at school every day and or pick them up. We have to cook and clean and sometimes it does not seem as if there are enough hours in the day to perfect our gift and to birth our greatness in the mist of all the madness in our lives.

I know it is hard for you to find energy to go after your passion and to live out your purpose. But it is important for you to balance your mind, body, and soul. I know you are working hard to birth greatness, but not only do you have to find a balance to working, going after your dreams, but some time for yourself as well. "But Chris, if I was not working, I would have time for myself and my greatness." I have always said, "Allow your job to fund your passion, until your passion becomes your job." I think that was tweet worthy, @Chris_Empowers. But you must find time for self because this journey to birth greatness is long and taxing on the mind, body and soul. You will need a balance in your life.

When I was writing this book, I would write about 5-8 hours a day. Yes, even after an 8 or 9-hour workday. Some days my thoughts were not flowing and on top of that my life was a reck. I had bills creeping up and work was stressful because I was spending more time at work then the time I wanted to spend working on my craft. All of this caused a crazy, unnecessary amount of stress. My good friend by the name of Rodney Baber use to always tell me to take a week off here and there to detox. We found time to play pool or just relax. I would find time to hang out with my mother and go on dates with my lady I challenge you to find a balance between work and play, regardless of what that work might be. A balanced life equates to a healthy life, and remember your greatness only has one place to live and that is inside of you. If you are messed up then your greatness has no place to dwell, grow or develop. Remember to create a balance in your life.

LUKEWARM BELIEVERS

I know that it is a lot to take in. Sometimes when there is a lot going on, you start to feel hot. We all heard of hot flashes, mostly heard from women. Hot flashes are sudden feelings of warmth, usually most intense over the face, neck, and chest, and profuse sweating. Once again you are probably wondering how in the world does this have anything to do with being spiritually pregnant. First, let's go to the scripture, according to The Living Bible, in Revelations 3:15-16 it says, "I know you well, you are neither hot nor cold; I wish you were one or the other! But since you are merely lukewarm, I will spit you out of my mouth!" Some people are displaying what they believe is a balance life. They balance being of the world and being of Christ.

Unfortunately, you cannot do both. I am not saying you cannot enjoy the world. What I am saying is that you cannot enjoy the sins of the world and enjoy the greatness that God has given you. Hot flashes are like a light switch, it comes off and on. When it is on, sometimes it takes a while to cut off; at least that is how my mom puts it. You cannot be "wishy-washy" with God. You cannot show flashes of being with him and then other times you are being of the world. You cannot show flashes of your greatness and then wake up the next day being ordinary. You know the difference between extraordinary people and ordinary people? Extraordinary people do a little EXTRA. I know some of you all will catch that later. Tweet me!

The great thing about God is that He gave us the freedom to

choose. You know we do not have to be #TeamJesus, we can be on team other, but He wants us to choose. Do not be a lukewarm believer. Lukewarm means only moderately warm. Spiritually meaning that you have one foot with God and another in the world. Remember who gave you your greatness. Remember who brought you out of darkness. You have to be on fire with God. Does God burn within you? When people see you, do they see steam? Or are you one of those TV dinners that is hot on the edges but cold on the inside? Being lukewarm with God translates to being lukewarm with your life. Some of us are just satisfied with our life being ordinary, when we were created to be extraordinary. When we are satisfied without God, it is evident in our behavior. To be honest I do not want you to be satisfied at all with anything.

Remember stay hungry and on fire for God. Do not have hot flashes. Sometimes you are on fire for God and other times you are lukewarm. A lukewarm heart is what can disconnect you from Jesus. I can just imagine me telling my fiancé, soon-to-be wife, that I am kind of in love with her. Being lukewarm in a relationship is waste of time. Now the great thing about God is that it does not impact on how much He loves you. However, it does impact you birthing your greatness. Do not be a TV dinner, stay on fire for God. Here are 3 signs that you are a lukewarm believer.

You do not seek God before making decisions.

During your journey in birthing your greatness, one of the major aspects in this journey is that we are trusting God to lead us. His grace, love and Will over our lives should be at the forefront of our hearts.

This takes having faith and it does not require a lot of faith; according to God, it takes the faith the sizes of a mustard seed.

However, because some people are lukewarm, they really do not believe consulting with God before making a decision. Lukewarm believer has a habit of going and making their own decisions in life. They think it is ok to listen to Him only sometimes and other times act as if they were hard of hearing. If you truly want Jesus to breathe life into your greatness, consult with Him.

You want to know how far you can push the limit with God.

It is incredible that believers always want to push and put God to the test. They want to see if God is who He really say He is. They wonder what all the hype is about and test him to see if He would pass the "hype test." They do this because this gives them more time to live in the world and be of the world. They want to live with God, but do not want to give up worldly behavior.

They want to know how far I can get without him and still

be ok. Well allow me to answer that question; nowhere. A true believer does not want to experience any walk of life without God. Believers do not want to know how far they can go without him. The real question believers ask is how close they can get to God.

You do not take your walk with Christ seriously.

I really want you to understand that if you are a lukewarm believer you are fooling yourself if you think you are going to birth greatness. Birthing greatness takes commitment. There are many people that lose fire in their relationships and they decide to step out of that relationship. You have to be and stay committed to your walk with Jesus. Being lukewarm states that you are not fully committed to God. When you want to do things on your timing and your way, as well as not be committed to God, then you are committing to fail.

A SPIRITUAL BOOST

Trust me this birthing greatness takes a lot of energy from you. When it comes to being pregnant, remember it is suggested for women to take prenatal vitamins. Specifically, Vitamin B is key nutrient because they supply energy for the baby's development. Spiritually speaking, the baby or in your case your greatness is not the only one that requires energy.

We as the carriers of our greatness, need to be continuously charged on the inside by the Holy Spirit in order birth the greatness that God has given us. Make no mistake, God is working in you. "For it is God who works in you to will and to act in order to fulfill his good purpose", Philippians 2:13. Now it takes faith to believe that God is working in you and that you have greatness on the inside of you.

Faith is a tremendous gift from God, but through our reality and our busy lives it takes some extra effort to stay spiritually healthy as well as to keep spiritually energized to birth greatness. During our journey in birthing greatness there can be a lot of distractions and things that sometimes compete for our attention. Because of that, life can drain the battery during your journey. But there are a few ways to boost your spiritual health in order to keep you going in carrying and birthing greatness.

Bible Reading & Studying His Word

Regardless of what education you obtain, educating yourself is important. Meditating, studying, and educating yourself on God's Word keeps us focused and energized on this journey of birthing greatness as well as keeping us focused on God. Staying focused on God and His Word will give you a spiritual boost like no other.

When you focus on your problems and what your flesh desires you can easily, not only get distracted, but drained of energy in your quest to birth greatness. Keep your head in the #1 Best Selling book of all time, The Bible.

Fasting

Spiritual fasting involves denying your body of physical needs in order to move the focus away from your flesh but towards your faith. Spiritual fasting tests or in some cases, activates your faith. If we are to be totally honest, a lot of the food we consume takes more energy than it provides. You probably think that if you fast, you are using more energy and if you are thinking that, then you are right.

However, spiritual fasting redirects your energy to enhance other important parts inside your body including your greatness. Spiritual fasting also is a soul cleansing. The reason why some believers get drained mentally, physically, and spiritually is because their soul has not gone through its proper cleansing. When you cleanse the soul, you have energy to receive the Holy Spirit and become more empowered to birth greatness.

Fellowship with other believers

I know that you are probably saying that you do not like people, and I understand. But it is important to build or to be a part of a community that are on a quest of birthing their greatness such as yourself. Sharing and caring with likeminded people is a great energy boost during your journey. Support and encouragement from other believers while carrying greatness is a must have. When you have another believer that is willing to support and encourage you through your journey keep them close because they are needed.

HOME STRETCH

The home stretch is the concluding part of a racecourse or the last part of an activity. I am here to tell you to not give up. You are on the home stretch. I know there are somethings transpiring in your life but do not give up, you are in the home stretch. God says in Isaiah 41:10, "Fear not, for I am with you; be not dismayed, for I am your God; I will strengthen you, I will help you, I will uphold you with my righteous right hand." You have to not give up on yourself nor this process.

You cannot give up on what God have given you on the inside of you, because God have not given up on you. Your children are depending on you. Your family is depending on you. The world is depending on you. To your surprise you are almost there to birthing your greatness. How do I know? Anytime it hurt more than ever before, when you get more trials and tribulations, then your blessing is around the corner.

You are stronger than you think. You are stronger than the battles you go through. You cannot, I mean cannot give up on yourself when life gets hard.

I know during the journey of birthing greatness you get tempted to give up and throw in the towel as if it is the end. However, it is far from being over. Birthing your greatness is not the end rather it is the beginning to something magnificent. Greatness is not for a special person. Greatness resides in all of us, but it requires you not given up. The reason why people have not birthed their greatness is because they have given up. You have to make the decision to not give up. #TeamNoExcuses. Failure is a normal part of life. As I stated before, I know you have failed during certain parts of your journey.

There is no chance to birth greatness without experiencing failure throughout the journey. If you are anything like me, then we can agree that failure sucks. Especially when you put your all into something and it seems like the devil is not giving up and God seems like He is nowhere to be found. But it is important to know that the devil would be attacking you if you were not up to something great. God is there, He promised us that He will never leave us nor forsake us. I promise you that you are closer to birthing greatness than you think. A lot of people get caught up in the dreams of others. Sometimes they get caught in their own dreams and I am one of those people. My head might be in the clouds when in reality I need to be caught up in the process of birthing greatness.

Sometimes we do not realize how close we are to birthing greatness. You have come too close to birthing greatness; that is why you cannot afford to give up. Keep pushing, I promise you are going to birth something amazing that will change your life. Remember the world needs you and that which is inside of you. When you give up you put a dim on the light of your greatness.

Do not be like other people that believe success or greatness should be birthed overnight. You have a purpose over your life that is worth slow cooking for you as well as the world to feast on. And if you do not know your purpose do not stop looking. Do not stop asking God. You have only one life to live do not stop fighting and pushing to birth your greatness. The only limits you have in your life are the ones you put on yourself. Trust me you are stronger than you think. Stop reading for a second and just sit back and think of all what transpired in your life. And guess what? You are still here, alive, and well. It is not by accident that you are still pregnant with greatness and still alive to birth it. I do not care what the devil tries to throw your way, do not give up.

Please listen to me when I tell you that the best of you is yet to come. I promise you that what God has for you is going to blow your mind. The worst mistake you can do is give up while you are on this home stretch to birthing greatness. Giving up can change the whole trajectory of the process and journey in birthing your greatness. I am not giving up on you, but I need you to not give up on yourself. Promise me, pinky promise me that you will never give up. Promise me you will push all the chips in on you and your greatness. I love you too much to not tell you the truth, which is that you are AMAZING, STRONG, and BRAVE. You promised that you will never give up. You are on the home stretch to birth your greatness. DO NOT GIVE UP!

LET IT GO!

How do you feel right now? How was that last read? I really meant when I said, I love you and I believe in you. It is really important to me that you do not give up. Whatever you are carrying on your heart and mind that is not going to help you birth greatness, let it go. Naturally speaking, during a woman's pregnancy, she is advised to avoid lifting heavy objects while pregnant. Lifting heavy objects during pregnancy can possibly increase the risk of premature labor, which may result in low birth weight.

During your journey to birth your greatness I need you to not carry what happened to you when you were a child. I need you to let go of what did not happen and what could have happened. If you do not let go, you will put your greatness in harm's way. Carrying that heavy weight will harm you and your greatness. When it comes to your burdens, put them down and do not pick them back up.

The word burden means a load, typically a heavy one. I need you to not carry that, whatever "that" may be during your journey of birthing greatness; there is no room for it on your journey. The only thing your burdens do is weigh you down and slow the process up. If you are wondering why you having a hard time going through this process, it is because you are carrying unnecessary weight.

Remember, birthing greatness is a marathon, and it is not possible to win the race, let alone finish the race that is set before you when you have cargo load full of burdens. So, the question is, what is really in your spiritual backpack? What are you carrying that is weighing you down? In Matthew 11:28-30 God says, "Come to me, all who labor and are heavy lade, and I will give you rest. Take my yoke upon you, and learn from me, for I am gentle and lowly in heart, and you will find rest for your souls. For my yoke is easy, and my burden is light."

The things you are carrying in your backpack can affect your exercise. God is trying to work you out, but something is holding you back. The things you are carrying can affect your persona, professional relationships as well as your relationship with Jesus. I know that unpacking that spiritual backpack of what we carry in our hearts can be painful and challenging but I promise you when you empty it out, it can free you and energy for you. I know it can be hard. I dislike unpacking. When I travel my clothes usually stay still be in the suitcase for days and when I have moved in the past, the worst part was unpacking. But when you unpack the things that are weighing you down, it can lead to a new, healthier direction for your life.

Your greatness feels the effects of what is weighing you down. It feels the grief you are carrying. I lost my father in 2015 and it weigh me down so much that I got depressed. I did not eat, shower nor talk to anyone. Anytime that I was at home, I would sit in the dark on the floor in a corner and just cry. All of us carry grief for the people we love that is no longer with us. I also know that we all process our loses differently. However, we must know that grief can hold us back from birthing greatness.

I promise you that person that is gone would rather you to birth your greatness instead of grieving on their departure. I got myself together and allowed my father passing to push me to greatness than my life change. To be honest this book would have not been complete if I did not turn that pain into purpose.

Reach into your bag and take out that grief and turn what seemed to be bad on the surface into something great on the inside.

Now grief is just one thing that we carry that holds a tremendous amount of weight, but some of us also carry regrets. We wish we could have done things differently. I am here to tell you that everything happens for a reason. Now I use to dislike this phrase with a passion. But when I sit back and think about if I could have changed what I have been through or things that I have done, I would not have met the love of my life. Now some regrets do not have to be personal; it can be professional. Regardless, it can weigh you do and hinder you from birthing your greatness.

Do me this favor, acknowledge your regret and embrace it, now let it go. What has happened, already happened and there is no changing the past. If you keep that on your heart it is impossible for you to move forward in your journey to birth greatness. When you harp over your regret, it can lead to fear, which can lead to self-limiting beliefs. The weight of fear is so heavy that it can leave you paralyzed. The fear of making wrong choices or no choice at all can lead to complication to your greatness. They say lift with your knees when carrying a load this heavy.

However, when it comes to spiritually lifting, anything that is heavy requires you to fall on your knees in prayer. Fear destroys our sense of self-esteem and keeps us from birthing our greatness. It is time for you to go in your bag again and do a little spring cleaning. Before you sit that bag down, I need you to do yourself one more favor. I need you to take out worries because of unfulfilled dreams. Some of us carry on our hearts that we have come up short in some of our dreams. But in fact, we did not come up short because we were not capable or smart enough. No, it was because it was not our season to fulfill those dreams.

Sometimes God has something better than that little dream you were dreaming. Let go of those old dreams that God did not set in your heart. Remember, He has a plan over your life, I promise you He has something better in store for you. Letting go of unfulfilled dreams can lighten the load tremendously. Accept God's plan and let go yours. Do not carry what happened to you in the past. Let go of past failures, I promise you those failures was there to make you stronger. Let go of fear and self-limiting beliefs; you are stronger than you think. Let go of regrets; there is no such thing as regrets. You are awesome and I am excited to what God has placed on the inside of you. In your journal I need you to write everything you are letting go of for the rest of this year. Now is the time for you to feel free.

CHAPTER 17

17

SPEAK LIFE

If you do not already know, I travel across the country as an Empowerment Speaker. One day I sat back and wondered how to I developed this ability to captivate and empower as well as inspire people around the country. One day when I was having one of my daily conversations with my mom she began reminiscing about when she was pregnant with me. About one hour into the conversation she says, "I am done talking to you. I been talking to you for a whole hour." As we shared laugh, she begins to tell me that she was the reason why I talk a lot and that is why public speaking fits me. When I was in her womb, she always talked to me and sung to me, she says.

Did you know during a woman's pregnancy that the baby can hear the voice of its mother? It is important that you read, talk, and sing to the baby. It is even suggested that the partner do the same. During your spiritual pregnancy it is important that you talk to your greatness. I need you to speak life into what God has promised you. You need to read God's word to your greatness. You have to sing praises to your greatness. My mother and I use to have the greatness conversations ever and till this day we still do. She told me she uses to speak life into me before I entered this word. She use to tell me that I was going to be great and that I was going to change the world. I need you to take a page out of my mother's book and speak life to your greatness as if it exists. Isiah 55:11 says, "So shall my word be that goes out from my mouth; it shall not return to me empty, but it shall accomplish that which I purpose, and shall succeed in the thing for which I sent it."

You have to believe that things will come to past in your life. Roman 4:17 God says, "Call those things which are not as though they were." Now speaking things into existence is not magic. Speaking things into existence is a faith move more than anything else. When you speak into your child's or your greatness's life, I need you to be specific. Do not speak small specific things, speak big things. The average child dreams big with no boundaries, so do not do your greatness a disservice by speaking small things in your greatness's life. If it were not for my mother speaking big things into my life, I would not be able to speak nor write books for people across the world. She was intentional in speaking over my life.

I need you to be intentional with what you are speaking over you and your greatness life. I sit back and now see how intentional my mother was even when I entered the world. When she sent me off to school, she not only told me that she loves me, but she intentionally told me that I was smart and that I was going to have a great day. How are going to send your greatness off? Your greatness will become what you profess with your mouth. I know it will feel awkward at first that you are speaking to something you cannot see, but that is the beauty in having faith. You have to see it before you can see it. I would not be able to write about greatness if I did not see it transpiring in my life. However, before I seen greatness happening in my life, I first had to see it with my vision lenses. What I am telling you is no magic formula.

This is no scientific nor math equation. No, it is simply believing in what God has placed on the inside of you. Your words are incredibly powerful. We can bring life with our words. When you truly understand that and believe that, then there is only one thing left to do and that is to speak life into your greatness in order for you to give your greatness life.

Psalm 127:3 says, "Children are indeed a heritage from the LORD, and the fruit of the womb is His reward." Your greatness is a reward that is going to change your life. My mother told me that being a parent to me is the most fulfilling and rewarding job. My mother was not just focusing on my present, she was speaking into my life for my future. She was not in the business of encouraging, she was in the business of providing faith and hope. She knew the importance of speaking life to me because she knew I was carrying something great on the inside. But what I love the most about my mother is that she wanted me to put in the work. She made me practice over and over again, speaking life into my greatness every morning and ever night before I went to sleep. She wanted me to be as prepared as I could possibly be for my future. Most kid have fun memories that will never leave their mind. However, for me, my favorite memory is my mother training me to be a dream catcher, a go getter and someone who knew who to speak life in their own lives. Speak life to your greatness because your greatness depends on it.

SPIRITUAL INVENTORY

Welcome to the third trimester! I promise you that God has some more exciting developments in store for you and your greatness. I know that you have been through a lot of ups and downs, and a lot of twist and turns during this journey. Even with that being said, you and your greatness are still standing. That is why I corelate this book to a woman's pregnancy, because women go through a lot during their pregnancy.

We can define pregnancy as many things, and while I believe it is about progression, it is more importantly about the gift of life. During a women's pregnancy, development is occurring. Yes, even while you are in your third trimester, your greatness is still developing. To be honest, you will never stop developing even after you gift birth. Speaking of developing, before we move on, this is a great time for you to begin tracking your development. This is what I like to call spiritual inventory.

Your spiritual growth and development are necessities for your life. If you are the same person you were last year, then you still have some spiritual growing up to do. One of my goals for you is to be a different person after reading this book. Your growth and development within yourself and in Christ should be different; it should have progressing overtime. You should always strive to grow daily; spiritually and mentally. I believe it is extremely important to take a spiritual inventory, not only during your journey to birth greatness, but also in your life. You need to take some time to identify what is contributing to your growth or what is stunting your growth. If you are not developing, then there is no way possible that your greatness is growing on the inside of you. If you are wondering why it is taking you so long for you to achieve success and to birth your greatness, the answer is quite simple; you have stopped growing in Christ. Here are a few areas that I believe you should examine in your spiritual inventory to make sure growth and development is taking place:

Shame

It is probably safe to say that you were not expecting that. However, shame is one of the leading causes of stunted growth. No matter what walk of life you come from, we all suffer from shame. We all have a desire for connection and acceptance at some point in our lives. Not only did I desire connection and acceptance from people in my personal life growing up, but also during my career as a public speaker as well as a businessman. More importantly, I desired a connection and acceptance from God. Through my life I sinned, and I came up short many times.

Sometimes I felt like I let my parents down, and especially God at times when I did not unwrap my gift and live in my purpose. When I failed in areas of my life, I felt as if I was not going to be accepted by my parents nor God, which, made me feel as if I lost a connection with my parents, which triggered shame. Shame even stopped me from connecting with God, but I am not the only one that suffered from shame. In Genesis 3:9, Adam and Eve sinned, and then hid from God. Essentially, they were ashamed that they were disobedient. In this Scripture God responded to them after they had sinned and ran off to hide by saying, "Where are you?" Now, God is an all-knowing God, and He did not ask them this question as if He did not now their physical location. No, He asked, "Where are you?" because He wanted to know what their spiritual condition was. Shame is not from God; it is a trick that the devil plays with our emotions. Shame puts us in a hide and seek game with God, but without God playing. Shame tells you that you are no good and that you are a bad person. Adam and Eve hid because of shame because they believed they were bad people. But I learned during my journey that Adam and Eve making a bad decision does not make them bad people. The decision they made just indicates they made a wrong choice.

I know that this journey to birth greatness was not and is not easy. And you probably made some bad decision along the way but trust me when I say that God knows your heart. Do not be ashamed. Do not let shame take the life out of you nor the greatness out of you.

Do not allow shame to stunt your growth. This particular item in your spiritual inventory, called shame, stunts people's growth. Do not be ashamed of any mistakes that transpired in your life. You are not perfect, none of us are. Yes, you have sinned, but you are valuable and what you have on the inside of you makes you a world changer. Do yourself a favor and eliminate shame out of your spiritual inventory.

Comparisons:

One of the hardest battles you will ever have to face on this journey of birthing greatness is comparison. Birthing greatness is a process that requires you to focus. However, it is challenging to focus when you are comparing yourself to others. Comparing yourself with others will cripple your belief that your greatness is worth birthing. God made you on purpose and He made sure it was only one of you that will ever walk this earth.

I know that it is hard when you are on your journey to birth greatness because when you look over at the next person's life, it feels as if they are passing you by, while you are stuck in a traffic jam. Not focusing and comparing yourself to others creates a level of jealousy, which sometimes is hard to get rid of. But you have to understand that what you go through in your season is for a reason. I know it does not seem like others go through a struggle, but I am here to tell you that in order to access success or to birth greatness you have to go through in order to get through. Focus on your greatness but more importantly focus on Christ and watch what God does in your life.

Forgiveness:

While you are doing a spiritual inventory, I need you to check on your ability to forgive people. Yes, leave the hatred at the front door and remove it from your heart. I am talking about the ones that hurt you and did you wrong; forgive them. Resentment will hold you back from birthing greatness. You must make the decision, which is a hard one, to no longer allow what people to have said or done in your life to stop you from birthing greatness. What you went through in your past is just an indication that your future is bright.

There is not one successful person that has achieved success without someone trying to delay or hinder them from that success. Forgiveness is not for the person who hurt you, remember that. Forgiveness is 100 percent for you. Your willingness to be forgiving allows your greatness to be brought into this world with confidence that your past and enemies will not affect your future.

The more mature I got during my spiritual pregnancy, I was convinced that our spiritual health, wellness, physical, emotional health, as well as a spiritual inventory check is important in order to birth greatness. As you start your third trimester, keep in mind that even though you are towards the end of your pregnancy it is not going to get easier from here nor does it stop here. The devil knows that you made it and you are on your way to greatness. He is going to try you, while God is putting you through a test. However, I want you to know whatever the devil throws your way and whatever God has is in store for your life, you can handle it.

CARRYING EXTRA BAGGAGE

Tired? I know you probably thought that starting your third trimester was going to be way easier than this. You probably did not think that you would have to start off doing a spiritual inventory check. Listen, I am sorry. I wish I can tell you that birthing greatness was going to be a breeze. For a woman to give birth it requires her to go through a process. A few things must be done in order for the birth to be a success.

During the third trimester it becomes more important that the mom-to-be follow the direction given from the doctor and do the necessary steps in order to prepare themselves for the last few weeks in their pregnancy. There is no difference when it comes to you giving birth to your greatness. I believe there is a very important first step when you enter your third trimester that is going to help you not only in your last few weeks of your spiritual pregnancy, but also for life. That particular step is for you to go through a spiritual inventory to do some possible adjustments in your life. By you doing so, cleansing takes place emotionally and spiritually.

It lightens the load mentally, physically, and spiritually, so that you can be capable of finishing strong in your last trimester of your spiritual pregnancy. However, if you still do not feel quite right, then you probably ran into an issue that I ran into during my spiritual pregnancy: carrying too much unnecessary baggage. Remember, this spiritual pregnancy is a journey and even after you birth your greatness the journey continues. When a mother gives birth, it does not stop there. Their next journey right after birth is motherhood. There is no difference on your next phase of birthing your greatness.

So, the question you should be asking is, "What do I need for my next journey?" What should I take? What should I leave behind? During trips we all have experience overpacking. We all are victims of taking things we just absolutely do not need. We do not realize that overpacking costs us. It is embarrassing to be running late to catch a plane because of a heavy suitcase. When I sit back and think about it, I laugh. I laugh because if you have seen me in person, I am five foot five inches tall and I weigh about 135 pounds soaking wet. I have no business having a heavy suitcase because it is probably going to weigh more than me, if not the same weight as me. Nevertheless, I believe we all have some baggage of some kind that is holding us back from getting us to our destination.

Maybe for you it is *relationship baggage.* You have put your all into someone that betrayed your trust in your personal relationship or even in your business relationship. Now your heart is frozen, and you will not allow people to enter in. You have convinced yourself that you will not allow yourself to be vulnerable nor in a position to get betrayed. That is cool and all, but on your trip to birthing greatness you must leave that relationship baggage in the past. You cannot allow what happened in your past business or personal life to hinder you from birthing your greatness. Those individuals are not hurting, it is you suffering and hindering yourself from birthing greatness because you cannot let go of that baggage.

Or it may not be relationship baggage problems that are holding you back, you might be carrying around the *baggage of abuse.* First and foremost, no one deserves to go through abuse. The statistics about victims of abuse are horrifying. I need you to know that what transpired between you and the abuser was not and is not your fault. I know getting over abuse cannot happen overnight. If you are experiencing the trauma that has happened between you and your abuser, I encourage you to go seek some help. There is nothing wrong with talking to someone. And remember you can always lay your burdens before God. No problem is too big for God; go talk to Him.

I want you to know that regardless of what abuse you have experienced, I am here to tell you that you are beautiful, smart, strong and deserving to carry and birth the greatness that has be given to you. When you birth the greatness that God has placed on the inside of you, watch how you are going to be able to articulate your story with confidence and help other individuals that have experience abuse get over the trauma. Your story, confidence and strength will help others birth the greatness that God has given them.

By the grace of God, I never experienced abuse. However, during my journey to birth greatness I carried a lot of baggage that delayed me to getting to my destination. I carried relationship baggage, but I also carried one baggage that was hard for me to let go and that was *self-image baggage*. Many people experience self-image baggage, and I would not be shocked if you are one of those people as well. In my many failures I use to tell myself that "I will never amount to anything." I had moments that I really thought I was not going to be an author or a public speaker and that I was not cut out to be successful. I even thought I was not going to birth the greatness that God gave me. Sometimes during your journey, you might feel as though you are worthless or that you are not smart enough. You might even lack confidence or assurance that you will ever amount to anything, let alone birth greatness.

These are just a few things that people believe, myself included when I looked in the mirror while on my journey to birth greatness. You must break free from the negative thoughts that you have placed on yourself. Many of us carry wounds of brokenness and pain in our heart unnecessarily. You are amazing. I need you to know that no weapon formed against you shall prosper. Put the spiritual baggage down. Your baggage is preventing you from not only birthing your greatness but also from having a meaningful relationship with God. I understand that you have a past; we all do. But you have a choice: to carry around that baggage with you or leave it in the past. You cannot walk into the door that you have been asking God to open with unnecessary baggage.

I need you to leave that baggage behind but use your experiences as a learning lesson to get you one step closer to your destination which is to birth the greatness that God has given you. Jesus states in Matthew 11:28, "Come to me, all you who labor and are burdened, and I will give you rest." We all struggled with carrying too much during our journey to birthing greatness.

However, if you bring your baggage to God, He will set you free. God never interrupts your free will from picking up the baggage. You packed it and picked it up, that means you have the same ability to put it down and leave your baggage in the past. I know it is not easy. That is why God will always help His children. Bring those things that weigh you down to baggage claim and God will do the rest. I know it is easier said than done. We all have found it difficult to hand over our excess baggage to God; I know I have. It is a struggle, because sometimes it is embarrassing and sometimes it is a crutch. However, when we do not hand our baggage over, we will become spiritually cast down. In Psalm 43:5 it says, "Why, my soul, are you downcast...?" This is not a question you should ignore.

When your spiritual life feels "heavy" which makes you feel as if you are slowing down during your marathon, then that is an indication that you are spiritually cast down. When you feel sad more than happy, then that is the indication that you just took a spiritual and emotional hit. You become accessible to the devil's plan when you carry around baggage. You need to unload that heavy backpack of your failures, mistakes, and so much more. Unload those negative thoughts. Free yourself because your plane cannot handle the load. Allow God to take this load off you and your life so you can be free to be able to birth greatness.

FINISH STRONG

I hope I have not scared you. I am far from trying to scare you, trust me. However, I mentioned earlier that birthing greatness is a marathon. With that being said, during this marathon to birth greatness you will experience shortness of breath. In the natural, moms-to-be experience shortness of breath occasionally, especially during their third trimester. The position of their baby on the inside their womb can place pressure on their lungs. There is no difference when it comes to you being pregnant with greatness. Greatness places pressure on you and sometimes it can make it hard for you to breathe.

The greatness that is sitting on the inside of you can cause you to experience shortness of breath on your journey. But do not worry! Doctors suggest that women who are having trouble breathing to be mindful of their posture and stand up straight to give their lungs a bit more room to expand. In your case, I suggest you do not give up on the marathon.

You are on your last lap and I need you to stand up straight with confidence and push through to the end. You got this, and God's got you. During my journey I was surprised I made it as far as I did, but I would be a fool if I told you that I got there on my own. The main culprit who helped me to the finish line, is the one and only Jesus Christ. When I tell you that I still find myself in shock sometimes to be where I am today, it is far from exaggeration. I would not be surprised if you also encountered a shock.

This marathon is probably the farthest you have run in years, especially during your spiritual journey. When you approach the finish line, which is giving birth to your greatness, you will begin to feel a rush of emotions. This journey will start to become one of the greatest passions of your life. I do not know about you but when I realized I was approaching finishing this race, it took over my mind in such a breathtaking way. Those thoughts and emotions are what got me out of bed in the morning. I wanted to birth greatness and change not only my life but the world. You have been chosen for this race. God sat back and wanted a dream player and created and choose you for His plans. I know you probably wondered why He choose you and

why it feels as if you are on this journey alone. Can I tell you a secret?

This race is unique and was created specifically for you. You and only you must go through what you have or will experience, so you can be groomed for your greatness. God created a distinctive race for you, that as you know took you on an interesting adventure. While the destination is the same for everyone, and that is to birth greatness, the journey is different for everyone. And just like many races, at some point you will experience shortness of breath. You will also experience obstacles that sometimes get the best of you. However, you cannot give up. Those obstacles may slow you down and sometimes throw you off track, but you cannot, and I mean cannot give up. You run this marathon to win. You came too far to give up now.

You promised me earlier that you were not going to compare yourself, nor your gift and journey to the next person. Keeping that promise sets yourself up to win the marathon. However, I need you to know that winning does not mean beating others that are on their own personal journey to birth greatness. The finish line is to birth the greatness that God gave you. The goal is not perfection nor beating others, but the goal is progress. A mom-to-be does not care about what another mom-to-be is doing in the next delivery room. A woman must sit for hours in pain and anticipation. Then in a snap of a finger they must prepare themselves to push with substantial energy in order to give birth. I can only imagine how exhausting that may be. And for you, during your spiritual pregnancy I know the progress of birthing greatness is tiring and you have probably experience shortness of breath through this journey. I want you to know I am proud of you. However, it is important for you to know that in order for you to win this race, it requires persistence and endurance. You must push through. You will need to persevere on your way to birthing greatness.

I cannot say this enough; it is important for you to know that during this spiritual marathon you cannot stop running. You cannot give up. Promise me you will never quit. I do not care what happens to you nor what obstacles that come in front on you, it is important that you do not give up. Trust me, I know at some point you have, or you will trip, you might even fall; but you cannot give up. I know you have failed and probably will fail again at some point during your third trimester, but you cannot sit there in your mistakes. Remember, learn from your failures, and allowed them to propel you to your goal, which is birthing your greatness.

One of my favorite lines that my track coach once told me was, "Run through the tape, young fella." I need you to run through the tape, but I need you to run with faith. Running without faith is equivalent to jogging because jogging is comfortable. Faith is uncomfortable. It takes a different type of person to run a spiritual marathon with a faith blind fold on. That is one of the reasons why not everyone has given birth to their greatness, because marathons make you uncomfortable. It becomes uncomfortable to the body and mind and who wants to be uncomfortable?

Although a faith marathon is uncomfortable, the only way you can get through is by realizing who you are running for. Identifying who you are running for gives you a level of motivation and confidence to push through. Remember, you trained for this. A mother will take on a lot in order to give birth. She realizes why and who she is giving birth for. You are running for not only yourself, but more importantly God. Isaiah 40:31 says, but those who trust in the Lord will find new strength. They will soar high on wings like eagles. They will run and not grow weary. They will walk and not faint." Finish strong! And like my track coach says, "run through the tape, young fella."

CHAPTER 18

18

KEEP STRETCHING

How has this continuous journey, marathon, and battle in order to birth greatness been for you so far? I know saying it "finish strong", is easier said than done. Listen, I know it is tough, but I need you to keep clawing and scratching until you reach your destination which is birthing your greatness. "How, you ask? One word. Effort. Effort is the last step of the cycle before accomplishment. You should know all about effort. You know when that hard-to-reach spot on your back starts to itch.

The question is are you willing to do everything it takes to scratch that itch? Or are you going to give up? It takes effort to reach accomplishment. You are almost there to birthing your God given greatness, but you must apply effort in order to give birth to your greatness. How bad do want that itch to go away? How badly do you want to birth greatness? Are you willing to claw and scratch your way to birthing your greatness? No one said that spiritual pregnancy was going to be easy and if you ask any mother, they will tell you that natural pregnancy was not and is not easy either.

The reason why people give up on birthing greatness before they even try, is because birthing greatness requires a down payment. And no, I am not talking money. I have never witnessed someone give up on that itch in that hard spot to reach on their back. They put in maximum effort to accomplish that itch. However, when it comes to birthing greatness not everyone is willing to put in maximum effort in order to birth greatness.

Some think they can replace effort with being educated. What if I told you that you do not have to be smart in order to birth greatness, or to achieve success? There are a lot of really not smart people that have birthed their greatness, as well as, accessed success in their life. So, what is the secret to people achieving success and birthing greatness in their lives? It is the one thing that no one can give to you and the one thing that no one can take away from you that makes the biggest difference.

That word is effort.

One of the keys to birth greatness is a deposit of effort. Can you imagine a mother not putting forth any effort when it is time to give birth? In order for her to become a mother, she has to put in the maximum amount of effort. Putting in effort gets her to the other side and on the other side is motherhood. Your other side of effort is greatness. Effort is everything. Anything and everything worth doing in life is an effort. People fail to make the effort to succeed. Birthing greatness is not for everyone, that is why you see others that have all the potential in the world not birth their greatness. Bestselling author Rory Vaden said, "Success is never owned; it is only rented, and the rent is due every day." I look at greatness the same way.

You must put in the maximum effort every day in order to keep greatness. Champions give their maximum effort every day of their lives, even when they do not feel like giving it. Orison Marden summed it all up perfectly when said, "What keeps so many people back is simply their unwillingness to pay the price, to make the exertion, the effort to sacrifice their ease and comfort." My question to you is, "What effort are you willing to give to evolve, grow, develop, practice, overcome to birth your greatness?" Some days will be more tiring and challenging than others.

Trust me, I know it will be hard some days to put in the

maximum effort to get you through. But implementing effort every day to be the best version of yourself so you can birth greatness is worth it. If you fail to put effort into birthing your greatness, change will not occur. Maximum effort equals success. Everything that you want to happen in your future will come to pass if you are making and putting in maximum effort now.

I have witnessed many people swing back and forth when it comes to their spiritual growth; I am one of those people as well that once could not make up my mind when it came to my spiritual life. One of the expectations is that God will do everything if only I have faith and wait patiently. So, to be honest I did not put forth much effort in my process nor when it came to my growth and development. Now there is some truth that waiting patiently and having faith in God will make a way out of no way. Although in this journey, people forget this key element: that they still have to put in some level of work, *effort.* Take some time to read James 2: 14-26. In this passage it states that faith without work is dead. Many people are not willing to put in the work. We all are working with the same number of hours in the day; it is what we do with them that make the difference.

Your journey is far from a competition. When you focus on yourself and have consistent effort, with a sprinkle of persistence, determination, and commitment then and only then will you put yourself in a position to birth greatness. Birthing greatness is not going to happen overnight, but it is not going to happen at all if you are not committed to deposit maximum effort in your journey. Remember, that it is not about perfection, it is about effort. When you bring that maximum effort to the table and apply it every single day to the process, then only great things can happen. That is where transformation happens. That is how change occurs. That is when greatness is born. How bad do you want it?

STRETCH MARKS

The dreaded stretch marks. Stretch marks are an indication that rapid weight gain has taken place or from weight changes. Stretch marks are hard to embrace. They are continuous reminders of heavy weight changes. It starts to affect the confidence. Guys become self-conscious and women avoid bathing suits and any situation where they must show skin. Some might even think they become damaged goods and believe their stretch marks are imperfections. People have the wrong idea about stretch marks. They focus on how they make the body look instead of focusing or knowing what stretch marks represent. Stretch marks represents growth. When the body grows it causes the skin to stretch and tug resulting in stretch marks.

Unbeknownst to some women during their pregnancy, stretch marks are taking place before they are even seen. In other words, growth is taking place. There is no difference when it comes to a spiritual pregnancy. Spiritual stretch marks represent growth as well. However, in order for growth to take place, it requires us to be stretched. If you have ever played any physical sport, you know that being stretched is not always easy nor pleasant. But stretching is necessary if we are wanting to grow during our journeys to birth greatness and in Christ. Stretch marks are unsightly. They were not invited to enter in us or on us. I look at stretch marks not for what they are on its surface. I look at stretch marks as battle scares, as growth marks.

God is more interested in our growth and development. He is looking at our willingness and effort to grow up and He is our comfort. Growth is not always pleasant. That is why it is a such thing as growing pains. Growth can be painful, but it is necessary. I do not know about you, but I want to show off my imperfections. I want to show off my battle scares and my growth marks. I want and embrace my spiritual stretch marks. It is a reason why God chose you.

Like I told you in the first trimester, I am a G.P.S for God; God's Personal Servant. I love being a billboard for God. I want my spiritual stretch marks to show that I am being stretched, that I am growing and developing. I now have a Paul mindset that he had in Galatians 6:17 (NIV) which he says, "For now on, let no one cause me trouble, for I bear on my body the marks of Jesus." Do not be ashamed about your spiritual stretch marks. Those marks are an indication that you have been through a lot, but you are still standing. Those spiritual stretch marks remind you that you have been stretched, developed, and grown up.

I know growth is painful. You have stretched for quite some time, but I need you to walk in your growth and shine in your light. Your spiritual marks show that you are not perfect, because if you were then growth, development or change would not need to occur. Stretch marks can be found on roughly 80% of Americans. Many of those men and women pay hundreds of dollars for creams and serums to minimizes and hide what they believe is God-awful imperfections, whether out of fear or shame.

Spiritually speaking, there are individuals that feel as if showing their growth is a sign of weakness. But I am here to tell you that it is ok that you are not who you once were. We should always seek growth. Yes, there are going to be seasons in your life where the growth is difficult but do not hide it. Do not put cream over your spiritual stretch marks to minimize or hide your growth. I encourage you to embrace your spiritual stretch marks. They are a friendly reminder of a hard change that occurred in your life. Your marks are a representation of how you were stretched uncomfortably. Do you want to know the beauty of it all? It shows how you managed to grow through the difficulty. I say that it is worth showing off. Embrace the imperfections. From now on, look at your spiritual stretch marks as beauty marks. Now show the world what God is working with within you.

SPIRITUAL CONTRACTIONS

Before we move on, I want to take this time to salute every single woman that walked this earth. There is no doubt in my mind that you all are the true definition of a wonder woman. It is amazing that God chose a woman to be the vehicle of giving life. All of you incredible women put your body and lives on the line to be able to bring life into this world and for that I want to thank and appreciate each and every one of you. Fellas, if you are a male reading this book, I want you to take some time and salute the amazing women that are in your life, especially the one who brought you into this world.

My appreciation for women and the significance of pregnancy helped spark the idea to write The Birth of Greatness. Pregnancy symbolizes progression, growth, development, and the ability to be used to give the gift of life. The Birth of Greatness is just that; progression, growth, development and giving life to your purpose, passion, ideas, vision gifts and greatness. I believe it is important that I state the obvious; I never experienced given birth.

However, I do know one of the hardest things to experience during the journey of giving birth is CONTRACTIONS. Now you have contractions that prepare your body for labor, which is called Braxton Hicks contractions, and then you have the "real" contractions that indicate that the body is preparing itself to go into labor. Spiritually speaking, spiritual contractions are an indication that you are approaching the next phase in your life or a that a transition is about to take place in your life. If you ask any mother, they will tell you that contractions are not a pleasant feeling.

Even though that feeling is the indication that you are about to birth the greatest joy in your life, those feelings are still no fun. During a contraction, the muscle becomes or is made shorter and tighter. Spiritually speaking when you have contractions, shrinkage takes place. What shrinkage is taking place you ask? Allow me to explain.

During your journey to birth greatness, especially when you are in your third trimester, the devil feels as if he is losing this fight because you have come this far. And because of your commitment of not giving up, he feels a level of defeat. He feels as if his back is against the wall and none of things, he is throwing at you are working. Just like anyone, when your back is against the wall, you begin to give all you have to not lose the fight. One of the last punches the devil will try defeat you with, is with your ego. That is one of the reasons why God allows you to experience spiritual contractions.

God puts you through spiritual contractions to shrink your ego. Since the devil knows that everyone has an ego, he starts trying to convince us that we made it this far without God. I believe one of the major tasks of spiritual maturity is recognizing, but also letting go of the ego in favor of birthing greatness. Now contractions can be excruciatingly painful. To be honest, letting go your ego is no better.

However, when we do not go through the contractions or the process to allow God to shrink our ego, it hinders the ability to birth greatness. The ego needs to feel special and is reluctant to give God praise or credit. That is what the devil wants you to feel. He wants you to believe that you made it to the third trimester on your own. Your flesh starts to convince you that you do not need anyone but you and yourself alone. During this time in your life the devil knows that he must pull all the tricks out to defeat you. He starts shining a spotlight on your ego. The ego starts to say, "Look at what I have done. See what I have accomplished." Egos want attention, even the attention from God. The ego wants you to believe that you have something to prove during your third trimester, when in reality during this time God want you to trust Him and allow Him to guide you.

Contractions are painful, I get it. Usually, when anyone experiences pain, their first extinct is to eliminate the discomfort anyway possible. The ego believes and tries to convince you that you can experience God without discomfort. Contractions are one of your biggest opponents the devil tries to throw your way during your third trimester. Contractions triggers your faith, because contractions are also there to see if you are going to trust God during your last lap on your marathon to birth greatness. To be honest, there is some level of discomfort during that process. This excruciating pain called spiritual contractions requires faith and effort. It is going to make you feel uncomfortable and your ego is going to tell you that going through this is not worth birthing your greatness. I am here to tell you that you have been through too much hell to give up now.

Most people like everything about Jesus, except when it is not beneficial to their ego. Like losing your friends or significant other that you wanted to spend the rest of your life with, although they were no good for you. Or seeing others becoming successful, but you are sitting there with your ego hurt because you believe that should have been you. Trust me, I understand, I am guilty of being one of those people. See, the ego is sensitive and can be easily offended. Question, how easily are you offended? When your ego is active it becomes your boss, it takes over and when that happens your opinion has little to no value when it comes to birthing your greatness. Experiencing contractions is a great need during any pregnancy, naturally or spiritually. Contractions are necessary in order for your labor to occur.

The devil knows that, and he will try his best to have your ego take over you. When your ego pushes, it does so without instructions or without permission. However, when a woman is in labor the doctor indicates when to push. The same applies during your spiritual pregnancy. Your doctor which is doctor G-O-D is the only one who can instruct you to push. The ego's greatest fear and weakness is change. The ego hates when you make up in your mind that it is time for a change to take place. Your ego does not want you to grow or change. Your ego does not want you to let it go and stretch your hands to God. You cannot stretch your hands to God when you have both of your hands full.

You are approaching the next phase in your life or a transition is about to take place in your life that is why spiritual contractions are and will take place in your life. That is what you call *change*. You must make up in your mind that you will not allow your ego nor the discomfort that contractions put you in, from going through the necessary process to birth your greatness. Giving birth is an incredible risk but this is a time to implement all that you have learned from God and your experiences.

More importantly this is the time for you to activate your faith. But I must inform you that activating your faith requires you to be patient and to trust God to get you through this. Stretch your hands to God and allow Him to guide your feet and your path.

OFFER UP YOUR PAIN

I told you that it was not going to get any easier from here. As you are witnessing, the journey to birth greatness is difficult. Usually, during this journey to birth greatness there are two things that becomes the most difficult. Two things that prevent individuals from birthing greatness. The first thing is the starting line. Some people have trouble starting the process or trouble getting out the gate to reach greatness. We all know someone who has a great idea and limitless potential, but they never start. If you do not start, there is no way you can finish.

Now not everyone has trouble starting. Some run into the

second thing that prevents individuals from birthing greatness and that is finishing. At one point in my life, I used to have the biggest trouble finishing projects for numerous reasons. The main reason why I had trouble in the past finishing ideas and projects is because I dislike, and I mentally thought that I could not handle the process. When I was on the journey to birth my greatness, I had trouble getting to my third trimester, let alone finishing the pregnancy. The pain of the whole process was so excruciating that it took a toll on me physically, mentally, and spiritually which made me want to give up.

However, I am here to tell you to offer up your pain to God. This process of birthing greatness is no joke; I get it. However, I want you to prepare yourself now and pray. Get in the habit of praying and offering up your problems to God, especially this battle that you have been experiencing. Do not be afraid to ask God for help. When you approach your due time to birth your greatness, it is important to prepare your thoughts so you can focus on breathing and pushing. The devil knows that you are close to giving birth to greatness, and he does not want you to change nor win.

I know during this journey you have experienced aches and discomforts, but remember you have a secret weapon that the devil cannot defeat and that is God. Offer up your aches, pains, trials, and tribulation to your Heavenly Father. Allow Him to be the great doctor He is. This trimester comes with what will seem like unbearable challenges from the start of your third trimester to the end. But what the devil does not understand is that you have already been through hell and you have God behind you every step of the way. If you have forgotten, God will not leave you nor forsake you during this journey.

I believe in you. You already have proven that you are strong. How do I know, you ask? Well, you are still here correct? As far as I am concerned, that indicates to me that you are strong and amazing. God knew what He was doing when you created you. God chose you for an incredible reason.

Again, I know it is not easy. I know you have been through a lot, more than you probably can explain. Trust me, I know the feeling of being at your breaking point. I know you want the Lord to show up and show out, now. Trust me I know you cannot take this anymore. You are tired of contractions. You are tired of crying at random times of the day. You feel like giving up because your flesh is tugging you one way and the Holy spirit is tugging you the other way. I promise you that I know that you have prayed and cried, and then prayed and cried some more, and this process still seems as if it is not getting any easier. You are human, so it is ok that you have questions or have been questioning God. I do not know about you, but I had my share of questions and concerns about the direction that God had me on. Sitting there wondering how I should go about what is happening in my home, career, business, gifts, and passions.

Life is difficult and attempting to birth greatness does not make it any easier. Life will feel, if it has not already felt as if it is ganging up on you, as if it is not aware that you are trying to birth greatness on top of trying to survive. Trust me when I say this, God is working in your life and again, He will not leave you in this thing called life. But I am here to remind you that God will never leave you nor forsake you. I have repeated that phrase numerous times is this book. I need you know that believe that and trust that. God is a loving God, and He has you in His hands. This is the third trimester; you think God lead you all the way here to leave you now. I know you have experienced pain throughout this process, especially during your third trimester.

However, this is a time to smile and rejoice because you made it to a place in your life where others struggle to make it to. It is time for you to rejoice. You should be excited. God has placed a gift and a whole lot of greatness on the inside of you. Those gifts must be cultivated, and your greatness must be birthed. Now pain is required in order to give birth and if pain is what you are experiencing then your delivery date is soon approaching. You are carrying something that the world needs.

Do not be alarmed or ashamed; it takes a special person to

be pregnant with greatness. You have been chosen to deliver God's message and to live out the plans He has created for your life. During this pain you are experiencing you must find it in your heart to rejoice. Offer up that pain and let go. Rejoice because you are about to have a baby in the spirit. When you give birth to the greatness that God has given you, then you will see that all of the preparation was worth it. All the trials and tribulations, the ups and the downs, the headaches and heartaches were worth it.

I learned that women during their natural pregnancy have no control of their weight gain, morning sickness, mood swings, appetite, nor their pain. The baby inside of her essentially controls all of that. Spiritually speaking, you do not have any control over what God has in store for you. However, you can prepare and during your preparation it is important that you do not get distracted. Oh, and by the way, you cannot give up, but you already knew that. This is the time that you must get in position to prepare yourself to push. I need you to offer up the pain and push through. We are going to talk about pushing shortly, but I need you to know that you are not alone in this process, God got you.

STAY ALERT

1 Peter 5:8 says, "Be alert and of sober mind. Your enemy the devil prowls around like a roaring lion looking for someone to devour." I know you are looking forward to the journey being finished, but devil seems to not give up. Allow me to inform you of why the devil has not given up yet. You are carrying something that is extremely valuable and that is greatness, which needs to be protected at all cost. Your greatest enemy is the devil and his workers. 1 Peter 5:8 warns us to, "Stay alert!" The devil is in the business to crush dreams, destroy passion, hide gifts, devour purpose, and kill greatness. He has tried it before and accomplished his goal with many people. I am not only here to warn you but also to educate you on how to protect your dreams, passions, gifts, purpose and more importantly your greatness, especially during your third trimester.

The first important piece of information you need to know in order to protect what God has given you starts with subtraction. We discuss offering up your pain and getting rid of your ego. However, there are a few other things that the devil will try to activate to prevent you from giving birth to your greatness. Things such as, entitlement, jealousy, insecurity, selfishness, and this is just to name a few that you will have to subtract out of your life, especially during this process. The process of subtracting these things out of your heart can be challenging and tough, but if you are serious about protecting your greatness you must submit to God's process of subtraction. All of these toxic elements can hinder your ability to birth greatness. These can be poison to your greatness. These toxic elements can consume you from the inside out and place you in what is called in the natural an "at risk pregnancy." When you allow these things to take over your life it can be cancerous to your body and spirit.

It becomes important to place boundaries in your life. Proverbs 4:23 says, "Above all else, guard your heart, for everything you do flows from it." Your greatness needs your heart to be pure. You not only have to subtract entitlement, jealousy, insecurity, and selfishness just to name a few. You also must be in the business of guarding your heart from bitterness, unforgiveness, resentment, and pride.

Placing a boundary around your heart is important. You cannot allow any of these things to gain any access to your heart. Boundary means guarding. You must keep not only you heart but your greatness free and clear from these negative and toxic elements. But it does not stop with just placing boundaries over your heart, you also must place boundaries of your mind. The enemy loves to rest himself on your thoughts. He tries to place in our minds the spirit of defeat and discouragement. He will try to tell you and place thoughts in your mind such as you are too old, too young, too inexperienced or have made too many mistakes to birth your greatness. One of the ways to take back control over your mind is replacing every self-limiting believes with affirmations and the word of God. Remember, life and death are in the power of our tongues. You must decree and declare God's promises over your own life. You must let the devil know that he is not welcome in your heart or mind. In Philippians 4:13 it says, "I can do all things through Christ who strengthens me."

To stay alert requires work and work requires time. You must also put boundaries around your time. In the natural, pregnancy has a time frame. During your journey to birth greatness, it requires time. You must protect your time. Do not allow the devil to hinder your time nor distract you. Time is a precious commodity. Time is something no one can get back. We all have the same 24 hours in a day. However, how we invest the time will greatly determine our ability to achieve success and to give birth to our greatness. You see others who have achieved success and have worked hard for it They put in the maximum effort and time to become successful. The devil loves going after your time because he understands that time is what people who are on the quest to birth their greatness value.

You have reached the final stage of your pregnancy, the

third trimester because you have been obedient, you have put in the effort and because you have put the time in. You are due at any moment, but you still have a little more time left. The devil believes if he can interrupt the time you have left, he has won the battle. But I am here to tell you that the devil cannot win. The devil is prowling because he knows that God is up to something great with you. The devil is aware that you have something great on the inside of you that the devils know he cannot destroy without your help. But to the devil's surprise, he does not know how bad you want this. Satan cannot destroy what God has given you. Stay alert!

PREGNANCY BRAIN AGAIN?

You probably saying to your self that this "pregnancy brain" seems to not leave you alone. I know we spoke on this earlier, but "pregnancy brain" occurs occasionally throughout a woman's pregnancy. Well, pregnancy brain is not an official medical condition; rather, it is a term for a few symptoms that affect many if not most moms-to-be at some point during their pregnancy. Now some of those symptoms vary from woman to woman, and can include memory lapses, general spaciness and the inability to concentrate. Spiritually speaking, during your journey to birth your greatness these symptoms can occur sporadically as well and sometimes all at once.

Pregnancy brain can strike when you attempt to take the time and evaluate your spiritual inventory, when you are trying to let go of some of that extra baggage, on top of that trying to stay alert and fight the devil tricks off; the inability to concentrate or general spaciness can set in. Which can cause you to sometimes get exhausted, which also can cause you at times to space out, memory lapse, or enables you to concentrate. We must watch out for pregnancy brain, especially when you so close birthing greatness.

Spiritually speaking, what also is one of the big factors that causes pregnancy brain is a shift. When you shift your focus from the greatness itself; meaning the process and nurturing of the greatness, to protecting and playing defense all the time, it can allow fatigue set in. When fatigue sets in you start to lose your footing during this marathon. In the natural women go through this during their journey in giving birth; they start to be unstable on their feet. When this happens to mom's-to-be it is an indication that their center of gravity has shifted, making it easier for them to lose their balance. During your journey there is no difference.

When your greatness is growing so much on the inside of you, it starts to weigh heavy on you. The pressure to be great, to start that business, finish that degree, ignite your passion, unwrap your gift, live in your purpose and birth your greatness. It sometimes become heavy on your shoulders and causes you to be off balance. On the other hand, for some, that hunger to unleash and birth your greatness and so much more brings a level of fatigue which can bring a shift in the spirit and causes you to lose your balance or focus. To keep yourself steady on the purpose, the goal, your greatness, and more importantly God. Do what David did in the book of Psalms: Cry out to God.

I know that seem like the easy answer, but it is the best answer. When you cry out to God you allow God to place your feet on solid ground. In Psalms chapter 40, a shift took place which caused David to cry out for some help. Who better to cry out too than God? Psalms 40:1-3 (NLT) David said, "I waited patiently for the Lord to help me and He turned to me and heard my cry. He lifted me out of the pit of despair, out of the mud and the mire. He set my feet on solid ground and steadied me as I walked along. He has given me a new song to sing, a hymn of praise to our God. Many will see what he has done and be amazed. They will put their trust in the Lord."

Your inability to concentrate is the devil trying to knock you off course. An idle mind is a devil's playground. I know you are tired of playing defense when it comes to this battle with the devil. I understand you are tired of the trials and tribulation. Tired of people passing you by and some not believing in you, but I am here to tell you that God hears your cry, and He will lift you out of that pit of despair, out the mud and the mire. He will set your feet on solid ground. I know it feels shaky and it feels as if you are losing your balance during this journey, but trust in the Lord. Stand with conviction. Get rid of those heavy burdens. Avoid accepting negative thoughts that others or even you have placed on you. Just like David, God will give you a new song to sing. And when it is time for you to birth your greatness many people will see what God has done and be amazed. God is using you for His glory and when you have your coming out party which is birthing your greatness the world will witness and put their trust in the Lord. I promise, you are getting closer and closer to meeting your newborn spiritual baby, which is your greatness.

Now I want you to know you are not alone when it comes to getting spiritual pregnancy brain; it happens to all of us especially in the latter stage of your journey to birth greatness. No matter what causes the brain fog, it is important to have some tools to help you gain and stay focused on your journey to birth greatness. I stated this before, but I want you to get sticky notes and place them on your bathroom mirror or even the front door and write affirmations on them. I need you to know that you are great, and greatness is upon you. I need you to know what is on the inside of you makes you a world changer.

It is a must for you to know that you are smart, brave, beautiful, more than enough and so much more. These many sticky notes are reminders of what you are and whose' you are. These sticky notes will allow you to stay focused and not allow pregnancy brain to be activated or to continue.

Now sticky notes filled with affirmations may not be enough for you to deactivate or prevent pregnancy brain. Since we all have our phones on us constantly, make it useful and set a reminder for you to pray to God. Again, I speak on prayer a lot throughout this book. You must pray on it, pray over it and pray through it. It is a must for you to set time out every day to talk to God. William Law once said, "Prayer is the nearest approach to God." I do not know about you, but I yearn to be close to God and if prayer gets me there, I am on my knees daily talking to Him.

It is beneficial for you to take the time and pray every day. I know this might be new and even challenging for some of you. I learned everything I know about praying from my mother. She started as a little prayer warrior since I was four years old. When I got older and life started to get busy, she informed me about putting an alarm on my phone to remind me of the time to talk to God. She sets the example of setting her phone everyday around 6pm, which indicates that it is her pray time. She taught me to never forget about prayer in your daily life, because God did not forget to wake us up every morning. Her leading by example taught me to prioritize prayer in my daily life. And if you're anything like my mother and I who pregnancy brain kicks in from time to time and memory lapses sets in, then it is ok to set a reminder to step aside from everything and pray to God.

Now, not only do I have sticky notes on my bathroom that are filled with affirmations and a reminder on my phone so can I dedicate time to talk to God, but I also make time to relax and meditate. You must take time to do some self-maintenance if not every day at least a few times a week. Earlier in the book I mention a prayer closet, but this is far from a prayer closet. I take some time out of each day to actually relax and meditate. That means, no TV, no phone, or interactions with people. It is just me, myself, and I, and I encourage you to do the same.

The more relaxed you are, the less likely you are to become confused, fatigue, or stress. I use meditation to focus not only on the mission to birth greatness but as well as, my well-being. I encourage you to do the same. If done correctly, you then should have a clear mind, a freshness to yourself and a great amount of energy. You take that clear mind, freshness and energy and use it to start prioritizing the tasks in your life that matter. We all have a lot of our plates in our daily lives.

When you have too much on plates our pregnancy brain

kicks in. We get tired and we struggle to concentrate, memory lapse kicks in or just general spaciness sets. If we prioritize, we can now prevent those things from happening and it will help our daily lives out tremendously. Trust me when I say this, one of the ways to prevent your pregnancy brain is by prioritizing. You have a lot going on in your life and when you add the process and journey to birth greatness then it can be overwhelming. If you prioritize your task from least to greatness, I promise you it will eliminate stress and prevent pregnancy brain.

I do not know about you but not only was the lack of prioritizing challenging for me, but it was also exercising. And no, I am not talking about physical movement. I am talking about exercising my faith. Exercising your faith offers a number of benefits during your spiritual pregnancy. When you exercise your faith, it increases the blood flow throughout your body that connects you to greatness, but more importantly God. Just like your brain, your faith is a muscle. When your muscles are active, strength is being built. There is no room for pregnancy brain to settle in because you are exercising your faith muscles. Your mind is not spaced out or isolated. It is fully focused on your faith muscle. I was weak and allowed the devil to not only creep in my mind but also, I allowed him to control me to some degree. If I was doing my faith push-ups and faith jumping jacks, then I would have built a level of strength that the devil could not defeat.

In 1 Timothy 4:8 (NIV) it says, "For while bodily training is of some value, godliness is of value in every way, as it holds promise for the present life and also for the life to come." Greatness is the life to come and you cannot birth greatness with pregnancy brain is present. You have control over your life. Use these tools and watch how you can eliminate pregnancy brain. Tweet me at @Chris_Empowers and let me know your progress.

Finally, do your best to be patient as you go through this journey to birth greatness. Pregnancy brain gets activated because we want to rush the process. And when we rush, we lack concentration. When rushing does not go our way then our mind becomes spacious and that is when the devil laughs and attacks. You must be patient. God has perfect timing. I know you thought you should have been successful. You might even have thought your business should have grown or you should have been birthed your greatness by now. But if you did not know God is an all-knowing God and His detail to timing is outstanding. Trust in God's timing. It is better to wait a while and have things fall into place than to rush and have things fall apart.

When pregnancy brain strikes, and you start to lose focus it becomes harder to concentrate. Then the feeling of wanting this to just be all be over settles in. Trust me when I say, God is never late. Matter fact He is always right on time. We all desire control, but the truth is that we simply do not know what is best for us. If we are not careful, anxiousness can get in the way of God's intended blessing for us. Spiritually speaking, pregnancy brain is sneaky dangerous. It sneaks up on you and we do not realize how it is detrimental to our ability to give birth to our greatness. From this time forward you will pray and invest time to get more patients. If not, pregnancy brain will come in allow you to be anxious and miss your blessing. You come too far, worked too hard to allow pregnancy brain to make you lose out on your blessing and birth your greatness.

CHAPTER 19

19

PRESSURE CREATES DIAMOND

How has the journey of carrying greatness felt like so far? You feel the kicking, the pain, the agony that carrying greatness requires? How does it feel? You did not expect to go through what you have been through to birth greatness, did you? How does it feel to go through this journey of carrying greatness and people not believe in you?

How does it feel when people do not believe and understand your idea and passion? How does it feel when your lights, gas, and rent bill is past-due, because your greatness is now due? How does it feel to lose people out of your life you thought was going to be there forever? How does it feel to be a single mom that is working a 9 to 5 to keep a roof over their children's head, clothes on their back, food on their table, while trying to give birth to your idea and greatness to make a better life for you and children? How does it feel? How does it feel to be a wife, a student, and a mom while trying to give birth to your greatness?

How does it feel to be man, a provider, a father while trying to give birth to your idea, passion, and more importantly your greatness without sacrificing your family normal? How does it feel to be young and full of ideas, passion, gifts, and potential but being told that you are too young? How does it feel when you have identified your passion, purpose, greatness, then being told to go get a job? How does it feel to have lived a long life and finally gotten pregnant with greatness, but someone tells you that you are too old to start a business, too old to have a passion or too old to give birth to your greatness? How does it feel that you have to go through hell to birth your greatness? How do you feel? How does it feel to carry greatness? Is it pain you feel? Is it agony you feel? How about confusion, lostness, hopelessness, or even disappointment? Again, I ask, how does it feel? I do not know about you, but I felt the pressure.

But the question is, how do we respond to pressure? Two things can be true, pressure can either make you or break you. If it were not for my father telling me that pressure creates diamonds, I would have allowed pressure to break me. Now pressure is no small task. Pressure affects our ability to work and get things accomplished. But it will be a horrendous mistake to believe that pressure only negatively affects us. When moms-to-be feels pressure on their stomachs, specifically in their third trimester it is an indication that something is about to transpire. The hope is that something positive will happen such as a successful birth, but if they allowed pressure to get to set in, they will never find out what is truly inside of them. I applaud moms-to-be. They make up in their minds that the pressure that they experience is forming the greatest joy: their baby or what I like to call a diamond, because a diamond is valuable and there is nothing more valuable to a mother than her a baby.

Diamonds are incredible, because even though diamonds are nothing more than a clump of carbon and coal that refused to give in to pressure. If my mom or your mom for that matter, folded and crumbled under the pressure that was placed on them in any trimester, especially in the first trimester, then we would not have had the opportunity to breathe the breath of life. I would not have had the opportunity to write this book. You would have not been able to be in the position to birth your greatness.

In order for a diamond to manifest itself, it cannot fold under pressure. Your greatness is relying on you to not fold under pressure but allow the pressure to push you to give birth. Your greatness is ready to unleash itself to the world. I know life it hard and it puts pressure on you to be great. I know your parents have certain expectations on your life. I know achieving success is difficult. I understand you may not have the resources that other individuals have nor in some cases the opportunity that others have to put yourself in a position to be great. But I am here to tell you that you are still a valuable diamond even if that diamond is in the rough. Even through the incredible pressure

we face during hardships, trials and tribulations, bad relationships, failures and so much more, deep down there is a hidden treasure within us ready to emerge. God uses us to show others that in our imperfections we are still worthy to birth greatness. Yes, it may take a process, but at the end, glory will manifest itself.

Speaking of process, in order to get a diamond from a rough stone into a faceted gem it requires cutting. Now you cannot cut a diamond without specialized knowledge, tools, equipment, and techniques because of its extreme difficulty. When it comes to birthing greatness is also extremely difficult. So, how and what does the Lord use to cut us and polish us in our lives? In your case, for your greatness to emerge from a rough stone into a faceted gem you need to get tips and tools and knowledge from mentors.

You must learn from your past experiences. Learn and gather information from books such as *The Birth of Greatness.* God puts you through a process because for a diamond to be formed it must go through necessary stages or processes. Let me make something clear right now. A process is not always ways pretty, but the process holds a tremendous amount of worth and value. Remember, a diamond starts with coal and carbon. Success starts, with a dream, idea, passion and when pressure sets and you refuse to allow yourself to fold or crumble, birthing greatness is the result. I learned this during my time of carrying greatness, that everybody wants to be a diamond, but very few are willing to get cut.

The word "diamond" comes from the Greek word *Adamas*, which translated means "unconquerable, unalterable, unbreakable, and untamable." Any gift from God, in this case, your greatness, He makes it so that it becomes unbreakable, untamable, unalterable, and unconquerable. You are God's treasure. You are His workmanship which was wonderfully and fearfully made. Whatever pressure you are experiencing it will bring out the best in you if you allow it. Pressure can make you or break you, which one are you going to allow to manifest? Yes, I know problems will occur during a time such as this. Most moms-to-be will tell you at some point during their pregnancy problems occurred. I am here to tell you on the journey to carry and birth greatness, problems will occur. However, I learned that problems are not signs, they are guidepost along your journey. Problems are essential to the process and problems excite change. Transformation or change is far from easy, but for a diamond to emerge change must take place in the process.

No matter the trials and tribulations, the cuts and the brushes that you have or will experience during this journey to birth greatness, God will cause you to prevail if you allow Him to be God in your life. Incredibly, God must break us down for us to prevail. But to build anything new, the old must be destroyed first. The word prevail means to be stronger, to have greater power, to be successful and efficacious. To determine the diamonds brilliance, it must go through several cuts and or facets. You will go through peaks and valleys, bumps and brushes, different cuts and facets, but you will prevail if you trust God's process. You will shine bright like a diamond. You are built to handle the pressure that comes with your greatness. Pressure is not formed to break us; it is designed to make us.

NO PAIN, NO GAIN

Yes, when there is pressure there is pain. However, we have all heard the phrase, "No pain, no gain!" Pain is what moms-to-be go through during their time of carrying a baby. Sometimes that pain can be identified as abdominal cramping or abdominal pain. The abdomen is that part of your body which is above your hips and below your ribs. I will never know the pain moms-to-be endure when carrying and birthing greatness. But what I can tell you that in life you sometimes must go through pain to gain what you want or need.

I know that it is a hard concept to grasp, but one day soon the pain that you are enduring will make sense to you. When I gave birth to my greatness, I started to understand that some of the greatest changes come from pain. If I did not endure the pressure or pain, I would have not given birth to my greatness. Jeanette Coron said something powerful that fueled me to birth my greatness even through my pain. She said, "Often the things that bring you the most pain is the very thing that will lead you to the most gain and your breakthrough."

I have realized that pain is necessary to access and to give birth to greatness. Most people that have not birthed greatness are unable to because they were not able to endure the pain. Zion Lee said it best, "Everybody wants happiness, and nobody wants pain, but you cannot have a rainbow without a little rain." So, my question to is, in the words of New Edition, "Can you stand the rain?" In the natural, one of the reasons why abortions take place is because of the amount of pressure or pain the idea of having a baby or the expectation in carrying, birthing, and parenting a baby brings. When you are on your journey to birth greatness the only way to get from Point A to Point B is to go on what I like to call a "faith ride".

Now I must warn you, there are no fast routes, no shortcuts, and you are often not in control. You will go through trials and tribulations, ups and downs, peaks and valleys on this faith ride. In other words, you have to go through it in order for you to get through it. There is pain in pregnancy, and you cannot get over pain in a snap of a finger. Faith is your Apeldoorn. During a woman's pregnancy, specifically during the third trimester when giving birth is approaching and pain is increasing the doctors may give the mom-to-be Apeldoorn. When it is your time to give birth to greatness you must go through the pain. The only help you have is your faith. The pain you are in is developing the strength you need tomorrow. Life is full of pain, but pain possesses your greatness.

Have you ever heard of growing pains? When I was younger, I experienced growing pains and it was not a pleasant feeling. It is impossible to grow in life nor in Christ without pain, so you might as well get a reward for your pain. You have gone through too much to get here. You have lost too much to quit now. You have taken too many L's (loses) to shut the door now. You have endured too much pain to give up now, so you might as well get your reward for your pain. Trust me, I know it hurts but pain is temporary. You better get something from all that hell you been through. When a woman is giving birth pain strikes, but it does not last forever. She has gone through too much pain during this pregnancy to give up now in the third trimester.

Birthing greatness is on the other side of your pain. How bad do you want to birth your greatness? The more pain you feel is an indication of how close you are to birthing your greatness. The devil attacks when you are a fingertip away, but you are too strong to give up. You cannot give up now. Ask God for endurance so you can finish the marathon even when pain tells you to give up. You must have the courage to say yes to temporary pain so that you can have the ability to achieve long term gain. Pain today. Greatness tomorrow. Even though it is hard, that pain is gaining your strength. I am here to tell you that greatness is upon you. Every successful person has a painful story. Every painful story can have a successful ending. Accept the pain and get ready to birth your greatness.

MY WATER JUST BROKE!

I do not have a child yet. However, I can just imagine being at home and my wife telling me the infamous words, "CHRIS!!! My water just broke!" O-M-G! I can see it now, my hands shaking and legs trembling. Nervous because water breaking is so unexpected. Similarly, when your water breaks in your life or during your journey to birth greatness, you will have to face an unexpected difficulty. Being laid off from your job, a breakup with whom you thought was the one, trails and tribulations and so much more. Now it is easy to be discouraged, angry, and frustrated.

However, you must have a different perspective when it comes to those difficult things that transpire in your life. When it comes to spiritual water breaking, look at it as God is about to do something new in your life. In the natural or in the spirit, water breaking is a sign that change is about to take place. Spiritually speaking, without the water breaking there is no way you are capable of giving birth. You would not be able to see the fullness of what God has in store for you, which is giving birth to your greatness if water breaking does not take place.

Such as what transpired in my life in 2015. My water broke when I stepped into my God-given assignment to become a public speaker. There was a flood of disappointments, bills were due, and rent was due. I was surviving on peanut butter and jelly sandwiches because I did not have any other option. Walking everywhere because I had to be mindful of how much gas to use because I was low on funds. On top of all of that, I was battling depression because of the loss of my father and because there were no instructions on how to carry this "greatness" that was given to me. What I did not know during this season in my life was that my water was breaking. Water serves numerous purposes for the body, one of those purposes being cleansing. The word breaking means to interrupt. Your water breaking is an indication that God is cleaning and breaking old things in your life so that new life can be birthed out of you.

God is preparing you for something greater. He has something new prepared that He not only wants to birth through you but in you. Greatness is upon you. Remember, birthing greatness is not for everyone. Not everyone can endure the pain and process it takes to birth greatness. Moms-to-be do not choose when to endure the pain, nor when or where her water breaks. You cannot choose when or where trials and tribulations will strike. You do not decide when you going to give birth to your greatness. That decision is in God's hands. Doctors indicate to the moms-to-be when it is time to prepare the body for labor. When she endures pain, she may want the doctor to deliver her baby at that moment.

During our journey of carrying greatness, we endure pain, and we want God to get rid of the pain at the moment we endure it. I learned that God may not come when you want Him, but He is always on time. We may not understand His plans for our lives and honestly, it is not our job to understand. But just know that God will never leave our side nor lead us astray. Now that does not mean along this journey to birth greatness that trials and tribulations will not happen. God does not allow you to go through without allowing that process to grow you. The pain, the pressure, the agony, the failure, the tears, the trials, and the tribulations are temporary. Your water breaking is giving way for your breakthrough. Something greater is coming. God is allowing your water to break because it is getting you in position for an increase.

The scripture says in Isaiah 14:27, "For the Lord hosts has purposed, and who will annul it? That is saying, "Who can stop what God has in store for you." Your water breaking does not mean defeat. No person, situation, obstacle, or devil can stop what God has ordained. Quit worrying about who does not like you nor what people say, or who does not believe in you. God is cleansing you and breaking off dead ends. What God has in store for you is bigger and more rewarding and fulfilling than you can ever imagine. You will not see it coming, but suddenly a good break or should I say a water break will occur. Get ready because God is about to take you where you cannot go on your own. So, it is ok to scream the infamous words, "My water just broke" because that is the indication that your breakthrough is approaching.

PUSH

OK! On the count of three, I need you to PUSH, ok? ONE. TWO. THREE. Push! Come on I know you can do it. ONE. TWO. THREE. PUSH! I need you to push through. I believe in you. ONE! TWO! THREE! PUSH!!!

We do not always understand why things happen to us. We sometimes do not understand why we must go through the things we go through. Or why we lose friends and family during our journey to birth greatness. We do not always understand why God puts us in a predicament or in a position to push. I need you to do yourself a favor, do not try to figure those things out. There are times, especially during our third trimester where God will stir things up, put us in an unusual, unfamiliar, or uncomfortable position. God's purpose was not and is not to place or push you into misery. He has placed you on the delivery table to put you in position so you can push out our greatness. If you talk to any mother, they will tell you that delivering a baby is far from comfortable. But God is not concerned about our comfort, as He is our greatness.

God places us in that uncomfortable position because He knows we would not go out without a push. Just sit back and think about how far you have come. Every painful breakup, every heartache and tears, every failure, every person who did you wrong and those who did not believe in you. Those experiences and seasons in your life were not there to defeat you but to put you in position to see if you were going to push. You would not be in this position to level up and to give birth to greatness if you did not go through what you had gone through.

Push means, to force someone or something to perforate, to penetrate or pass through. It is time to push and give birth to your greatness. In the natural order of things, at the end of pregnancy, labor begins. The trials and tribulations, the pressure, the pain that you have endured, the long days and long nights of hard work are about to finally pay off. During the journey of carrying greatness, you usually will start to experience an overwhelming amount of urge to push to give birth. The test is being patient and waiting for God's instruction to push. Now when God says "Push" it will be an unspeakable pain.

When I look back on what I have gone through, I realize

that nothing can defeat me when I have God on my side. I pushed my way to grow when it was painful. I pushed my way to becoming a motivational speaker when people did not believe in my gift because they thought I was too young or too inexperienced. I pushed my way to becoming an author when people counted me out. I pushed in order for me to birth my greatness. I would not be where I am and who I am if I did not push. I did not enjoy many seasons in my life that God put me through because it was uncomfortable.

It took me to step into my faith and trust God that He will close doors and push me into my purpose, which made me push out my greatness. God is about to use you and place you in positions that you may not like, you may not understand, but if you stay grounded in faith,

whatever is thrown your way will not defeat you. There is something bigger and something better on the other side of you pushing. Your obedience to push will not go in vain. When it is tight, uncomfortable and it feels like you are being squeezed, that is a sign that birth is about to take place.

I need you more than ever to activate your faith. Your faith is only as strong as the test it survives. I pray that I have encouraged you to continuously push through, no matter how difficult your situation may seem. Pain is daring you to push and do not stop pushing until your greatness has manifested. God has a purpose for your pain, a reason for your struggles, and a reward for your faithfulness. Do not give up! Those who are in great physical condition has pushed past the pain barrier to reach their goal. Successful businesspeople and even your favorite celebrity have overcome countless limitations, pressure, and pain to reach their level of achievement. These individuals realize that to achieve or birth greatness they must go through the thresholds of pain.

Going through pain is unavoidable unless you just do not want to become successful. God sometimes uses pain to push you to where and who you are intended and created to be. I know it may be hard for you to see what God is doing. I know what you are going through does not make much sense, but I need you to trust God. I need you to know that you and your greatness is in God's hands, you just have to push.

OK! On the count of three I need you to PUSH, ok?

ONE. TWO. THREE. Push! Come on you can do it. ONE. TWO. THREE. PUSH! Come on, I need you to push through. I believe in you. ONE! TWO! THREE! PUSH!!!

DELIVER ME

"THIS IS MY EXODUS"

Congrats! You have reached the end of The Birth of Greatness book. Now before you read any further, I want you to know that I am proud of you. Usually, the average person does not finish what they start. They give up because it requires such a commitment, discipline, and the will to push in order to finish what they have started. The same thing goes for when it is time to carry and birth greatness. They have trouble committing, they lack discipline and have a hard time pushing when times get rough. But what mostly hinders someone to finish is when it comes time to push. Pushing requires individuals to endure pain sometimes, and when pain settles in, they settle for giving up.

So, I am proud of you because from the looks of it, you are not in the business of giving up. I see you are in the business of finishing. It is clear to me that you have pushed yourself to finish this book. And it seems as if you are going to continue to push until you get what God has promised you. For that, amongst other things is the reason why I want to take the time to let you know that I am proud of you. Now even though the end is here this is the time when a new beginning is about to take place in your life. Your growth and journey do not stop after reading this book. In fact, your greatness is about to emerge. The time has come for you to receive what God has promised you. Now is the time for you to birth your greatness. I understand that is easier said than done but as we both know;

you did not come this far and endure much pain to not birth your greatness.

Now any mom-to-be will probably tell you that there is no true guideline when it comes to giving birth. That might be true, but what I do know to be true is that moms-to-be do all the necessary steps to prepare themselves to birth the blessing that God has placed on the inside of them with. Just like you, God blessed me with greatness and our assignment is to birth such greatness. But to be honest there is no true guideline to birthing greatness. Because of that, God blessed me with a few words to share with you in hopes to prepare you for what is to come. That is when "The Birth of Greatness" was born. My prayer is that you were blessed with the words that were written in this book.

The Birth of Greatness was written for many purposes, but the two most important reasons for its existence was to inform you that you have greatness on the inside of you that the world needs. The second important reason for this book's existence was to prepare you for the journey that you will embark on carrying and birthing the greatness that God has blessed you with. I pray I prepared you. Now it is time for you to birth your greatness. What you are about to read is titled, "Deliver Me" (This Is My Exodus) which was inspired by a gospel song written by a living legend Donald Lawrence. This is the last bit of information to prepare you to give birth to your greatness. Allow me to take you on this last journey where Exodus will take place. Before we dive in, we need to know the meaning and significance of the word Exodus.

The word Exodus is the name of the second book of the Bible where we can read the story in which Moses was directed by God to save the Israelites out of Egypt. Exodus is also where we get the popular story about the Red Sea where Moses took those same Israelites and guided them through the parted Red Sea to freedom. Now Exodus means; departure, set free, or deliverance. Hint, Moses "set free" the Israelites from the bondage that was taking place in Egypt.

Stay with me now!

When I see the word deliverance, I think of the word deliver. However, the word deliver means; to provide, hand over, launch, or assist. Hint, where we get the word delivery. "What are you trying to say, Chris?" I am glad you asked. Buckle your seatbelt, the preparation is about to begin. When it is time for moms-to-be to give birth, it is common practice that there only be three or fewer people in the delivery room.

The reason for that is to protect the mom and the newborn as well as to provide the mother with intimate support throughout the process. The same thing goes for you when it is time for you to give birth to your greatness. You cannot put you or your greatness in danger with unnecessary, unmotivated, unsuccessful people around you when delivery is taking place. I suggest you get what I like to call a, "Delivery Support Team." This team should have the best interest of you and your greatness. These individuals should be utterly reliable, the supportive type, tireless cheerleader, but more importantly someone who will not get squeamish when they see The Blood of God pouring out of you during your labor. Not everyone can handle blood, especially the Blood of God.

So, you must get individuals who not only can handle The Blood but have experienced The Blood. Now we all know that only the person carrying the child or carrying greatness can give birth to that child or greatness. However, it is ok if you need some support when it is time to give birth. I recommend you have a support team to encourage you, to make sure you stay focus on the task at hand, and to hold you accountable or to hold your hand for support when Doctor G-O-D instructs you to push.

Now, not everyone is qualified to be on your Support Team. Not everyone can handle what God has in store for you. That is why people fall off when you are on the trajectory to success or on your way to giving birth. Not everyone can handle what takes place throughout the journey to carry and birth greatness, let alone see what is about to take place in the delivery room.

The delivery room, in the physical and in the spiritual sense, is a sacred place. It is a place where a new beginning is about to transpire, a place where a new chapter or journey is about to open, more important a place where new life will emerge. That is why when times weigh on the tension becomes thick in the delivery room for a mom-to-be. If you ever been inside of a delivery room with a mom-to-be, you know her patience has begun to run thin, while the anticipation begins to increase. The suspense starts to get to her. Thoughts start to run through their head as time continues to tick. She beings to get frustrated, wondering when this baby of hers is going to come out of her, because the pain is starting to increase. Sounds familiar? We sometimes get frustrated with God because we been through so much hell carrying greatness and now is the due date, but we must wait.

We know what He has promised us, but we still must be patient and wait just a little while longer to retrieve what God has promised us. Just like moms-to-be, we must sit back in frustration just wanting as times tick for this baby or should I say our greatness to come out of us. To add on top of the frustration, the mom-to-be are then instructed to lay in what some moms define as, an uncomfortable position. It is amazing through our frustration about being uncomfortable God still is capable to do wonders in your life. We sometimes miss out on our blessing because we are to be busy being frustrated being in an uncomfortable position. However, to birth greatness, it requires us to be an uncomfortable position at times. It is incredible that during our frustration and uncomfortable state, God still finds it in Him to somehow display grace and love for us to deliver our greatness out of us.

But in order for God to deliver what He has promised us, we must go through a series of final progressions or a series of final events. I already hinted at what happens first. In the first final stage of birthing greatness, it starts with us being placed in an uncomfortable position. You know, making that uncomfortable decision to quit your job so you can put that full-time effort into your dreams and greatness. Or how about that uncomfortable position you must face to stay at your job a little while longer to fund your dreams. I got it! How about the uncomfortable decision you must make to leave that relationship that makes you comfortable to build a better relationship with God that seems uncomfortable.

The point is, "Life begins at the end of your comfort zone. So, if you are feeling uncomfortable right now, know that the change taking place in your life is a beginning, not an ending." – Neale Donald Walsch. God knows it is uncomfortable for you to quit that great paying job to birth your greatness. He knows it is uncomfortable for you to stay at that horrible job to fund your dreams. I promise you; He understands how uncomfortable it might have been for you to break up with a person you thought was going to be in your life forever. He knows how it feels to be looked down upon when you are trying to build a relationship with Him and to birth what He has given you. This uncomfortable state you are experiencing is a test to see if you trust Him to be God in your life. He wants to see if you will place your faith in His hands.

When moms-to-be are in that uncomfortable position the Doctor lays His hands upon them to indicate that they are in good hands and everything is going to be ok moving forward. The question is are you going to put what you have been carrying on the inside of you in God's hands and trust Him? If you answered yes, then are you going to have to trust Him when He unexpectedly tells you to push? Remember in your pushing you will experience pain. When a mother is lying there on the delivery bed pushing, her objective is to give birth to be set free of the pain she is enduring. In other words, she is looking for deliverance; (*meaning rescued or set free from.*) The same thing transpires in the natural.

Anytime we endure pain in life, the loss of a loved one, the pain of someone doing us wrong at a job or in life, or the pain we endure throughout our journey of entrepreneurship. We try to find a way to eliminate the pain. Even the pain that comes with our faith walk, or even the pain we endure carrying and birthing greatness. In the spiritual sense, that is called seeking deliverance. We go to God for deliverance, for God to set us free or to rescue us from the pain that we are enduring.

However, to be set free or for deliverance to take place, assistance is needed. Mothers go through nine months of carrying life to need assistance in the last few moments. We are aware that a woman cannot bring a baby into this world alone, nor can we bring greatness into this world alone. Moms-to-be cannot deliver the baby by themselves, she must put her faith in the doctor's hands. I know you are at the end of your rope and you want to birth your greatness, but you have to be willing to put your faith in God's hand to handle the rest.

I know it is scary and painful to be at the cusp of birthing your greatness and God tells you unexpectedly to push. I know those pushes hurt. I know it feels as if you have no more energy to give, but you must push through the end. I know it hurts that the more pushing God instructs you to do, the more crying out you display. But I am here to tell you that in your cry is Exodus.

You cannot experience labor without pushing and crying out. Deliverance might set you free of pain but to birth greatness it requires pain, it requires you to cry out. Moms-to-be realizes through their pushing and crying out, the pain gets them one step closer to delivery. Trust me, there is a reward for your faith and obedience to crying out to God. Just like when moms-to-be hear from Doctors say, "Push, I see the head!" You start to see God assist in launching your new business, because of your faith and cry out. Your start to see Him and over the keys to your new car or new home even when your credit says otherwise; that is because of your faith and cry out. You start to see Him provide and make a way out of what you thought was no way. What you are seeing take place or will see take place in your life is God being a deliver. You will start to see Him deliver your greatness. It just requires you to push and I encourage you to cry out while you push.

You must put your faith in God's hands for delivery to take place. This delivery is not going to be pretty. There is going to be sweat, tears, and the Blood during the transaction that God is about to do between you and your greatness. Now birthing greatness will have you looking ugly. People are going to judge and laugh but if they only knew what you have gone through to birth your greatness, they would find nothing humorous. However, they will find humor in how you looked trying to give birth to your greatness. You must stay strong in the midst of your pain, pushing and you're crying out.

Know that God hears you and understands your pain, so do not forfeit your greatness because of the pain you endure in birthing your greatness. Just breathe and listen because what is about to happen next in your life requires discipline. When Moses was required by God to free the Israelites out of Egypt he had to listen and display discipline. And I am going to tell you what God told Moses to tell the people, "Do not be afraid. Stand firm and you will see the deliverance the Lord will bring you today...the Lord will fight for you; you need only to be still." In other words, it is time for you to wait, listen, and be still. Allow God to fight for you and deliver this baby or should I say greatness for you. If you listen closely you hear God tell you to push no more and then watch how He hands over greatness like a newborn baby.

At this moment I decree and declare from this day forward that your greatness is set free. I pray that God delivers what He has promised you not when you want it but when you need it. This is your Exodus.

I Love You! – Christopher S. Williams

Acknowledgments

When I sit back and think about the journey it took for me to finally be able to say, "I am author", I start to get emotional. But I would be remorse if I said I completed this book alone. To my other half, my queen Briana Williams. I love you so much. You were my confidant, my shoulder to cry on, my accountability partner, and my biggest cheerleader throughout this tough journey. You pushed me and encouraged me when I wanted to give up. You never took anything less than my best from me and for that I love you with all my heart. You are such a wonderful person and I thank God for you, and I am blessed and honored to be able to call you a best friend and a wife. This book would not have been completed if it were not for you. I love you and I truly thank you for just being you.

CHRISTOPHER WILLIAMS

www.ingramcontent.com/pod-product-compliance
Lightning Source LLC
Chambersburg PA
CBHW021849090426
42811CB00033B/2195/J